Praise for *More Than*

T0031891

"*More Than Your Number* gently and assuredly provides the perfect entry point for novices and practiced students alike into a truly understandable yet profound journey of self-awareness and change."

Ian Morgan Cron, Author of *The Story of You: An Enneagram Journey to Becoming Your True Self*

"Beth and Jeff McCord are paving a path for so many people to truly experience freedom in their lives through this amazing new resource. *More Than Your Number* is a book that will revolutionize the way you see yourself and experience the world around you."

Jackie Brewster, Author, certified Enneagram coach and experiential specialist

"As a family therapist, I have long believed in the wisdom of the Enneagram. I've seen the game change with parents who know their number and are willing to allow the Enneagram to influence their journey as mothers and fathers. In *More Than Your Number*, Beth and Jeff McCord act as the trusted guides they have been for so many years, helping us use the Enneagram to transform our relationships."

David Thomas, Author of the bestseller *Wild Things: The Art of Nurturing Boys & Are My Kids on Track?*

"*More Than Your Number* is truly more than another Enneagram resource. The McCords have described with gracious detail the inner tension that exists within all of us in a way that leaves no one out in the cold. I wish I would have had access to these truths years ago, but I'm grateful for them now."

Jamie Ivey, Author and host of *The Happy Hour with Jamie Ivey* podcast

"Though they would never say it, Beth and Jeff stand among very few people atop the peak of gospel-based Enneagram knowledge and practice. In *More Than Your Number*, they draw us into their own lives and experiences while also leading us to a completely new and innovative approach through the advent of the Enneagram Internal Profile. The EIP will redefine the very topic of the Enneagram for years to come."

Ben Allison, Chief Executive Officer of the American Association of Christian Counselors

"Applying the Enneagram to my life and relationships has helped in so many ways. Beth and Jeff McCord continue to dive deeper and bring such impactful principles to the surface for all of us to take in. I'm so thankful for this book!"

RACHEL CRUZE, *NEW YORK TIMES* BESTSELLING AUTHOR
AND HOST OF *THE RACHEL CRUZE SHOW*

"*More Than Your Number* is truly more than another Enneagram resource. It is full of scriptural principles and truths that will help you understand your struggles and your need for God's grace—and how you can become more and more like Jesus in your everyday life. Our friends Beth and Jeff McCord put the gospel front and center in everything they do, and in this book you will be drawn into not only a better understanding of your unique God-created design but a deeper walk with the Lord."

JEFF & SHAUNTI FELDHAHN, SOCIAL RESEARCHERS AND BESTSELLING
AUTHORS OF *FOR WOMEN ONLY* AND *FOR MEN ONLY*

"The Enneagram is one of my favorite tools in therapy with both adolescents and adults. Beth and Jeff McCord not only explain the Enneagram in an accessible way; they infuse it with the truth and hope of the gospel. I trust the voices of the McCords to guide us all into what the Enneagram does best, giving us a foundational understanding of ourselves and others that brings more grace to all."

SISSY GOFF, M.ED., LPC-MHSP, BESTSELLING AUTHOR
AND DIRECTOR OF CHILD AND ADOLESCENT COUNSELING
AT DAYSTAR COUNSELING MINISTRIES

"With the growing popularity of the Enneagram, many people fall into the temptation to hide behind their number as an excuse to stay stuck. The McCords shine an important light on how you can understand the Enneagram and at the same time grow as a person, grow in your faith, and most of all take hold of the freedom you were created for."

CHRISTY WRIGHT, NATIONAL BESTSELLING AUTHOR OF *BUSINESS
BOUTIQUE*, *TAKE BACK YOUR TIME*, AND *LIVING TRUE*

"I just love that Beth and Jeff have given us another tool with this book that we can use to better understand ourselves and others and how we interact! We are so much more effective for the kingdom of God when we understand and honor how God wired us. Bravo!"

JENNIFER ALLWOOD, BUSINESS COACH AND AUTHOR
OF *FEAR IS NOT THE BOSS OF YOU*

"Discovering your unique Enneagram Internal Profile is a game-changer and takes the power of the Enneagram to the next level. Beth and Jeff McCord will give you the tools, understanding, and encouragement to unlock deeper self-understanding through the lens of the gospel. *More Than Your Number* is a must-read!"

ALLI WORTHINGTON, LIFE AND BUSINESS COACH, AUTHOR
OF *STANDING STRONG: A WOMAN'S GUIDE TO OVERCOMING*
ADVERSITY AND LIVING WITH CONFIDENCE

"Reading this book is like taking a good, hard look into a crystal-clear mirror. While that can be intimidating, Beth and Jeff McCord beautifully reflect to you not a sterile personality type but the beloved child of God you were created to be. Their wisdom, frameworks, and gospel-centered guidance is a balm to our weary, tension-filled souls."

GEORGE KAMEL, RAMSEY PERSONALITY AND COHOST OF *THE RAMSEY SHOW*

"*More Than Your Number* is truly more than another Enneagram resource. It's a beautiful guide through the often-neglected terrain of the inner world. The McCords describe with gracious detail the inner tensions that we all face and provide a clear path to integration and soul health. Above all, they point us always to the Good Shepherd as our steady, faithful guide into deeper healing, joy, and life-changing growth."

DR. ALISON COOK, PSYCHOLOGIST AND AUTHOR OF *THE*
BEST OF YOU AND *BOUNDARIES FOR YOUR SOUL*

"Self-awareness is an important part of maturity. We change and grow best when we know God and understand how He made us. This book blends the insight of the Enneagram and the wisdom of God's truth to help you understand that you are indeed more than your number."

JILL SAVAGE, AUTHOR OF *NO MORE PERFECT MOMS*
AND HOST OF THE *NO MORE PERFECT PODCAST*

"Since I live with an Enneagram expert, I thought there was not much left for me to learn, but Beth and Jeff did an incredible job helping to uncover new truths about this powerful tool that were revelations to me. If you are someone who knows a lot or someone just getting to know about the Enneagram and how God can use it to help you learn more about yourself, you are going to love this new book from the McCords."

STEPHEN BREWSTER, CREATIVE AND LEADERSHIP CONSULTANT

"Beth and Jeff are the real deal, truly seeking to experience the love of God and allow it to define who they are and change them from the inside out. *More Than Your Number* is a personal, heartfelt look at how they are overcoming their own woundedness to find identity as a beloved child of God. This gift helps us go deeper with the Enneagram and understand how our Enneagram Internal Profile guides us and our relationships."

JOSHUA STRAUB, PH.D., COFOUNDER AND PRESIDENT OF FAMOUS AT HOME

"Thank you, Beth and Jeff McCord, for continuing to move the Enneagram into the broader cultural narrative while aligning it with the gospel! *More Than Your Number* will be an invaluable resource for my students and clients. Personally, with every new book, I find more and more enlightenment as to who I am, how I interact with others, and how to further live as a healthy, authentic believer."

DEVON MILLS, PHD, LPC, ACS, CLINICAL DIRECTOR, RICHMONT TRAUMA CENTER, AND ASSISTANT PROFESSOR OF CLINICAL MENTAL HEALTH COUNSELING

"The gift from *More Than Your Number* is spiritual freedom. The McCords graciously guide the reader on how to navigate life as a beloved child of God, aligned with the gospel. If absorbed and activated upon, these words will transform communities to bring God glory."

HEATHER MACFADYEN, AUTHOR OF *DON'T MOM ALONE* AND HOST OF THE *DON'T MOM ALONE* PODCAST

"The Enneagram has been an enlightening tool for my ministry, largely thanks to the gospel-based approach of Beth and Jeff McCord. *More Than Your Number* is an invitation for readers to bask in the warmth of God's revealing light, confident of His continued work in each of our lives. This book resonated so powerfully as it revealed the tension and uncertainty that I (as a Nine) often interact with. My heart soared as I was called to rest, knowing that God has equipped me for every good work. I am so grateful that Beth and Jeff would gift us this resource to help us make sense of our inner wiring and call us to the truth of our identity as beloved children of God."

DORENA WILLIAMSON, MINISTRY LEADER AND BESTSELLING CHILDREN'S AUTHOR OF *COLORFULL*, *THE CELEBRATION PLACE*, AND *CROWNED WITH GLORY*

"When the McCords speak and write, the gospel is always at the center. *More Than Your Number* offers a Christ-centered approach to understanding your internal wiring. If you want to learn more about why you think, feel, react, and relate the way you do, I highly recommend this book. I will definitely share this with our church family."

TED CUNNINGHAM, PASTOR OF WOODLAND HILLS FAMILY CHURCH, BRANSON, MO, AND AUTHOR OF *FUN LOVING YOU*

MORE THAN

YOUR

NUMBER

MORE THAN
YOUR
NUMBER

A Christ-Centered Enneagram
Approach to Becoming AWARE
of Your Internal World

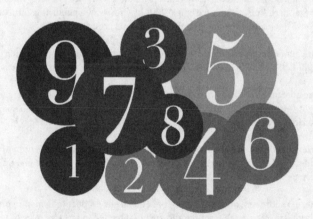

BETH AND JEFF MCCORD
WITH JOHN DRIVER

W Publishing Group

An Imprint of Thomas Nelson

More Than Your Number

Published in Nashville, Tennessee, by W Publishing, an imprint of Thomas Nelson.

Published in association with the literary agency of Wolgemuth & Associates.

Thomas Nelson titles may be purchased in bulk for educational, business, fundraising, or sales promotional use. For information, please email SpecialMarkets@ ThomasNelson.com.

ISBN 978-0-7852-9100-8 (Softcover)
ISBN 978-0-7852-9099-5 (HC)
ISBN 978-0-7852-9101-5 (e-book)

Library of Congress Control Number: 2021952943

Printed in the United States of America
23 24 25 26 27 LBC 5 4 3 2 1

To Jesus Christ.
To our son and daughter, Nathan and Libby.
To our parents, Bruce and Dana Pfuetze
and Jerald and Johnnie McCord.
To our readers: May you come to know the love
and care that you have received from Christ.

Contents

CONTENTS

Introduction

My Good Shepherd

"You are not enough!"

"You are too much trouble!"

"Your voice doesn't matter, so why are you surprised you feel this way again?"

These devastating messages were flooding my mind—and I (Beth), an Enneagram Type Nine and an expert in the Enneagram for over twenty years, was somehow still drowning in the wake of these harmful messages yet again. *Why does this keep happening?* I wondered. In that moment, I truly thought I was a failure as a wife. Jeff had never said as much—he never would say it out loud, and I know he didn't believe it. But I certainly believed it because the messages within me were louder than the messages around me. They left me feeling quietly withdrawn and adrift. I was exhausted from living this way, losing my way every time Jeff and I had to face certain conflicts in our relationship. If I were a better wife—a better person—this wouldn't be happening.

Amid this particular crisis, I remembered a book my parents had given me: *A Shepherd Looks at Psalm 23* by W. Phillip Keller. Reluctantly, I picked it up and began to thumb through its pages. What I read began creating seismic shifts in my internal world. I was instantly captivated by descriptions of a Shepherd I had met, but whose actual care for me seemed foreign.

I was so moved that I began googling images of sheep and shepherds—and that's when one particular photo divinely captured my attention: a little lamb being held tightly in the arms of a shepherd. While my family is so very important to me, when I pick up my phone to unlock it, their beautiful faces are not the first image I see. It's this photo of this lamb with its little eyes shut as she nuzzles herself closer to the heart of the one who is keeping her near and safe. She is experiencing complete contentment, safety, and peace. For her, all is well, and all will be well.

This photo encapsulated not only tens of thousands of words we have spoken during coaching sessions, events, and podcasts—but also the ones you are about to read. It affected the way I hear, react, and respond to the intense messages that so often flood my heart from seemingly different places within me. How is it possible to have different places within me? Does this mean I'm crazy? Maybe you can relate to this feeling—and the answer is: no, you are not crazy.

You are more than only one thing.

In an indirect yet significant way, this image on my phone represents me—that is, the part of me most reflective of my truest identity in Christ. I am the sheep, and Christ is my Shepherd. I am His beloved. He has brought me close. I am safe. I am secure. I am seen, known, loved, cherished, provided for, and protected. I belong. My presence matters. I am neither distant from Him nor too much for Him.

For some reason, though, parts of me still need to be constantly reminded of these elemental truths. That is why I need to look at this background screen—and other tools—so often: to help me reawaken again and again to my true inner reality as Christ's beloved. The psalmist David recognized the same divided state within himself, which is why he asked himself searching, vulnerable questions about his forgotten identity—questions like: "Why, my soul, are you downcast? Why so disturbed within me?" (Psalm 42:5).

Maybe you're like David. Maybe you're like me. Maybe it feels like you often lose sight of who you are—and more importantly, Whose you are. Maybe you keep losing your temper when a certain person pushes your buttons. Maybe you freeze up with anxiety when you think about your child's future. Maybe you keep talking over a certain situation when what you really need to do is just listen and be present. Maybe you've asked yourself the same question I ask: "Why do I keep forgetting what is true so often that I need reminders of who I really am?"

This question lies at the heart of this book.

All of us struggle here. We get stuck and lose sight of who we are, wondering why this keeps happening. Like sheep, we wander toward the same thorn patches, pitfalls, quicksand, and cliffs—and this repetition brings up feelings of shame, fear, and self-condemnation.

Even in crises of faith, purpose, or relationships, the truth is that my identity remains unchanged. I am Christ's beloved. That matter has been settled, and the most important lingering question of my life has already found its joyful conclusion: "You also are complete through your union with Christ, who is the head over every ruler and authority" (Colossians 2:10 NLT). The end is already mine: I am already complete in Christ. But on this journey between beginnings and endings, the middle is generally where we get stuck—somewhere in the patterns and pressures of real life.

In the chapters to come, my husband, Jeff, and I will reveal stories that will be familiar to you. Even though we are Enneagram experts, you will see from our own journey and marriage how we have tried and failed—and you will join us in exploring why. Then, using a new and revolutionary application of the Enneagram called Enneagram Internal Profile (EIP), which Jeff and I developed while doing our own internal work, we will introduce you to your unique EIP.

Through this process, we hope to help you become aware of how to get unstuck—just as David worked through his own difficult questions and found a path to better, hope-filled pastures: "Put your hope in God, for I will yet praise him, my Savior and my God" (Psalm 42:5). He began with our same questions of brokenness, but he found hope in divinely revealed answers. So will we.

Our journey ahead in this book begins and continues with our true identity in Christ. This is about continually being aware of who you are as a beloved sheep in relation to your Shepherd. It's a reality that already is, even when it feels like it isn't. At the end of our lives and the end of all our searching and crawling and reaching and striving, we anticipate that we will experience in heaven a holy awareness that will suddenly bring a holy relief. We will finally fully know, without forgetting or foreboding, who we really are. More importantly, we will fully know and rest in Whose we really are.

But what if I told you that eternity has already begun? And that, in fact, you're smack-dab in the middle of it right now? In other words, what will someday become fully evident in our future is available to us in our present. We just often fail to see it in the fog of life. Instead of striving for a future awareness, Jesus invites us to rest in a present awareness, one that doesn't wait for us to get unstuck before we can know it. Our souls can—and should—live presently aware of our ultimate hope in Christ, which releases us from the old patterns harming our souls and relationships in ways that the Shepherd does not intend for His beloved.

If we are truly already this near to the Shepherd, we must learn to remain aware of it, even if we feel like we've wandered away.

We Have Parts That Need a Shepherd

A main reason I so often forget the true nature of my relationship with the Shepherd—that is, the reason I get stuck—is because there is more than one thing going on inside me.[1] You see, *I have parts*. This small statement is a monumental concept that we will soon map out in greater detail. For now, just try to accept this idea that you are more than one thing. You are made up of parts. Have you ever said, "Part of me wants to go to the party, but part of me wants to stay home"? We already speak in these terms without realizing it. For those of us who have put our faith in Jesus Christ, there are parts of us that believe we are divinely loved. Yet so much of us doesn't actively believe it at any given moment.

Because of the fallen state in which we live, some parts of me become negatively activated by situations and circumstances—and they tend to lose sight of or stop fully believing who I really am in Christ. They get lost, angry, and confused. They begin to panic and think that the Shepherd has forgotten me—that He is distant, disappointed, and standoffish. When this happens, I become derailed by the fears and reactions of my parts. I get stuck in these false messages. Like a sheep, I feel lost. Maybe you can relate.

Dane Ortlund, in his book *Gentle and Lowly*, helps us move from sheep in the arms of a shepherd to a beloved child embraced by his Father:

> "It is one thing, as a child, to be told your father loves you. You believe him. You take him at his word. But it is another thing, unutterably more real, to be swept up in his embrace, to feel the warmth, to hear his beating heart within his chest, to instantly know the protective grip of his arms. It's one thing to hear he loves you; it's another thing to feel his love. This is the glorious work of the Spirit."[2]

Whether we use the Enneagram or any other tool of self-discovery, the inner work of the Holy Spirit helps us hear the heartbeat of the Shepherd so we might also see and relate to the Good Father. These concepts go together, and each speaks to us in different ways.

Speaking of different ways of speaking, this is also a timely moment to introduce you to the other author of this book. Throughout these pages, you will hear from each of us individually, which will be easy to recognize because a section will begin with "I (Beth)" or "I (Jeff)." And at times, we speak together in a collective "we."

We pray that the journey ahead will help you not only become aware of who and Whose you are, but also help you learn how to stand in His grace as the beloved lamb—His beloved child—each and every moment of your life, even when you get stuck. We want you to know what it means to be a sheep under the care of the Shepherd and a beloved child under the care of the Father.

PART ONE

Seeing the World Within

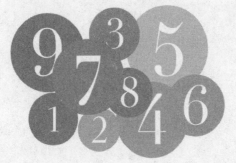

ONE

The Wounded Child and the Beloved Child

As I (Jeff) gazed out the window at the lights of the cars passing by, a part of my five-year-old heart was convinced (and was very convincing) that my adoptive parents were never coming back to get me.

This is part of a story to come, but for now, it suffices to say that each of us has a story to tell. Mine includes the fact that I was adopted. As a result, there have been many times in life when I have suffered from an intense fear of being abandoned, which also corresponds to some of the essential motivations of my Enneagram type. You may not yet know what all that means, but for now, I simply want to express that I know what it feels like to be wounded.

Woundedness is universal, yet when it is so personal and unique to you, it can feel as if you are the only one broken this badly. This is why it is so helpful to explore the central motivations and issues that each of us shares with many other people. Each of us is uniquely made and even uniquely broken, but there are commonalities within our uniqueness that can help remove our sense of loneliness and isolation. You may know what it feels like to be wounded, but you don't need to stay there alone. Using the tool of the Enneagram helps invite Christ into these real places—places you may not fully realize, much less name—and guide you closer to healing. Closer to Him.

To begin this journey to healing, the good news is that you don't have to know your Enneagram number (that is, your type) or already have your head fully wrapped around wings, the varying layers in the Enneagram, or a dozen other things that may sound like Greek to you at present. If you're an Enneagram novice, please relax. We have you covered.

In part 2 and throughout this book, we will help you gain a deeper understanding and practical application of the Enneagram. For now, feel free to visit yourenneagramprofile.com/resources to take one of our free assessments to begin the process of determining your type. Or maybe you have been studying the Enneagram for a while now and understand your internal motivations, but you are searching for practical ways to apply these insights more deeply to the areas of your life. Whatever the case may be for you, this book is exactly what you need to take the next steps in applying the principles of the Enneagram to your real life in new and effective ways.

No matter where you are in your level of Enneagram exposure or understanding, this idea of being wounded is a key concept on which everything else in this book is constructed and furnished. Don't worry about all the specifics, but simply open your mind to another simple idea: you have a primary Enneagram type (your way of relating to the world) that always functions in one of two ways. In fact, the Bible references the fact that we always live out of one of these two divergent places in our interior world. We call these two places the Wounded Child or the Beloved Child.

Try not to get hung up on the semantics of these terms. The concepts they represent can be named in multiple ways in both biblical and psychological expressions. Some may struggle with what they call a "fear of man" (Proverbs 29:25), while others struggle with the same thing, though they call it codependency. We will lean more into the biblical terms, but this doesn't mean that you should be limited by them—feel free to add terms that help you grasp the concepts.

To that end, a few terms of noteworthiness that we will use are the words *adoption* and *wounded*. For our purposes, *adoption* is a biblical term (Romans 8:15) that helps us more deeply identify with our true state of existence and value in the eyes of our Father. When we talk about the Wounded Child and the Beloved Child, this is the context of these terms; as adopted children, we are wrestling to know and believe our place in the heart and the household of the One who has brought us into His family.

When we say "wounded," do we mean that everyone should approach this process from the mindset of victimization? Not at all, though each of us certainly has our own respective stories about which we should be sensitive and respectful. Even so, our use of "Wounded Child" refers to the ways each of us have engaged certain strategies in attempts to manage our own fallenness and sin—strategies that only leave us more broken and stuck in places we don't want to be.[1]

The concepts of the Beloved Child and the Wounded Child are not novel or worldly ideas. Scripture expounds on these over and over. Remember that Scripture is mainly written to those who believe, which is why they are willing to read and accept it. In other words, God is clearly speaking encouragements and challenges to believers, but to modern ears, some of these encouragements and challenges can sound more like something nonbelievers would need to hear. We somehow assume that believers should always be thinking and acting as Beloved Children, but if that is the case, why are there so many references that indicate otherwise?

Wounded Child		Beloved Child
WALKING IN THE FLESH		WALKING IN THE SPIRIT
The parts of our heart that seek to live independently from God and others	vs.	The parts of our heart that have been indwelled by the Spirit are living in reliance on God and in genuine relationship with others (Romans 8:4; Galatians 5:16)

Wounded Child		Beloved Child
THE OLD SELF The parts of our heart that choose self-serving and unhealthy autonomous patterns	vs.	**THE NEW SELF** The parts of our heart that daily align themselves with the redemption and communion of life with the Father and His children (Ephesians 4:22–23; Colossians 3:9–10)
PARTAKING IN THE SIN NATURE The parts of our heart that lean into the fallenness within without bringing their desires and impulses into the light of confession and community	vs.	**PARTAKING IN THE DIVINE NATURE** The parts of our heart that lean away from self and into the life-giving resources of God's Word, God's Spirit, and God's people (Romans 7:25; 2 Peter 1:4; 1 John 1:5–7)
OLD CREATION The parts of our heart that focus on the scarcity and death of our past and our seemingly hopeless patterns of sin and weakness	vs.	**NEW CREATION** The parts of our heart that live aware of God's grand plan of rescue and redemption into which we have been grafted and which offers us daily hope for today and eternity (2 Corinthians 5:17)
SLAVE The parts of our heart that feel powerless to break the chains of addiction, apathy, and avarice and thus are constantly running away from the Father we don't trust to have our best interests at heart	vs.	**HIS CHILD** The parts of our heart that humbly yet boldly turn and return to the arms of the Father because we trust that His strength is for our protection, not our harm (Romans 8:14–16)

Regardless of how we explore it or name it, when our primary Enneagram type is functioning as a Wounded Child, it becomes the part of us that holds tightly and carries closely all the pain, fear, and shame related to the tragedies we face from living in a sinful and fallen world. This causes us to hold on to negative beliefs about ourselves and our world. These are false messages, as Beth will expound on in the next chapter. Though the Wounded Child is the part of me that longs to run away or fight against the acceptance I need, it is also the part of me that Christ most tenderly invites to come near—to be welcomed, heard, and redeemed.

The Wounded Child's role in each of us is to operate within our primary Enneagram type's "core motivations" to protect us from future pain and rejection, influencing us and relating to us through our longings, fears, desires, and weaknesses. (We will more fully explore these core motivations in part 2.) When our main type is functioning as the Wounded Child, it also becomes the chief interpreter for everything that has happened, is happening, and will happen to us. This wounded way of relating to the *external world* becomes a lens through which we see everything in our own *internal world*. More accurately, the way we see our internal world shapes how we relate to the external world. One is the root, and the other is the fruit. These create a cycle of external and internal realities reinforcing and feeding one another.

This cycle causes us to lead or coach our other parts accordingly (usually unaware we are doing so). We coach ourselves into self-protective or demanding strategies so we don't face more of the same pain. Much like the sheep who runs from the Shepherd, the Wounded Child runs from the Father and the one place where everything it is so desperately searching for is not only already found but also already fully bestowed.

Simply put, the Wounded Child is unaligned with the truth of the gospel—that is, from the realization that there is a Father who has given us a Good Shepherd who always welcomes us with open arms, even when we are stuck in painful or sinful places.

There is good news, though. Our main type can also function as the Beloved Child. This is the same concept of the sheep being held—or as Beth puts it, knowing both who you are and Whose you are. Romans 8:14–16 speaks to the possibility of such a drastic transition from functioning as the Wounded Child to the Beloved Child: "Those who are led by the Spirit of God are the children of God. The Spirit you received does not make you slaves, so that you live in fear again; rather, the Spirit you received brought about your adoption to sonship. And by him we cry, '*Abba*, Father.' The Spirit himself testifies with our spirit that we are God's children."

In this passage, Paul was describing what happens when we begin to relate to the world not through the Wounded Child but through the Beloved Child, who realizes that though it is being drained by the pain of this world, it is also being filled by the Spirit. This part of us is free because it realizes we're no longer slaves to fear. (Fear is one of the core motivations of the Enneagram, as we will learn.) Furthermore, verse 16 promises that we have inner assurance because God's Spirit now testifies with our spirits to the fact that we truly are children of God. Why would we need such assurance unless there are times in our lives when we feel stuck and unassured?

This lends evidence to the fact that sometimes we function as the Wounded Child and sometimes we function as the Beloved Child. The good news is that Christ offers us a path to move from one to the other in real time. By depending on the Holy Spirit and learning to recognize when we are functioning as the Wounded Child, our heart can more easily choose the divinely forged path that leads toward living as the Beloved Child. There is so much more to come, but for now, here are a few clues to decipher between the Wounded Child and the Beloved Child in your own life.[2]

Recognizing Your Wounded Child and Beloved Child

Wounded Child	Beloved Child
• Acts as if God is disappointed	• Knows that the Father is pleased and delighted
• Has self-made rules and focuses on willpower	• Believes and trusts in the finished work of Christ

• Has insecurity around identity, appearance, and reputation	• Has inner peace
• Motivated by guilt and shame in relationship with others	• Motivated by gratitude and authenticity in relationship with others
• Has an ongoing sense of self-rejection	• Finds comfort in the Father's presence
• Comforts and seeks relief through all types of coping behaviors	• Seeks comfort and relief in the Father's love and provision
• Is defensive, justifying, and constantly hides	• Accepts both inner glory and depravity—accepting character defects in light of the Father's love and forgiveness
• Judges through comparing unique gifts to others and measuring oneself against others who have the same gifts	• Appreciates God's design
• Is guarded and distant	• Is warm, hospitable, and engaging
• Lives in bondage	• Lives in freedom
• Fights to meet personal needs	• Trusts that personal needs will be met

The Path Ahead

This book is not just about the Enneagram, and it certainly is not about using the Enneagram to fix ourselves. The Enneagram Internal Profile (EIP) can help novices and seasoned students of the Enneagram learn to lead their internal parts back to the Shepherd, but our goal is not merely to equip you to get yourself unstuck by your own means. In Christ, the end you most desire is already yours because you are already His. There are Christ-centered, practical ways to lead the various parts of your internal world back into this state of awareness so you can once again fully lean into the grace and strength of your Shepherd, resting in the finished work of Christ and applying this daily as a way of living, not just a way of reacting to crisis.

Later, in chapter 8, we will introduce you to a very practical spiritual exercise for applying these principles in real time. It is based on the acronym AWARE, which stands for Awaken, Welcome, Ask, Receive, and Engage. Though we have yet to unpack these ideas, they may seem very simple, but trust us—learning to become aware changes everything. It is not a party trick that suddenly makes everything better. When certain parts of us become negatively activated over an issue with our toddler or teenager, or in the business we lead, becoming aware of what's happening will not necessarily keep these things from happening, or at least happening for a time. But awareness does allow us to reorient our souls back to a place where we can, time and again, embrace our true identities in Christ. In that place, we are reminded of who we are . . . and Whose we are.

But how do we come to our senses when we've yet again become stuck? How do we avoid the shame cycles that so easily beset us? And why do we get stuck so often and in so many different ways unique to who we are? These questions will help us begin the journey of becoming aware.

Throughout the chapters ahead, we will explore the foundational principles of the Enneagram from a gospel-centered perspective. We'll show you how using the Enneagram with EIP will help you accomplish these key milestones:

- You will recognize the conflicting messages and internal dynamics that take place inside you and how they produce your own unique protective strategies and vulnerabilities, leading you to function as either a Beloved Child or a Wounded Child.
- You will identify and name your different "parts" using the Enneagram, including the driving force (core motivations) behind why each of them thinks, feels, and reacts to life in particular ways.

- You will recognize when your parts are operating from places that are misaligned or aligned with the gospel truth.
- We will help you see how the gospel enables you to align your heart with truth, which brings deeper growth and transformation, even as it reduces reactivity, defensiveness, and blaming—and equips you to pursue the positive engagement you are uniquely created for.
- For each Enneagram type, we will help you map out your EIP so you can clearly see and know how to welcome and lead the parts of your inner world toward health, security, and joy.
- You will be able to honor how God has uniquely created you as you apply the finished work of Christ to every part of your life.

The journey ahead will be filled with self-discovery because self-awareness is essential for transformation. You can't change what you're not aware of. This is why Jesus put a special emphasis on being able to see yourself clearly when He invited disciples to be willing to recognize the metaphorical planks in their own eyes (Matthew 7:2–5). Self-discovery was the key to recognition, but it was not the key to transformation—to actually removing the planks. He wanted His disciples to see the problem, which would lead them to see their inability to change it on their own. The planks in our eyes are heavier than we think, but we must at least start with acknowledging their existence.

Self-discovery should never be the complete or ultimate goal of the Enneagram, EIP, or any other tool. As sheep who have often wandered, stumbled, and become stuck, we already know that life is not safe—and that merely learning more about ourselves won't make it so. What it can do, however, is help us, by the power of the Spirit, to deny our fallen instincts to wander and to instead keep coming back and drawing closer to Jesus our Shepherd, not out of guilt, religious duty, or shame, but out of a complete trust in His love, goodness, and purpose for us.

Throughout this book, we will continually remind you of your existing secure status with the Shepherd—and the Father. He knows you and longs for you to experience peace in your relationship with Him, peace in your relationships with one another, peace in relation to your work and circumstances, and peace in relationship to yourself. We hope you will allow Scripture and the wisdom that flows from it to realign your perspective in a way that transforms your life and relationships.

We've heard it said that Christians spend much of their lives trying to get into a room they are already in. We don't have to keep knocking on this particular door, the one that brings us into the good graces of our Shepherd and Father. The door has already been opened. In fact, we aren't the ones who knocked—Christ knocked first. "Here I am! *I* stand at the door and knock. If anyone hears my voice and opens the door, I will come in and eat with that person, and they with me" (Revelation 3:20, emphasis added).

All we long for in the end is already ours in Christ. Why, then, should we continue to live oblivious or stuck in so many areas of life, especially when God cares so much about these parts within us? As you read, we hope you become aware of the following:

1. You keep getting stuck in life because you have internal parts that respond to circumstances in varying ways (*introduction, chapters 1–2*).
2. These internal parts can be aligned or misaligned with gospel truth (*introduction, chapters 1–2*).
3. The Enneagram offers a GPS-style framework for understanding your main type and how it relates to and interacts with the respective types of your other internal parts, which include your main type, your two wings, and your two Enneagram paths (*chapters 3–4*).
4. By developing your own unique EIP, you can begin becoming aware in real time of the patterns that keep causing your main type to function as either a Wounded Child or a Beloved Child (*chapter 5; EIP templates for all nine types are provided in part 3*).

5. By implementing the AWARE strategy, you can lead your main type back to the gospel truth of its Beloved Child status so it can in turn coach, lead, and shepherd (in real time) your entire profile of internal parts out of misalignment and back into alignment and health *(chapter 6; EIP templates for all nine types are provided in part 3).*

Exploring the nuances of your own EIP will reveal once and for all that you are more than a number (or nine numbers, or a million numbers). Meticulously made in the image of God, your inner world is like no one else's—and each part of you is loved and welcomed to freedom. That's something worth the work of becoming aware.

TWO

Recognizing the Fog Within

AN INTRODUCTORY GLIMPSE OF THE PARTS THAT
MAKE UP YOUR ENNEAGRAM INTERNAL PROFILE

"Whoa, slow down, Jeff!"

At that moment, any motion felt dangerous. I (Beth) didn't want to move another inch, no matter how fast or slow we might try.

We had just begun to drive across the Natchez Trace Parkway Bridge, a magnificent structure resting on two enormous arches. If tall bridges make you nervous, just stay home. (Trust me on this one!) This concrete wonder is 1,572 feet long and 145 feet high. And if that isn't enough, its terrifying-for-acrophobics passage isn't even over a river or a lake. No, it towers over a heavily wooded valley and a highway, State Route 96, neither of which would make for a very soft landing in the highly likely case (or at least that's how it felt) that our car would soon careen over the low guardrail. On a clear day, the beauty of the Tennessee hills surrounding this magnificent bridge makes the drive worthwhile.

But on this day, I could not see anything because of the dense fog that had descended on the valley floor, and that's why I was pleading for

Jeff to slow down. Only a few moments before, I had been completely confident in the boundaries of the road, the safety of the car in which we were riding, and yes, even in Jeff's ability to drive. But now, with the fog surrounding us as we drove over this towering bridge, I felt suddenly, utterly, and completely lost and scared. In that moment, it seemed as if all options for safe navigation were gone. I just wanted us to pull over, stop moving, and wait for the fog to lift.

Of course, the road, the bridge, and all elements of the safe and reliable path ahead had not actually disappeared. They were only hidden from sight on that day and at that time. A part of me understood the truth, so I wanted to relax and believe the best about what might happen if we kept driving. Knowing myself, a part of me also wanted to be quiet, avoid conflict, and not upset Jeff. But there was another part of me that was anxious, imagining all the worst-case scenarios. Still another part of me wanted to correct Jeff's driving. (Jeff loves that part.) Another part wanted to protect us by getting more intense and trying to control his driving, while another part was afraid of looking foolish by revealing such deep anxiety.

Each of these parts was competing to get what it desired and to avoid its fears. These internal fights and dialogues can wreak havoc within my soul. This chaos often spills over into the ways I relate to others. I get frustrated with this internal tug-of-war between so many parts, even trying to ignore them, but that tends only to make things worse. They tend to get louder and more demanding. When these parts are ignored, dismissed, or shamed, they dig in their heels, sending me deeper into disorientation and disintegration. I then become angry with these competing parts, wishing they would just go away and leave me alone. I see them as the problem.

Before learning that I am more than my number, I lived as many of us do. We often fail to realize that our unawareness of our internal parts and our misaligned ways of approaching their needs are the greater problems. Especially in moments, events, patterns, or circumstances that activate things within us we wish weren't there, we lash out, clam up, or run away. We tend not to recognize that each of our parts is a gift from God, and that when all our parts are aligned, they reveal strength, creativity, security, beauty—and a million shades in the kaleidoscope of wonder and peace that the Father desires for us.

When I live unaware of these things, it can keep me from navigating the effects of the internal fog that each of us faces within. Our densely clouded internal worlds disenfranchise our souls from the healthy, authentic versions of ourselves that we know we were divinely created to be. For me, there are times I want to avoid dealing with my issues because they seem too big or too overwhelming. I often don't know where to begin—that is, how to take the first step without being swallowed whole by my emotions or distress.

When implemented through the lens of the gospel, tools like the Enneagram and our unique EIP can equip us to recognize—that is, to be aware of—what we can and can't see so we can navigate the fog differently. We can walk forward according to who we actually are in Christ (His Beloved Child) and not who we feel like in moments of stress (an orphaned, Wounded Child). We don't have to remain paralyzed—or angry, controlling, reckless, or whatever unhealthy pattern characterizes our reaction to the fog—every time it sets in.

I often don't recognize when my parts are misaligned with the truth of the gospel because they speak very convincing but very false messages. When I live unaware, I tend to believe these false messages, even if I know them to be untrue from a theological or a logical standpoint. These false messages impede my growth and derail me from God's healthiest plan for my life. They shape how I relate to others and to myself—and they keep me stuck in the fog. Yet when my internal parts are aligned with the gospel, I experience peace and confidence in my relationship to God, others, and myself.

The Enneagram coupled with the strategy of an EIP has helped Jeff and me see more clearly what is happening within us so we can approach our painful, overwhelming, or confusing places in safe and effective ways, rather than avoid them altogether. This concept has given us the ability to break free in the moment from unhealthy patterns and to be ready if these patterns return later. Through this process we have learned how to be kind, gentle, compassionate, and patient toward the parts within us— to be friends with our whole selves in the same way Christ is a Friend to our whole selves. In turn, this enables us to extend these same healthy qualities to others.

By seeing how each of my parts compose the whole of me, I can now care for, guide, and even self-coach them toward health from a gospel-centered perspective. In short, I must better understand myself so I can lead my various parts through the fog that often hides God's truth I desperately need: that the gospel has declared me His Beloved Child.

Understanding and Leading Your Internal Parts

Especially in moments of stress, our internal fog can obscure healthy paths before us. We often do not understand ourselves or why we do what we do. Many people live unaware of why the fog comes, how it consistently derails them, or how to humbly and healthily lead their own souls through it. Even though the same things happen to them over and over, they are always a little shocked at the negative effects of their unawareness. They feel helpless to lead themselves, often thinking that doing so is some sort of self-help nonsense. After all, Jesus is all we really need, right?

But what if Jesus wants to help us respond to the Spirit's leading so we can align ourselves with truth? He does—and that is why when we say "lead ourselves," we don't mean "be our own saviors." Only the grace found in the gospel can transform us. Even so, as Christ does this transformative work through His Spirit, He intends for the fruit of self-control, which is being divinely nurtured and matured within us by His Spirit, to spur us on toward this transformation. He is not just enacting change upon us, apart from us. Rather, He is transforming us through our very lives, even the resistant, stuck, or foggy parts of them.

Through His work in us, we can understand and welcome our conflicting internal emotions instead of experiencing shame or anger over them, which leads us to either reject them or react negatively to their overwhelming influence. By grace, we can instead accept, listen to, and lead the parts that make up our own internal worlds, reminding each of them of what is most true in the gospel. In other words, when we learn to become aware of and lead our internal parts, we do not bypass the work of Christ; they are integral elements of that very work.

But is this work biblical, or is it just a religious spin on a worldly idea of self-appreciation and self-help? Paul pondered this line of questioning in Romans 7:15: "I do not understand my own actions. For I do not do what I want, but I do the very thing I hate" (ESV). The New Living Translation of the first few words of this verse expresses the whole of the matter in a way all of us can relate to: "I don't really understand myself."

Because of Adam and Eve, we are born into *fallenness*. And along the way, we each choose *sinfulness*. These two factors contribute to our inability to clearly understand ourselves. The psalmist referred to this when he said, "My sins have overtaken me, and I cannot see" (Psalm 40:12). This state of being keeps us from "seeing" clearly in the fog around us. But we weren't meant to stay there.

Christ is actively redeeming all things from humankind's fallenness, and we are invited to be included in this ongoing process of redemption. This means that though we will never fully arrive on this side of the fall—that is, have complete clarity on and self-control over every internal part in every situation—we can develop patterns for welcoming and rewelcoming the ongoing work of Christ in these fallen places, even when we fall yet again.

Scripture calls this being transformed by the renewing of our minds (Romans 12:1–2). This is a present-tense process, which indicates that we will constantly, actively need to be renewed. How can this be okay? Shouldn't we finally get it right? Remember, the heart of our Shepherd never tires of us. Especially in our foggiest moments—in our fallenness and sinfulness—He actually draws closer.

David seemed to already understand this nature of God, as well as his own lack of awareness of his internal world and its parts. He expressed his own journey into the vast, dense fog within himself by saying to God, "You formed my inward parts; you knitted me together in my mother's womb. I praise you, for I am fearfully and wonderfully made. Wonderful are your works; my soul knows it very well. My frame was not hidden from you, when I was being made in secret, intricately woven in the depths of the earth" (Psalm 139:13–15 ESV).

If you are a Christ-follower, you are probably already familiar with this passage. Its most common modern application references the wonder and beauty of God's formation of the trillions of coalescing variables that make up the body and brain of a precious, unborn child being developed in her mother's womb. So many miracles happen in this environment, sometimes minute by minute. This is certainly an accurate way to apply these verses.

But we can also think of this in much broader terms than just the body or the brain. Specifically, we can also ascribe to God the unfathomable number of less-observable aspects of His creative genius. If you're a parent, you've already had a front-row seat to the divine development of these other "inward parts"—that is, the completely unique characteristics, personalities, and dispositions that accompany our children at birth. Yes, most babies are blessed with the same set of internal organs and outward extremities, but each is also uniquely, "intricately woven" by God into his or her own distinctive self. We often fail to acknowledge that this weaving is more complex and miraculous than mere sinew and synapses.

All your parts, including the unseen parts of your internal world, reflect the beautiful and gracious complexity of God's handiwork.

Yet David didn't just point out the fact that he had parts he didn't understand. This was only the first step on his journey to becoming aware. He also invited God to help him see these parts accurately, as well as help them become aligned to God's ways. "Search me, O God, and know my heart; test me and know my anxious thoughts. Point out anything in me that offends you, and lead me along the path of everlasting life" (Psalm 139:23–24 NLT).

We tend to read this in a modern context and assume that David is asking God to know his "heart" as a singular thing. In our culture of extremes, this is how we see people and the world. "This guy is good, while that guy is bad." "This viewpoint is perfect, while that viewpoint is garbage."

But pay attention to David's prayer: "Point out *anything* in me that offends you." This speaks to the fact that David assumed there was more than one part of his heart that needed God's interventional care. He didn't just say, "Fix my heart in one fell swoop!" Yes, that would be great, but David seemed to know that there was more than one thing going on inside him. He also seemed to know that he could seek God's help in learning to recognize those parts for himself, which is why he invited God to "point out" what was going on in all the parts of his internal world, even those that were repeat offenders.

We've already acknowledged that we all have areas of repeated offense, but *discovery* of these parts is not *recovery* from their patterns. Stepping on a scale is a very important component of beginning healthier patterns toward physical fitness, but merely weighing yourself doesn't cause you to lose weight. There has to be more than just the knowledge of what needs to change. We must walk a continual path so change can occur consistently and incrementally.

As we learn to understand and lead our parts closer to Christ by the strength He affords us, the Holy Spirit does the heavy lifting of transformation *within us*—but He doesn't do it *without us*. An ancient quote often attributed (though unproven) to Saint Augustine sums it up nicely: "Without God, I can't. But without me, God won't."[1] In other words, God desires relationship, and relationships require mutual participation.

Much of the "change" language Paul used in Ephesians 4:21–24 tells us that we should constantly be tending to our internal parts.

> Since you have heard about Jesus and have learned the truth that comes from him, *throw off* your old sinful nature and your former way of life, which is corrupted by lust and deception. Instead, let the Spirit renew your thoughts and attitudes. *Put on* your new nature, created to be like God—truly righteous and holy. (NLT, emphasis added)

Take note of the active, present nature of these verses. "Throw off" and "put on" indicate something you are invited—even compelled by grace—to do today. Right now. In this very moment.

In moments of misalignment, if you believe you are only one thing ("I'm just an idiot," "I have good reasons for incessantly screaming," or the like), throwing off whatever seems "bad" leads you to condemn, shame, or ignore only one thing: yourself. This is "all or nothing" thinking.

But since you are intricately, miraculously, wonderfully woven as a whole person with multiple parts, there are elements within yourself that can be identified and shepherded when they become misaligned. You are of infinite value to your Father, and your heavenly Brother, Jesus, has not only died to redeem you but also lives to constantly intercede and advocate on your behalf. This frees you to focus on your misaligned parts not so you can condemn them, but rather so you can understand them and once again become aligned with the grace and truth of the gospel.

Welcoming Our Parts

Many people reach a point when they realize that while a part of their soul wants to fully embrace Christ's call to continual newness in the gospel, other parts keep protesting, acting out, or otherwise going to war against them—and against God. We often end up hating these parts of our inner selves for their constant troublemaking.

This divided feeling also makes some of us feel unsettled, unsure, or ashamed—and we don't know why we keep experiencing these same pitfalls. In fact, knowing that these derailments are coming and yet not being able to avoid them only erodes our confidence even more. Even if we know at our core that we are the Beloved Child, why is there such a disconnect between what we believe and how we react in certain situations? Why is there so much distance between what we know to be true and what we experience in our internal world?

In the next several chapters, we will use the principles of the Enneagram as our own internal GPS to help close the gap between the false messages of our inner parts and the truthful embrace of our Shepherd. Then, by using our unique EIPs to zoom in on who God created us to be, we will develop an adaptable map for understanding and navigating the complexities of our internal dynamics. This process will help you see your own internal parts as members of an internal team who can win, lose, and do a hundred things in between.

Another way to think of it is in terms of family.[2] Just as each of us has a family on the outside—healthy, unhealthy, known, or unknown—each of us has the same on the inside. The goal for every member of an external family is to find roles that work well for the individual and for the good of the whole family unit. Likewise, your own unique internal Enneagram "parts" can be identified, addressed, and led into healthier reactions and interactions within the various parts of your heart.

The Enneagram offers uniquely effective insights into this process of identifying and addressing these parts. It reveals how our primary types relate to our other EIP members, each as different Enneagram types themselves. Even though each of us use all nine types to varying degrees, our thoughts, feelings, and reactions stem mostly from six distinct parts of our personality revealed through the Enneagram.[3] We will more clearly define these six parts in part 2.

For now, just know that it can feel as if these parts are competing for control and attention to ensure that their needs are provided for. Our parts do not necessarily operate autonomously, but they do express their particular type's strategies as they relate to our main type, either protecting the Wounded Child (when we are misaligned with gospel truth) or being led by the Beloved Child (when we are aligned with gospel truth). When our parts are trying to protect the Wounded Child, the fog sets in and we become unclear on who is right or who to listen to.

While we haven't yet mapped out our EIP members or explored their core motivations or strategies in relation to our main type, it is imperative that we first realize that our EIP does not lead us to resent the internal parts within us. When we do this, we alienate our own souls, because condemnation and shame do not lead to change. Only frustration. Actually, it's not knowledge, discipline, or force—but "God's kindness [that] is meant to lead you to repentance [change]" (Romans 2:4 ESV). By the grace extended to us through the gospel, we can learn to be kind to our internal parts—to welcome and listen to them rather than deny or betray them.[4] After all, Christ has already redeemed them, so why should we condemn them?

This is not to say that we don't willfully sin—we do. Despite this, each of our parts is well meaning, though often misguided. Many sins are the result of bad actions taken out of desperate intentions to make something better. Understanding this intention is the key to not overlooking their often-sinful approaches, while extending to them the same grace given to us through our Good Shepherd. We can extend kindness to them not out of self-justification or overt neglect to acknowledge sin, but rather because we acknowledge that the price of our sin and fallenness has already been fully paid in Christ.

The fact that our parts are sinful should only compel us all the more to extend to them compassion, grace, and love. This is the way of Jesus. His kindness to those who did not deserve it earned Him the title "friend of tax collectors and sinners" (Matthew 11:19). Obviously, neither we nor the biblical writers are suggesting that kindness toward our sinful parts gives us a license to sin (Romans 6:1–2). We simply mean that Christ is kind to sinners, so in His grace, we can approach our sinful parts with His kindness (which has been fully imparted to us) apart from condemnation.

In this context, we can understand that each of our parts intends to work toward the purpose of helping us, even when their patterns hurt us instead. Each part is influenced by their own type's core motivations, but these never override or replace the core motivations of our main type, which is why understanding your main type is so critical.[5]

Regardless, when we are operating as the Wounded Child, our parts see, interpret, and react to life through their own unique lenses and demand that we meet the Wounded Child's needs according to their ways of interacting with the world. If these needs or desires are not satisfied, their type's defensive strategies activate thoughts, feelings, and behaviors to get these needs met and protect the Wounded Child—that is, to protect us. Each part feels that its perspective and approach will prove most effective at meeting the needs of the core motivations of its main type. Therefore, each part that is activated within us fights to fulfill our core motivations, using whatever means necessary to tilt our mindfulness in their direction. Each part is fighting to help us feel safe and content.

In this internal fight during foggy moments, each "family member" has its own defensive approach reflective of their Enneagram type's unique makeup—just like your external family! Since each member believes its perspective is the correct one, when these parts are not healthy (not aligned with gospel truth and not being led well by your main type functioning as the Beloved Child), they draw us into familiar pitfalls that ultimately lead to personal, relational, and professional harm.

In other words, in trying to help us, our parts often end up sabotaging us. Again, this is why awareness is so crucial. What doomed and sank the *Titanic* was a failure to see what lay beneath the surface. We all have mass layers, or parts, below the waterline that need our attention. The Enneagram can help us become more aware of each part's defensive patterns so we can effectively shepherd each part back into gospel health—that is, we can engage each part of ourselves in what we call "gospel self-talk." Once our parts are realigned with the gospel, it is impossible to overstate the value they bring to our lives. The Father made us to reflect His image, and it is in these aligned parts of our inner worlds that we see infinitesimal nuances of His divine soul reflected in the prism of our human soul.

These are the general concepts of understanding and leading the parts of your own internal world that we will build on in the chapters to come. For now, it may help to see how we once became seriously lost together in a fog—and how these basic concepts of EIP contributed to our surprising journey toward clarity.

THREE

Waking the Beloved Child

How Your Aligned or Misaligned Self
Relates to Your Internal Parts

I (Jeff) am a Type Six, also known as the Faithful Guardian. While some Sixes resource themselves by seeking outside guidance to avoid fear, some dive right into it. I'm the second kind—I generally process fear by trying to overcome it. This expression of my type is called a counterphobic Type Six. My go-to move in my own internal fog has never been to stop moving but rather to forge ahead. But throughout my life, this has not been because I have no fear; rather, I have always tried to outrun my fears rather than sit in them or live truly aware of all their nuances. No matter what appearances may seem, I am often quite scared on the inside at a very real level, which is based on the core motivations of being an Enneagram Type Six, as we will soon explore.

As a husband and a pastor, I have spent much of my life in the same patterns—appearing to be one way and even performing to a certain standard on the outside, but never really inviting the inner part of me that was always scared to share the reasons it felt that way.

When Beth and I first found out about the Enneagram, I latched onto the idea that I was a Type Eight: the Passionate Protector. I wanted to elevate the concept of myself as someone who was powerful, self-confident, decisive, willful, and even confrontational. I didn't want to recognize the fear and anxiety that was underneath it all.

I portrayed a tough yet charming exterior that was both provocative and playful, which often came out in the form of passive-aggressive sarcasm. But there has always been a younger, childlike part of my heart that feels much different. Though you heard how I drive in literal fog, my inclination to drive faster through my own internal fog is not because I'm instinctively brave but because I'm instinctively scared.

This life in ministry with Beth and our team is so fulfilling, but if we're not careful, the pace and expectations can overwhelm us in our lives and our marriage. We can spin out and misfire with one another, even though we're not really apart. In these moments, this inner part of me expresses itself in declarations of abandonment and loneliness, despite Beth never abandoning me or even walking away.

As a Six, these times find me searching for something outside of myself that will help resolve this internal scarcity—something that will assuage the fear, insecurity, or anxiety. I long for something to calm my heart. I sometimes find moments of serenity in my relationships with Beth, the kids, or my friends. But even when their presence settles my soul for a moment, it promotes the feeling that I may someday lose them all. My heart is not actually being calmed; it is merely being pacified. But deep down I live in constant fear of losing these relationships. This is one part of my internal world that continually leaves me feeling lost and on the edge of disaster.

But why does this part of me often cloud every good thing in a constant fear of abandonment? Why does it protest so loudly in moments of stress, rendering the rest of my internal team overwhelmed and anxious?

For the first fifteen years of marriage, I never entertained what was bothering this part of me, but it just wouldn't stop vying for my attention.

It all came to a head when we were living in Normal, Illinois (yes, that is a real place, and yes, it is normal). The other normal thing was the familiar fighting between Beth and me; if you've been married longer than a honeymoon, you know what I mean. There are well-worn ruts in long-standing relationships into which friends, family, or couples constantly fall, causing seemingly new conflicts that are just reiterations of the old. I don't remember what specific event threw us back into that ditch, but we had been married long enough that I knew how it would play out and where it would lead. Yet I couldn't stop it from happening.

It was a familiar dance for us. I would lead by making myself very big—loud, boisterous, and intense. And this led Beth to become very small—quiet, wounded, and withdrawn. Her reaction activated certain feelings in me, mainly that she was trying to opt out of the conversation and not engage this conflict alongside me so we could find a resolution together. It felt like she was bailing on our relationship (or abandoning me), which increased my need to get bigger, only making her get smaller. Rinse and repeat.

On this day, the cycle was especially bad. In fact, Beth finally left the kitchen table and retreated upstairs to bury herself in the covers. Even though I was the anxious pursuer, when she left the room (and every time she would leave the room), it engulfed my inner world in flames of emotional abandonment (one of the greatest fears of a Type Six). She was only upstairs, but I felt a crippling fear that she was gone—like, really gone. I suddenly began weighing all that I had to do to get her back and to repair the situation. So I pursued her, as was my pattern.

In my state of panic, fear, and anger, I literally yelled the words "I love you!" at Beth, completely overwhelming her. She was balled up under the covers and weeping, just trying to figure out what was happening inside her. All the while, I was still intensely pursuing her, trying to sound compassionate but coming across harshly. It wasn't working. But as I prepared for my next step in this familiar pattern—to leave the room and slam the door—this time I felt God's Spirit leading me in a different direction. In a divine moment beyond my own ability to conjure, I instantly became aware of what my heart was so afraid of. It was something I had never before been able to articulate.

Exasperated, I turned to look at Beth, who was utterly destroyed. Talking this out with her looked impossible, so I spoke this new awareness in the form of a question instead: "Are you going to leave me now?"

I'll let her reveal her reply to my question, but this moment of awareness—of really hearing this internal part express what was bothering me—began a new journey toward change in my life. It revealed a core fear and some deep-seated memories from early childhood, especially surrounding the fact that I was adopted, which I will talk about in greater detail in the chapters ahead. I began to see how this internal part's fears—and one experience in particular—had, unbeknownst to me, been affecting everything I had ever done, from playing football to pastoring to communicating with family and friends to stepping into the entrepreneurial world in which we live now.

This is such a core memory and moment of change in my life because it's when I realized that I constantly bear an insatiable need to grip everything of value in my life, keeping it from slipping away. This burden is always there, though not always as heavy. It contracts and expands within my soul like an accordion; at times I have a deeper fear of abandonment, while at other times it's a more surface-level fear. But it never leaves, and no matter what good comes to my family or career, I am always waiting for it to all come to an end—to be abandoned by those who love me and to lose everything that matters to me. Not that I have ever suffered on Job's level, but I at least have a basic understanding of what he meant when he said, "My inward parts are in turmoil and never still" (Job 30:27 ESV). Stillness in my inward parts is hard to come by because each part is vying for something—and sometimes, one or two parts try to take over so much that I lose sight of my authentic self.

Welcoming the part of me that was terrified of abandonment was the beginning of a long journey. But becoming aware of which parts of me needed to hear the reassurances of the gospel in my scariest moments changed everything. Now I had a way to stop recklessly running headlong through a blind abyss to find safety and escape. Instead, I began to see steps to navigate toward the next point of actual transformation of my inner world.

How deeply grateful I was for this new reality.

What's Behind Our Dance?

When I (Beth) say that this argument with Jeff was a dance we both knew, I mean that we could have won *Dancing with the Stars*. Instead of dancing with celebrities, though, we were in a pattern of misunderstanding and hurting one another. (Not sure what that show would be called, but I doubt it would be renewed for a second season.)

When Jeff finally asked me, "Are you going to leave me now?" I was shocked. He had no idea what was going on inside me at that moment, but none of it had anything to do with leaving him.

"No, dummy! I'm never going to leave you!" I said with all the grace I could muster amid the gathering tears.

At that moment, he had finally revealed a key clue to why we had been engaging in this dance for so long. But he wasn't the only dance partner on the floor. In fact, there were more than two of us. There were many dancers—many members of each of our EIPs—who were contributing to each stepped-on toe, twisted ankle, and yes, full-out collapse into the punch bowl. Each part was playing . . . well, a part.

I am an Enneagram Type Nine, also known as the Peaceful Accommodator. The way I view foggy moments like my argument with Jeff is to fixate on the fact that he is getting more intense, more passionate, and more filled with emotional energy. For a Nine, these things signal trouble. Even when I sense trouble that's not directed at me, such escalation feels like a thick, heavy, wet blanket over me. Being under that blanket is emotionally suffocating to a Nine.

At that moment, I didn't understand why everything had to get so big because, in my Type Nine internal world, big means bad. Big means the potential of conflict or of losing connection. Big means that I've done something wrong. This is why I generally attempt to reposition a heated conversation in a way that lowers the intensity, which often leads me to not saying anything at all out of fear that it will only agitate or frustrate the other party more. In this case, I wanted to bring calm and peace, but to Jeff, my reactions felt like I was not being honest or authentic with what was really going on. When he escalated and I tried to de-escalate, each of us activated negative cycles and negative reactions from our internal parts, even as we were both trying to solve the problem at hand.

As I learned my own EIP, I found that it helped to actually name my parts. No, this does not mean I literally have other people living inside my psyche. It is merely an applicable strategy that helps us to not only name but also understand the motivation and patterns of these various parts.

One part of my heart is a member I call "Little Bethy." She is the part that always feels threatened or wounded, which are common feelings for everyone, but especially Nines. She is the Wounded Child part of my main type. In my case, Little Bethy fears not making people happy and that people might be upset with her. She tends to feel that her presence doesn't matter—that her voice doesn't matter either. She worries that she'll be overlooked and will not maintain good relationships with others. She just wants peace and harmony—and for everyone to have a place at the table so they can all be seen and heard, respected, and cared for.

In moments that feel like they are ramping up or escalating, Little Bethy begins to feel anxious. She wonders, *What did I just do? Why is he so upset? Why can't I get this right?* Nines work hard to clearly understand and respect the perspectives of all the other types—that is, we get people. We know how to accommodate and navigate conversations in such a way that will bring peace and stability. When this assumption fails, we don't understand, and we can fall apart. We try to accommodate, but sometimes it just doesn't work.

Little Bethy will often tell me that I must not be good enough, or else Jeff wouldn't be so intense or raise his voice. He would positively respond to my requests to lower the volume, but this only makes him angrier instead. So I figure this must be my fault. For Nines, it's like there's a two-liter soda bottle inside with the lid screwed down tight on life's circumstances. When people begin to shake it up with their intensity, passion, or anger, it feels like they are shaking our internal worlds—and the pressure and tension begin to painfully build. Yet we're afraid to release our feelings or to finally blow everything up because that will only make things worse, proving that we're not good enough to calm the situation.

It's easier to just exit the situation to reduce the pressure. If we can't physically leave, we may simply withdraw emotionally and go inward, which looks like being quiet or disengaged. For me, I might even dissociate or numb out completely, which, in this case, makes Jeff feel even deeper feelings of abandonment and only intensifies the whole dynamic. Can you see how all this plays out and why this was a familiar dance we did for so many years?

As we will continue to learn in the chapters to come, in addition to our main type being either aligned as the Beloved Child or misaligned as the Wounded Child, there are four other parts that show up the most in our internal worlds. This is our first mention of these parts, so there's no need to fully understand them. Just know that these other four parts function as four different Enneagram types related to our main type through our two "wings" and our two Enneagram "paths," which the EIP will help us to discover. As we learn more about the Enneagram type of each of our parts, we will better understand what each part feels, thinks, and does during moments of distress. For me, each of them shows up and tries to help me deal with the fog. I will identify each of their Enneagram types, but only as examples of how this works—again, you don't yet need to know what these types mean or how they work.

As we've seen, when Little Bethy, the Wounded Child, has been activated, she can become sad, distraught, or withdrawn. That is often when my Type Six part (whom I will name later in the book) begins to chime in. This part begins to think through and offer a vast array of opinions about all the possible outcomes that could result from this situation. When healthy, this part is a such a gift because it is so dependable and brave, able to foresee possible pitfalls and help me avoid them from a place of wisdom and caution rather than crippling fear. But when it is not operating in a healthy way, it focuses on worst-case scenarios in my relationship with Jeff. If I make a move this way or that, it lays out hundreds of possibilities—and of course, since I don't know which one to choose, I withdraw even deeper.

That is when my Type Three (the Admirable Achiever) part shows up. When aligned, I need this part to show up because it is such an efficient and capable go-getter, even affirming me through the struggle. But when my Wounded Child is activated, this part does not show up aligned. Seeing where I am, it agrees that I'm not good enough, but also points out that I'm failing to some degree, which is causing it to panic. It begins with my failure in my relationship with Jeff, but then moves on to my deficiencies as a mom, pastor's wife, and ministry leader. It tells me that I'm not good enough because I can't perform or excel in these areas.

The next part to show up and add its two cents is my Type One (the Principled Reformer) part. Since I am already vulnerable and dealing with all the banter between the Six and the Three as they try to manage various protection strategies, the Type One can really cause me harm. Everything is black and white to it, which can be so helpful when my internal world is in alignment, helping me see the best path to take that can get so easily lost in the grays of the fog. But since I'm misaligned, it immediately begins trying to fix this situation so I can finally get out of it. Of course, since Little Bethy is still paralyzed and won't receive this bombardment of advice, this part becomes more vicious than the other two and really dives into all the reasons that I'm a bad wife and a bad mom. It produces a black-and-white list of my missteps—not just what I've done to fail, but also how I'm fundamentally bad at a heart level.

This Type One part is trying to whip me into shape so I will do better, but its criticism feels like someone is beating me with a baseball bat. It hopes I will shake myself free and get on the right track, but these tactics rarely work. At this point, none of my parts know how to fix me—and all of them have only pointed out that I'm not good enough. Hopelessness begins to set in. When each of them is not healthy or aligned with gospel truth, their thoughts and ongoing input into my mind reinforce the core lie of a Nine (my main type): that my voice and my presence do not matter and will not make a difference. I should not assert myself. Since I only cause harm, I should leave and disappear.

When I reach the floor of hopelessness, my Type Eight part makes an appearance. And let me tell you, it's flippin' mad when it shows up! Since I'm misaligned with gospel truth, instead of its wonderfully bold and powerful approach to fight for the right cause, it now wants to protect Little Bethy at all costs. As it sees the onslaught of the others, it steps in and tries to plow over everyone else's insight—and not just over my internal family members, but also my real family members. It tries to plow over Jeff and sometimes even the kids. After all, enough is enough! My Type Eight part can be passive-aggressive, or it can be aggressive-aggressive. Regardless, it tries to burn it all to the ground to salvage what little life remains.

Finally, as the relational dynamics are getting worse, Little Bethy suddenly makes it clear that she has had enough. Even though the Type Eight may talk the biggest game, Little Bethy is the most powerful, and her final defensive strategy is to act the quitter. She knows how to shut everything down and shut everyone out—for good. If this whole scenario were a bank robbery and we were in danger, where my Type Eight part has failed through its anger and bravado to neutralize the emotional threats by force, Little Bethy's quitter defensive mode activates the fail-safe option, in this case locking all of us in the bank vault where no one can get in and no one can get out. This is why Jeff usually leaves the room and slams the door; he knows that when Little Bethy has activated the fail-safe, I'm now unreachable.

While trapped in the vault alone and isolated, my other parts also continue their attempts to help with their own unhealthy Enneagram defensive strategies, which feel to me like attacks. It is here that Little Bethy is all alone, yet she is tormented by so many parts that point out her failures. It is a damaging and painful place for Little Bethy.

How does she get out of this dark fog?

The great news is that there is a path that can help her become aware and find the healthy, gospel-aligned self that Christ has made her to be.

Waking Coach Beth

I call my healthy, gospel-aligned self "Coach Beth"—my Enneagram Nine part who is functioning as the Beloved Child. Coach Beth can see the good intentions of all these parts and can help guide and navigate them toward healthy ways of relating to one another and others. But when Coach Beth doesn't show up, all my other parts can and will run amok. So where the heck has she been this whole time, when we all needed her the most?

In *Boundaries for Your Soul*, counselors Dr. Alison Cook and Kimberly Miller MTh, LMFT, liken this phenomenon of the healthy part being absent in key moments to a bus being driven by scared kids while the adult is asleep on the back seat.[1] When we are not aligned as the Beloved Child, we are unaware of what our parts need. Since no one is at the wheel, they take over and do their best to drive, but from an immature and ignorant position that ultimately leads to destructive outcomes. In my case, Coach Beth needs to wake up, show up, evaluate the situation, gain clarity, find insight, and ultimately bring encouragement and direction to everyone on the bus (all my parts).

In each of our internal worlds, we must wake up and see that the kids (the unattended, misaligned parts within us) are afraid and desire a mature adult to drive the bus so each of them can get to their desired destination safely, calmly, and enjoyably. To bring stability to these parts, we must take charge of our lives and inner worlds with the courage and compassion God offers us through the gospel and His Spirit. We must calmly and lovingly take over the wheel, reassuring our parts that we are now in control and that we understand why they were so frightened.

Whenever we are not internally experiencing or expressing love, joy, peace, patience, kindness, goodness, gentleness, faithfulness, and self-control (Galatians 5:22), our inner parts are not being led by the Spirit empowering our Beloved Child. This means someone else is driving the bus—and someone is always at the wheel.

When our Wounded Child is driving instead of our mature and healthy self, we are usually headed for a ditch. But when we surrender and depend on the Holy Spirit to help our Beloved Child drive the bus and lead our parts, we will display that love, joy, peace, patience, kindness, goodness, gentleness, faithfulness, and self-control—the very fruits of His Spirit. When this happens, our parts calm down and enjoy the ride, trusting that our mature, healthier self has their best interests in mind.

The big questions are: Why do we leave the driver's seat and go to the back to fall asleep? Why did we let the kids (the less healthy parts within us) put the Wounded Child behind the wheel of the bus when we know it is incapable of safely navigating to the correct destination? It's not that we're always asleep in the back of the bus. Sometimes, our parts don't fully trust our leadership, so they try to take over out of desperation and fear. They feel it is up to them to save themselves and their desires.

This is why not being attuned to our internal parts' needs leads to personal and relational harm. We must learn to be both courageous and knowledgeable when addressing each aspect of ourselves. We must listen to their concerns and reassure them, meeting them where they are most scared with loving truth. Tenderly addressing them will calm them down. They will *take a seat* rather than *take over*. They are well meaning but still capable of sin, so they need healthy boundaries. Thankfully, God has given us wisdom and truth in the Holy Spirit to help us grow and establish these essential boundaries for our internal parts.

The Enneagram provides us with clarity and insight into what is happening within us so we can become more equipped to lead our parts with wholeheartedness as the Beloved Child, even when our hearts feel divided by their motivations and strategies. In Christ, they can all be led with joyful security in the same direction because the Beloved Child is behind the wheel.

In our online community focused on clarity, connection, and growth, we hear from thousands of people just like you who long to wake the Beloved Child within their inner worlds. I empathize with them because my daily struggle is to wake up Coach Beth and keep her actively guiding my internal team. We want to help you learn how to continually awaken your Beloved Child as well.

For Jeff and me, this journey has led us to new awareness. Becoming aware of our EIPs continues to revolutionize the ways we approach our old patterns that used to land us lost in the fog with the Wounded Child at the wheel and scared kids in the seats. These concepts are not just relevant to our individual selves or our marriage. These apply to friendships, parenting, professional interactions, and so much more. Anywhere you are and God is, your internal world is at play and can be either aligned or misaligned with His truth.

We now have a better path: applying the gospel as we utilize the tool of the EIP. But before we can dive deeper into your EIP, we must explore the basics of the Enneagram itself.

PART TWO

Exploring the Enneagram and Your Enneagram Internal Profile (EIP)

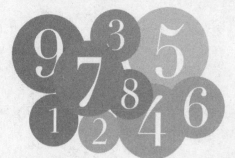

FOUR

Activating Your Internal GPS with the Enneagram

An Enneagram Primer for Everyone

Regardless of your previous level of exposure or your lack of familiarity with the Enneagram, this chapter will provide a brief overview. If you are already familiar with these concepts, we invite you to read through this content not only as a refresher but also to help you become better equipped to explore your own EIP in the coming chapters. If you are a newbie, then this chapter is crucial for you as well, for obvious reasons. Don't forget that you can also visit YourEnneaPath (https://www.youren-neagramprofile.com/resources) for additional tools and resources for understanding and applying the tool of the Enneagram in your own life.

We learned in the last chapter that false messages often derail us, leaving us lost in the fog of our familiar circumstances and reactions. To become healthier and more like Christ, we must become aware of these false messages, turn from them, and live in gospel truth instead. Romans 12:1–2 describes this process as presenting ourselves to God as a spiritual act of worship, which leads us away from agreeing with the false messages of this world and into an intentional pattern of transformation where our minds are constantly being renewed in alignment with God's true message of grace. This pattern will include asking ourselves key questions that we may have overlooked for most of our lives, perhaps chalking up our derailment as merely the way it has to be. But if we're willing, these questions can begin to bring clarity to why we derail from healthier paths of living.

We opened this book with several relational paradigms and metaphors: Sheep being held in the arms of the Shepherd. The Beloved Child being held in the arms of the Father. Our internal parts functioning as a well-meaning team or family. These concepts help us keep the end in mind as we progress through various levels. But as we mine the shallows and depths of the Enneagram itself, we will employ other, nonrelational metaphors to help us grasp the basics of these concepts. As we build on these more concrete ideas, we will see them mature back into more relational analogies.

Along these lines, what false messages create the fog of unawareness within us?

That question leads to another: What if you had an internal GPS tool that could bring clarity to your heart condition so you could recognize familiar, dangerous pitfalls? That tool exists—it is a gospel-centered approach to the Enneagram. It is our internal GPS. It reveals *why* we think, feel, and behave in particular ways so we can steer our internal life where God's Spirit is leading—to the best direction for our personality type, which reflects the way God has uniquely created us.

In the last chapter we asked, "Who is driving the bus?" We will continue to find the concept of driving quite helpful in understanding the Enneagram and our internal parts. Now, while most of us have and use GPS in the modern world, including extra features like lane-departure warning systems, these technologies hearken back to a rudimentary tool that predates GPS but accomplishes many of the same goals: the roadside rumble strip. A rumble strip is a series of slotted lines cut into the pavement near the edge of the road that produces an unmistakable sound that is impossible to ignore when your tires roll over it. It warns you that you are veering off course and nearing very real danger, which is especially important when driving on a foggy highway. (Hey, rumble strips might be simple, but don't let any tech snobs fool you: they still get the job done.) Regardless of how you prefer your lane-departure warning, the Enneagram is an effective tool that alerts you when you begin to once again believe the false messages that so often land you in the ditch. Knowing doesn't cause you to course correct, but it is an irreplaceable first step. In these tenuous moments, the gospel equips you to turn back to the reality of your soul—back to the place where the Beloved Child is steering as you follow the truth revealed by the One who continually loves and redeems you.

Uniquely Alike

Personality tests are all the rage these days, providing seemingly endless memes and constant entertaining fodder for conversation at social gatherings. Most personality tests help you categorize patterns of response that people share in common situations. But the Enneagram works differently than other personality tests or profiles because it reveals not only *what* we are prone to do but *why* we do it. The *why* is the key, and the Enneagram helps us both recognize the fog and realize why we are in the fog in the first place.

From the Greek words for nine (*ennea*) and drawing (*gram*), the Enneagram is represented by a nine-pointed geometric symbol. The Enneagram symbol is merely that: a visual representation of nine types and how they relate to one another. Each point represents a basic personality type—a specific pattern of thinking and interacting with the world. The Enneagram reveals nine valid perspective types that exist among all people.

This doesn't mean all people of each type are the same, and it doesn't put individuals into boxes where everything about them is known or predictable. If you've ever been to Sherwin-Williams or any other professional paint store, you know that you can't just ask for a can of "blue" paint. Lining the walls are seemingly endless shades of blue from sky to cobalt to lapis (yes, that is a real color) with every imaginable hue of blue in between. The same rings true for your personality and makeup—you may be a primary type, but your particular shade is one of a kind.

None of us likes being summed up or boxed in, which is fortunate because the Enneagram rightly applied from a gospel perspective does not seek to do either of these things. In fact, even though we each have one central perspective (or type) that dominates why we do what we do, we use all nine perspectives to varying degrees. Furthermore, discovering the nuances of your own EIP will only further demonstrate that you are more than one number or nine numbers . . . or even a million numbers. Marvelously created in the image of God, you are completely unique, with a story and an inner world that is like no one else's. When we understand there are nine main valid perspectives from which these other infinite variables flow, we can have more compassion, kindness, mercy, grace, and forgiveness for ourselves and others.

We can clearly see that God did not create us all to see and experience life in the exact same way. In fact, He reveals in 1 Corinthians 12:12–27 how He loves diversity and has created each of us differently to reflect and glorify Him in a unique way, all while being unified as a single body—the "body of Christ." In this body, there is both unity and diversity. Finding your unique perspective, or Enneagram type, helps you access the internal GPS that will bring clarity to your path as a unique part of this body.

To that end, we must heed this warning: others will often try to help by advising us to follow their GPS coordinates, but they are not necessarily intended for us. We must find the direction that fits who we are, not who everyone else is. Others share your type, but that doesn't mean your path is identical to theirs. Even so, knowledge about your type will bring clarity to many aspects of your unique journey. After all, people with the same types do share commonalities.

Regardless of our individual journeys, we all experience relational discord, despair, or personal shame along the way. We find it hard to understand others, much less ourselves. Deep down, it feels as if we possess longings that are never satisfied. We know this to be true, but have you ever wondered what those longings truly are, or why we feel them in the first place?

The Garden and Our Core Longings

You are not alone in feeling an unmet longing within. All humanity shares a deep longing for more. "He [God] has made everything beautiful in its time. He has also set eternity in the human heart; yet no one can fathom what God has done from beginning to end" (Ecclesiastes 3:11). The stuff of eternity beats in our heart, but the stuff of earth breaks our heart at the same time. This creates tension because we can't fathom God's beginning-to-end big picture—it's as if we're in a movie, but stuck on a single frame of human limitation. This is why "the whole creation has been groaning as in the pains of childbirth right up to the present time" (Romans 8:22). This groaning is because we live with two divergent realities within us and around us. "We are God's children *now*, and what we will be *has not yet appeared*" (1 John 3:2 ESV, emphasis added).

How is it possible that everyone could be in this same state? In the beginning, God created man and woman in His image and placed them within His grand creation, calling it—and the humans living on it as His greatest masterpiece—"Very good" (Genesis 1:31). Every person is still fashioned by God with this inherited image created to uniquely reflect Him and His attributes. In other words, you reveal the character of God. You are a part of the story that He began writing an eternity ago.

When God created the first man and woman, He placed them in a perfect garden—a place of complete beauty, abundance, and safety that puts any modern beachfront resort to shame. But in this perfect place, they knew no shame. Every day they walked with God and lived free not only of shame, but also of fear, guilt, and death.

They didn't just sit around all day eating grapes. Their divinely assigned work in cultivating and tending to God's new creation only heightened the contentment and real purpose they were already experiencing in their identities as Beloved Children of the Creator. They walked in perfect joy in all their relationships—with God, with one another, and with the world around them. In the garden, they were free to be their true selves.

It's clear that we're no longer in the garden, but instead of jumping straight to all that keeps us from such a divinely blissful existence today, let us simply pause to point out a longing for it. This longing emerges in many different forms, but ultimately it originates in an echo of our beginnings—we long to return to the garden, even if we don't believe such a garden once existed or if we can't name it as such. We instinctively know we are missing something vital.

This shared void of humanity's inner longing to return to Eden expresses itself differently through the personality types of the Enneagram. Humanity's collective yet singular core longing to return to the garden is expressed differently in core longings of each type. In other words, humanity's core longing funnels down to your own unique core longing based on your type.

Each type has four core motivations that function as the driving forces behind why we think, feel, and behave in our own particular ways. Everything hinges on your type's core motivations. Everything.

Your type's specific core longing is one of your four core motivations. This core longing is a type-specific message your heart longs to hear and experience. Every person and every type's core longings were fully realized and perfectly satisfied in the garden, so our souls ache to return to that state—to be free of shame, fear, guilt, and death. We long to feel contentment, purpose, joy, and freedom to be our true selves.

Since there are nine main types, the Enneagram articulates nine core longings, one for each type. If you don't yet know your type, read and pay close attention to each one; this is a key step in discovering which longing, if any, most deeply resonates with you. It may be helpful to make a note beside each one, jotting down how it reverberates within you. If nothing does, that's okay; it took Jeff nearly five years to find his type—and another year to accept it.

To use the Enneagram as your internal GPS, you will first need to find your main type, how God uniquely created you to see and understand the world. Core longings are a great place to begin the process of discovering your main type. As you read through these core longings and the other core motivations to follow, try not to get hung up on the language. Sometimes we get feedback that while these principles ring true, the vocabulary can feel somewhat off. Some Nines say they think in terms of "I am not enough," or "My presence or voice doesn't matter," while some Sevens say, "I will never be satisfied or content," or "I will always feel trapped and deprived." Focus on the principle, but feel free to add your own vocabulary as you go.

 The Core Longings of Each Enneagram Type

Type One, Principled Reformer
Your core longing is to hear and believe that
"You are good."

Type Two, Nurturing Supporter
Your core longing is to hear and believe that
"You are wanted and loved."

Type Three, Admirable Achiever

Your core longing is to hear and believe that "You are loved and valued for simply being you."

Type Four, Introspective Individualist

Your core longing is to hear and believe that "You are seen, known, and loved for exactly who you are—special and unique."

Type Five, Analytical Investigator

Your core longing is to hear and believe that "Your needs are not a problem."

Type Six, Faithful Guardian

Your core longing is to hear and believe that "You are safe and secure."

Type Seven, Enthusiastic Optimist

Your core longing is to hear and believe that "You will be taken care of."

Type Eight, Passionate Protector

Your core longing is to hear and believe that "You will not be betrayed."

Type Nine, Peaceful Accommodator

Your core longing is to hear and believe that "Your presence matters."

Which type or types do you most resonate with? If you don't yet know, it will help to continue reading through them, as well as other resources at yourenneagramprofile.com/resources. We help thousands of people explore their core motivations and types every day, so you are not alone.

Regardless of whether you know your type yet or not, we all instinctively know that we are missing something vital. We sense that we are created for more. Some people notice it when they are connecting with nature, others while they are listening to their favorite songs. Some people notice it when they finish a big project and don't feel the complete sense of accomplishment and contentment they anticipated, while others sense it as they experience glimpses of an otherworldly love with their spouse and children, yet still feel a deep longing at the end of the day that no human love can ever completely fulfill.

When do you most feel an ache for more? Can you name these instances? The truth is, apart from God, our core longings can never be fully satisfied. So how did we get here? What happened to the garden? And where is God in our story now?

The Fall and Our Other Core Motivations

The fog of life may keep us from seeing things clearly, but it is quite clear that when left to our own devices, humans are not experiencing the perfect peace, joy, and freedom described in the garden. We struggle through life's ups and downs. We experience relational discord, despair, and personal shame—at the root of the problem, our core longings are not being fully met.

Most people don't even know what their core longing is, so it's no wonder they don't know where to even begin looking for what might satisfy it. We desperately attempt to secure the desire of our heavenly core longing by trying as many earthly options as possible. The human life is like a giant, bottomless hole into which we continue to heave shovelfuls of experiences, relationships, and strivings—but a heavenly hole cannot be filled with earthly things. No matter what we do, the longing always returns.

God addresses humanity's insatiable search for satisfaction in Jeremiah 2:13: "My people have committed two sins: They have forsaken me, the spring of living water, and have dug their own cisterns, broken cisterns that cannot hold water." We desperately need to realize and experience our core longing, but instead of going to the real Source, Jesus Christ, the Spring of living water (John 7:37–38), to have this thirst quenched, we try anything we think will fill us up completely (that is, we dig broken cisterns) to attempt to quench our thirsty hearts.

How did we get here?

In the beginning, there was an Enemy of God who hated humans because they were created in God's own image. This Enemy devised a plan. He planted a seed of doubt in the hearts of the ones made to reflect the heart of their Creator—and this tiny seed sprouted, causing a harmful, false message to take root in them: *You are not really God's Beloved Children. He doesn't have your best intentions in mind, and you can't trust His ways. He's trying to keep you from what's good, so you must seek after what's good by your own means.*

Again, while the Bible describes the fallout of believing this lie as the rendering of humanity into a sinful state of being, we are still focusing on Paul's metaphor in Romans 8:15 that uses terms of adoption. From this vantage point, God's Beloved Children were deceived into thinking they were actually Wounded Children—and when they believed the lie and disobeyed God, bringing sin and death into the garden and all of creation, they ironically became the Wounded Children the Enemy convinced them they already were. For the first time, they felt shame, fear, and guilt. Becoming discontent, they stopped living in the truth of their Father's clearly articulated message that they were not only "very good" but also deeply and eternally loved by Him. They began living according to the false messages that had now taken root within them.

Even if you doubt everything about the creation narrative of Scripture, it is hard to deny the false messages we each feel so deeply rooted in our heart. There is so much we instinctively believe about God and about ourselves that simply isn't true—that we are not His Beloved Children and we are not the sheep our Shepherd so deeply cares about.

Each of us echoes the beautiful image of the Father who created us in love and for hope, but we also still feel the stark reverberations of the fall. We sense the longing for heaven, even as we fight against death here below. We are torn—and we know it, even if we can't articulate exactly how or why.

The first man and woman knew exactly why. Because of their sin, they became frightfully aware that they were suddenly no longer in right relationship with God, one another, the creation around them, or even themselves. They had always been naked, but now they truly felt it—and a deep shame because of it. They could not stay in the perfect garden. But even as they began experiencing the sad, divinely pre-warned consequences of their willful fall, God graciously clothed them and proclaimed over His Beloved Children—who had chosen to become Wounded Children—a tender yet powerful promise (Genesis 3). The promise was for them and for us, speaking straight to the unmet core longing within every human who has followed in their sinful footsteps: creation will one day be fully restored, and our Enemy will be ultimately defeated (Genesis 3:15).

They left the garden to toil on the land and to face a new thing that had never before existed: death. Yet, through their hardships to come over the millennia that followed, God's presence was always near. He faithfully guided humankind with laws and prophets, even as sin and death ruled over them, just as they had allowed when they chose to believe the ultimate false message. Along the way, humanity continued to try to fix their utter brokenness by their own strength, apart from God. They built towers, waged wars, fashioned new things to worship, manipulated one another, abused one another, exploited one another, and began desperately living to fill their pockets, minds, and stomachs. Their longing was great, but nothing could satisfy it.

Outside of the garden—that is, outside of an unbroken relationship between the Creator and His Beloved Child—we still try to fulfill our core longing in our relationships, self-talk, careers, advancement, and more. This reveals the three other components of our core motivations besides our core longing, namely our core fear, core desire, and core weakness.

Apart from health in our relationships with God, we are always running away from our type's core fear, running toward our type's core desire, and stumbling over our type's core weakness—all the while, trying to obtain our core longing.

- **CORE FEAR:** What you are always running away from or trying to avoid.
- **CORE DESIRE:** What you are always striving for and believing will bring you complete fulfillment in your life.
- **CORE WEAKNESS:** The issue you are always wrestling with, which will remain a struggle until you're in heaven.
- **CORE LONGING:**[1] The central message your heart is always longing to hear.

Spend some time reviewing the nine types' core motivations: core fears, core desires, core weaknesses, and core longings. Again, if you don't yet know your type, please read through each one to discover which most resonates with you. If you relate to more than one, take note and compare it to the core longings you felt connected to in the last section.

The Core Motivations of Each Enneagram Type

- Core Fear
- Core Desire
- Core Weakness
- Core Longing

Type 1 (Principled Reformer)

Being wrong, bad, evil, inappropriate, unredeemable, or corruptible

Having integrity; being good, ethical, balanced, accurate, virtuous, and right

Resentment: repressing anger that leads to continual frustration and dissatisfaction with yourself, others, and the world for not being perfect

"You are good."

Type 2 (Nurturing Supporter)

⚑ Being rejected and unwanted: thought of as needy, inconsequential, dispensable, or unworthy of love

☀ Being appreciated, loved, and wanted

⁇ Pride: denying your own needs and emotions while using your strong intuition to discover and focus on the emotions and needs of others, confidently inserting your helpful support in hopes that others will say how grateful they are for your thoughtful care

🔥 "You are wanted and loved."

Type 3 (Admirable Achiever)

⚑ Being exposed as or thought of as incompetent, inefficient, or worthless; failing or appearing unsuccessful

☀ Having high status and respect: being admired, successful, and valuable

⁇ Deceit: deceiving yourself into believing that you are only the image you present to others; embellishing the truth by putting on a polished persona for everyone (including yourself) to see and admire

🔥 "You are loved for simply being you."

Type 4 (Introspective Individualist)

⚑ Being inadequate, emotionally cut off, plain, mundane, defective, flawed, or insignificant

☀ Being unique, special, and your most authentic self

⁇ Envy: feeling that you're tragically flawed, that something foundational is missing inside you, and that others possess qualities you lack

🔥 "You are seen, known, and loved for exactly who you are—special and unique."

Type 5 (Analytical Investigator)

⚑ Being annihilated, invaded, or not existing; being thought of as incapable or ignorant; having obligations placed upon you or your energy being completely depleted

☀ Being knowledgeable, insightful, capable, and competent

 Avarice: feeling that you lack inner resources and that too much interaction with others will lead to catastrophic depletion; withholding yourself from contact with the world; holding on to your resources and minimizing your needs

 "Your needs are not a problem."

Type 6 (Faithful Guardian)
 Fear itself; being without support, security, or guidance; being blamed, targeted, alone, or physically abandoned

 Having security, guidance, and support

 Anxiety: scanning the horizon of life and trying to predict and prevent negative outcomes (especially worst-case scenarios); remaining in a constant state of apprehension and worry

 "You are safe and secure."

Type 7 (Enthusiastic Optimist)
 Being deprived, trapped in emotional pain, limited, or bored; missing out on something fun

 Being happy, fully satisfied, and content

 Gluttony: feeling a great emptiness inside and having an insatiable desire to "fill yourself up" with experiences and stimulation in hopes of feeling completely satisfied and content

 "You will be taken care of."

Type 8 (Passionate Protector)
 Being weak, powerless, harmed, controlled, vulnerable, manipulated, and left at the mercy of injustice

 Protecting yourself and those in your inner circle

 Lust/Excess: constantly desiring intensity, control, and power; pushing yourself willfully on life and people in order to get what you desire

 "You will not be betrayed."

Type 9 (Peaceful Accommodator)
 Being in conflict, tension, or discord; feeling shut out and overlooked; losing connection and relationship with others

 Having inner stability and peace of mind

※ Sloth: remaining in an unrealistic and idealistic world in order to keep the peace, stay easygoing, and not be disturbed by your anger; falling asleep to your passions, abilities, desires, needs, and worth by merging with others to keep peace and harmony

♦ "Your presence matters."

After reading the core longings, core fears, core desires, and core weaknesses, with which type do you most resonate? If you're still unsure, don't worry; not everyone finds their type right away. This is a marathon, not a sprint.

One more thought about our core motivations. When you begin to explore these longings, fears, desires, and weaknesses, it is common to feel as if a million-watt spotlight is being directed squarely at the most embarrassing and vulnerable parts of yourself. This is normal. Let us remind you that the Enneagram is a nonjudgmental friend—the GPS doesn't judge you for getting lost; it merely reveals that you are. It shines a light on your darker parts not to hurt you, but so you can become aware of the shadows that have haunted you your entire life and find freedom from them. When aligned with gospel truth, the Enneagram can become a very helpful friend—and "faithful are the wounds of a friend" (Proverbs 27:6 ESV).

No type is better or worse than another. Each has negative and positive qualities. Each can be aligned or misaligned. Each can function as the Wounded Child, but each can also live as the Beloved Child because we are all created in the image of God, deeply loved by Him.

As you can see, our constant efforts to meet our core longing only fail us, which leaves us feeling devastated, discouraged, and alone. This leads to increasing desperation to chase after our longing. Like one who drinks salt water while stranded at sea, our thirst only increases, but we keep reaching for what looks like it should quench it. These destructive patterns harm our relationships with God, others, and ourselves. These patterns will continue in an endless cycle until we wake up to—that is, become aware of—the truth: on our own, our efforts are futile. We need something else, Someone outside of ourselves who, through the Spirit given to us, already lives within us.

In what ways do you try to fulfill your core longing apart from God? Do you engage in unhealthy relationships, negative self-talk, unbalanced careers, distracting hobbies, or harmful habits? There is no shame here. We all struggle with destructive patterns. Thankfully, God knew all along that we couldn't break free on our own, which is why He proclaimed both a promise and a plan to rescue us. Jesus was to be both the Rescue and the Rescuer.

Redemption and Restoration

We have learned that our four core motivations—our core longings, core fears, core desires, and core weaknesses—reveal our Enneagram types and serve as a foundation for future Enneagram work. If you're still unsure about your type, we suggest you "try one on" for a few days to see if the motivations align with your day-to-day interactions with the world. Throughout your day, take note of your responses to your experiences and keep asking, "What was motivating that behavior? What do I really want?" Then "try on" another type and do the same thing. Eventually, you'll discover which type best represents your motivations—your main type.

Another way is to ask yourself: "Do I relate to the endless cycle of running away from a certain type's core fear, running toward a core desire, stumbling over a core weakness, and all the while desperate to hear a core longing?" Try to discover how these patterns show up in your life—and pay attention to how futile your own efforts have been in satisfying your core longing.

Our loving God knew we could never completely meet our needs, so He sent the One who could. Jesus came to earth as a man and lived among His creation. He put His hands into our dirt to uproot the lie of the ultimate false message the Enemy had sown into the heart of humanity:

that God isn't for us, but rather is against us. Since Christ Himself was the "the radiance of the glory of God and the exact imprint of his nature" (Hebrews 1:3 ESV)—that is, "the image of the invisible God, the firstborn of all creation" (Colossians 1:15 ESV)—the way He lived and interacted with a broken humanity, even dying to rescue them, revealed not only a better way to live but also the truth about the Father's disposition toward His creation.

We often wonder who God really is, so God sent a mirror image of Himself in Christ to forever solve the mystery: He is our Father. Jesus revealed the Father's love, compassion, and grace. He forever confirmed that God desires us to live as His Beloved Children, not as Wounded Children still feeling the shame of our own rejection as a rejection of the Father. In Christ, God made it clear that the sinful path from the garden was being repaved with grace at His own steep expense.

While on the earth, Jesus spoke out against sin, which angered the men who had learned to harness its power. These men devised a plan to silence Jesus, and thus He was betrayed and murdered by His own creation. Despair darkened the land, but this plot twist wasn't a surprise to God. The story wasn't over. Three days later, Jesus rose from the grave, conquering sin and death. And through Jesus, sin is forgiven and remembered no more.

Now the thirst within us that reveals itself in insatiable longings can be quenched through Christ Himself, the Spring of living water (John 7:37–38). When we turn to Him, He meets us at our core longing, fulfilling part of it here and promising to fully satisfy it in our eternal future. But we don't have to wait for heaven to experience fulfillment—He has offered us all we need through His perfect life, death, resurrection, and ascension. Not only did He remove all past, present, and future sins, but He also gave us his perfect righteousness so when God the Father looks at us, He sees His Son's righteousness credited to us. This is why we are Beloved Children—little sheep being held and protected by our Shepherd. We are redeemed.

The Westminster Confession of Faith asks three key questions regarding the benefits of redemption. "Can I be accepted by God?" The answer is yes, with God's *justification*. "Can I be loved by God?" Yes, with *adoption*. "Can I be changed by God?" Yes, with *sanctification*.

The redemption of Christ rings a resounding yes to all three questions. At the same time, the gospel benefits meet the three fundamental needs of the soul: to belong, to be loved, and to become. Christ's work puts us back in right relationship with God and allows us to have healthy relationships with others, with creation, and with ourselves. Each of us can now live as the Beloved Child, coheirs with the Father's Beloved Child: Jesus. Though we still get stuck, our higher reality is that we are no longer permanently stuck, lost in the fog, and desperate. Rather, we are free, found, and satisfied. We are no longer alone. We belong.

When you know, believe, and trust in who you are and Whose you are, you will be offered a deep peace and joy that settles your inner world. You now have the invitation to rest in God's care and move forward in new ways that bless others and bring glory to Him.

But as we've pointed out along the way, the reality of who we are in Christ still sometimes becomes incongruent with who we are in this world. Getting stuck without Christ was hopeless, but getting stuck as one in Christ is full of hope because we have access to the same path of redemption that brought us to Him in the first place. As we walk that path daily, we see Him heal the brokenness of our misplaced core motivations.

But we have to at least be aware of where we are. The Enneagram is like an X-ray: it can show you what is broken, but it cannot heal that broken place. Only the true Healer—Jesus—can restore your heart. The gospel transforms you; the Enneagram helps you recognize what's going on in your heart. Returning to our earlier metaphor, like a GPS locator, the Enneagram offers the exact coordinates of your anger, reactivity, lust, fear, critical attitude, or the like. It can also show you where you are joyful, peaceful, helpful, and courageous. The GPS doesn't define or change your location—it reveals it.

To the surprise of Jesus' followers, after His resurrection, He didn't remain on earth for long. Soon the time came for Him to return to the Father, but He promised that He would return again to fully restore the life we are destined to know in the garden.

In the meantime, Christ commissioned us to join Him in the restoration plan by bearing witness to His life, death, resurrection, and ascension (2 Corinthians 5:16–21). Along the way, just as He is the reflection of the Father, we are to be the reflection of Him—to authentically model love, joy, peace, patience, kindness, goodness, faithfulness, gentleness, and self-control. We are Jesus' image-bearers—the salt and the light (Matthew 5:13)—so others will recognize and receive God's free gift of grace. Many people don't realize that grace is free, much less that the false messages they have heard about the Father aren't even true. Christ's plan to help them know the truth about the heart of the Good Shepherd is to use us as examples of His love—broken, imperfect, sometimes misaligned *us*.

This is no easy task, and God knew we would need a Guide. After Jesus left, He sent us a Helper, the Holy Spirit, to live within our heart and to gently guide us down the correct path (John 14:26). The Spirit living within us is a key to understanding the mystery of why we are Beloved Children who still get stuck in the role of Wounded Children. We aren't yet in heaven, but through the Spirit, heaven is already in us. We're currently living in the tension of already, but not yet. This means that God has victoriously saved us, and we are fully His in Christ, but we also still live on an earth that is tainted with sin, death, and destruction. This tension will remain within us until Jesus returns.

It's challenging to live in tension. We all want a comfortable and easy life. We all long to be back in the garden. Because of this, we often become unconscious of our inner world where the tension plays out. We sleepwalk through life, unaware of our deeper motivations, failing to recognize the voice of the Holy Spirit. Most people live a great deal of their lives in a state of reaction to the sin and brokenness around them and within them that harms them and their relationships. That's why it is important to wake up and become aware of our current hearts' condition.

First, you need to become aware in real time of the false messages you are believing, which lead to "autopilot" reactions—things we all do out of a pattern rather than gospel-based intention. Next, we need to speak the gospel truth to ourselves, using our unique personality's specific language. The Enneagram, seen through the lens of the gospel, can help us do that. Speaking the gospel to yourself might be a new concept for you, but it can help you learn to shepherd your heart. In the pages ahead, we'll reveal how.

Proceed with Caution

Since the Enneagram reveals a person's inner world and their heart's condition, we must endeavor to use it with great care. We should never use the Enneagram as a sword or as a shield.

When we use it as a sword, we will find ourselves mocking, teasing, shaming, harming, or belittling others (or even ourselves) for their hardwiring. Again, the Enneagram is not just about memes or fun games at social gatherings. When using the Enneagram from a gospel-based approach, it is like a GPS system by which we become aware of our distance from Christ's best ways so we can call to Him to help us navigate back to health.

On the other hand, when we use the Enneagram as a shield, we will find ourselves excusing or hiding behind unhealthy tendencies through defending, ignoring, or blame shifting. Your Enneagram type reveals your motivations, but it is not a valid excuse for how you react to those motivations. The goal is to use it to know when you're lost in the fog so you can move away from the attitudes and actions of the Wounded Child, not so you can stay in the fog while claiming, "It's okay—I'm a Type Six, and this is what we do."

As we close this chapter, we hope you've become more familiar with the role of the Enneagram as a GPS tool to reveal where you are so you can move closer to the Father who loves His Beloved Children. If you still don't know your main type, don't panic, but also don't give up. Later in this book, we will include summaries of each type to help you gain even more clarity.

As always, you can visit yourenneagramprofile.com/resources to learn more about your type, including common areas of mistyping. Above all, be diligent to do the work of self-discovery while also inviting the Good Shepherd to help you see how you are made so you can invite Him deeper into those places. Knowing your main type is key, and in the next chapter, we will further explore how the Enneagram relates to your EIP, including how two other parts, *wings*, and Enneagram *paths*, round out your internal team.

FIVE

The Health of Your Enneagram Type

UNDERSTANDING LEVELS OF

ALIGNMENT WITH THE GOSPEL

We began this book introducing you to the concepts of the Beloved Child and the Wounded Child. While we will continue to observe on paper the obvious signs that you are functioning in one or the other, it can be less obvious when you are in the moment. We exist not just on the polar extremes of some number line. We exist on a continuum—and we move across this spectrum between levels of alignment and misalignment, often unaware we are doing so.

So while our goal for this book is to help you become aware of those moments when you are not functioning as the Beloved Child, we also don't want you to somehow think that it is always an either-or scenario. Just like life, spiritual health is a moving target. Just because you are not at your best does not necessarily mean you are at your worst—and vice versa. It happens on a sliding scale. Jerry Bridges says, "Your worst days are never so bad that you are beyond the reach of God's grace. And your best days are never so good that you are beyond the need of God's grace."[1]

In 1977, Enneagram teacher and author Don Riso introduced what he called the Enneagram Levels of Development. His goal was to establish some sort of strata by which people studying the Enneagram could evaluate their levels of health—in this case, as healthy, average, or unhealthy. We all advance and regress through these levels depending on our hearts' condition in that circumstance, season, or moment. It is not a static process but a dynamic one.

As we've developed these concepts from our own perspective, we refer to these shifting dynamics as "levels of alignment with the gospel." The idea that there can be levels of misalignment with the gospel is based in Scripture. One instance is when Paul confronted Peter because he and his Jewish Christian friends were refusing to eat with certain Gentiles, which meant that some parts of their hearts were still basing their righteousness not on the work of Christ but rather on their own abilities to follow certain rules. Paul lovingly called them back to a healthier place in the gospel in response to this evidence that they had drifted: "When [he] saw that their conduct was not in step [aligned] with the truth of the gospel" (Galatians 2:14 ESV).

We all need God's Spirit to do the work of Paul among our parts—to take them aside when they are worried, confused, angry, or otherwise activated to help them move further on the spectrum toward health. This is helping our internal parts keep up with where Jesus is going and wants us to go, which is why Paul said, "If we live by the Spirit, let us also *keep in step* with the Spirit" (Galatians 5:25 ESV, emphasis added).

While Riso developed three levels of health, the truth is there are infinite levels of health between each of these. Much like the uniqueness of your own internal world in relation to your main type and your other internal parts, you also move uniquely on the continuum of health. That being said, it is still advantageous to explore these three levels merely to become more aware of when our health begins to slide down the wrong side of the scale.

Adapting Riso's three-level paradigm for our purposes, we believe that you can be healthy, average, or unhealthy. When you are healthy, you have become aligned with the gospel and are living as the Beloved Child. When you are average, you have become misaligned with the gospel and you are living under your own strength in certain areas, but probably not all of them. When you are unhealthy, you have become out of alignment with the gospel in most areas. You are living as the Wounded Child in both states, but "average" is less severe than "unhealthy."

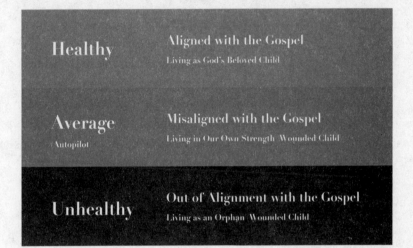

Healthy	Aligned with the Gospel
	Living as God's Beloved Child
Average	Misaligned with the Gospel
Autopilot	Living in Our Own Strength (Wounded Child)
Unhealthy	Out of Alignment with the Gospel
	Living as an Orphan (Wounded Child)

Aligned

Living as God's Beloved Child is being aligned with the gospel. This describes Christ-followers who are believing, trusting, and resting in who they are in Christ. Especially in moments of stress or patterns of unhealth, we each employ internal tactics to attempt to falsely soothe or fix our inner selves, attempting to come to our own rescue. This is a part of fallen human nature.

But when we are healthy, we no longer insist on using our personality strategies to meet our own desires. Instead, we go to our heavenly

Father because we truly trust that He loves us and will provide for us. We recognize emotionally and spiritually what we may already believe intellectually but can become fuzzy in the fog: that Christ has already accomplished everything we need. As we keep our focus on Him, we again realize what brings fullness in life and choose it over that which only promises fullness but ultimately leaves us feeling empty. When we stay aligned, Christ perfectly renews us every time.

Misaligned

On the other hand, living in our own strength and leaning on our protective strategies is being misaligned with the gospel. This is when we begin to live as the Wounded Child. Again, our hearts tend to wander away from fully trusting in what Christ has done for us. We do not as fiercely resist this drift, so we begin to depend less on Christ.

In this state, we still realize and believe that we are His Beloved Child; that is, deep down inside, we still know that God is loving and providing. Even so, we somehow cease to be certain that He will ultimately do what is in our best interest. We begin to trust only partially, so we think we need to take over some control of our life, even if only in minor ways. Becoming distracted by what we want (and even demand at times) causes us to be misaligned with the gospel, and we veer off our best path of growth. Again, this state varies greatly on a vast continuum—we can exercise different levels of control over own lives, depending on the situation and the patterns we follow.

Out of Alignment

Unfortunately, there is a moment on the spectrum when we cross more into a lack of health than a presence of it. In this state, we are completely living as the Wounded Child and as if we are all alone in life. Our internal parts organize to protect us, spending an inordinate amount of energy trying to cope and keep us safe. This is because we are living out of alignment with what is true about us according to the gospel, leaving us functioning like unprotected orphans without a Father to lead, feed, guide, and protect us.

The reality is that we're still God's Beloved Child, complete with all the same inheritances Christ gave us, yet we are no longer *experiencing* this Beloved Child status. This is the good news of the gospel: when we receive Christ as our Lord and Savior, we are always His Beloved Child. After all, our relationship status never changes, because "those whom he called he also justified" (Romans 8:30 ESV). Our justification is completely secured. This should render us "confident of this, that he who began a good work in [us] will carry it on to completion until the day of Christ Jesus" (Philippians 1:6).

No matter where we land on the levels of alignment, Christ's life, death, and resurrection have already accomplished everything required to render us forever safe in His arms—and also fully pursued by His affections. Returning to an awareness of this status is the goal—seeing where we are, rejoicing again at His work in our lives, and repenting if needed, all while returning to a place of resting fully in who we are in Him.

Self-Coaching Between Two Levels of Alignment

The goal is to become adept at coaching yourself as you become aware of these levels of alignment. Easier said than done, right? Perhaps, but paying attention to your levels of alignment can show you when you are not surrendering and depending solely on the finished work of Christ. For most of us, the moment when we need alignment the most, we desire to ask for it the least—we become more and more tempted to lean into our own strength. Yet spiritual awareness beckons to us through the fog.

The first step that begins to change everything is merely asking the Holy Spirit to take over our hearts and renew our minds. Admit your need. God always meets the humble and needy with grace and mercy (Matthew 11:28–30). Thus, it begins with the humility and courage just to ask; if you're asking, you're acknowledging awareness that you are not aligned in some way. There is a process to follow, but by asking, you've at least set it in motion.

Romans 12:2 reminds us, "Do not be conformed to this world, but be transformed by the renewal of your mind, that by testing you may discern what is the will of God, what is good and acceptable and perfect" (ESV). Because of the fall, there are ways of this world—patterns of thought and action not rooted in your higher, heavenly-based reality already secured in Christ. These are residuals of the sinfulness that still try to control you—to convince you of exactly what the serpent convinced humankind in the garden: that God can't be trusted, so His ways shouldn't be followed. Awareness begins by refusing to be conformed to this world—that is, the main lie of this world. This is the first step to continual transformation.

As we've laid out, the three levels are merely markers on the spectrum between being healthy and being unhealthy—again, there are infinite levels of dimming light as dusk sets in. Our place on the continuum is as infinitely varied as our personality itself. Any given moment, we can be anywhere between healthy (aligned), average (misaligned), and unhealthy (out of alignment).

For our purposes of creating an EIP reflective of your unique internal world, we will use two levels of alignment: aligned and misaligned. Recognizing elements of both is the key, even if you don't exactly know where you fall between the two in any given moment. Your EIP will help you discern where you might be, but awareness is the first step. This will help you coach yourself back to an awareness of your true reality in Christ as His Beloved Child.

Your main type can help you recognize many of the behaviors

and feelings that often indicate misalignment and alignment. For each type, it's easy to see how the fruits of misalignment are defensive self-protection strategies organized to protect the Wounded Child. On the contrary, notice how the fruit of alignment represents our same internal parts but operates out of our true identity as the Beloved Child. Rather than defensive patterns that rupture relationships, our aligned parts lead to love for God, others, and ourselves as we use our gifts in life-giving ways.

TYPE ONE

- When you are *misaligned* with the truth of the gospel, you struggle to trust in the Lord's timing and become more judgmental, reactive, opinionated, irritated, and resentful. You become rigid in procedures to ensure accuracy or perfection to appease your inner critic, who is never satisfied. You begin to convey this through both your body language and words. At your worst, you allow your inner critic to control you as you become intolerant, explosive, sharp, critical, punishing, judgmental, nitpicky, and inflexible, all in hopes of making things "right." Mistakes and imperfections are glaring at you, and the inner critic is excruciatingly loud.

- When you are *aligned* with the truth of the gospel, you understand that your inner critic doesn't actually have power over you. You choose to put your trust in God's truth instead. You choose to believe that there truly is no more condemnation because you have been justified in Christ (Romans 8:1). This allows you to be more accepting, noble, and respectful. Trusting that God has everything in control, you are more patient, allowing time for Him to make things right. This frees you from feeling that you have to police and judge everything. You trust that God is sovereign and is working all things for His good and glory (v. 28). You get to participate in life but realize that you are not solely responsible for perfecting things. God is in control.

TYPE TWO

- When you are *misaligned* with the truth of the gospel, you need to be highly involved with others. You begin to read people, searching for those who are in need. You start to communicate through flattery, giving, and affection so others will provide you with praise, affirmation, and gratitude. If you do not get the appreciation you seek, you can become aggressive, hover, and intrude into other people's lives with subtle or not-so-subtle gestures of unsolicited help. At your worst, you try to control others by manipulating, shaming, and playing the martyr or victim to secure what you want. You become blind to your unhealthy strategies, believing that you are being helpful, selfless, and giving. This inhibits you from listening to how you have hurt or intruded on others, which further isolates you from the relationships and affirmation you desperately seek.

- When you are *aligned* with the truth of the gospel, you recognize your feelings and needs, communicating them directly to others without shame or fear of rejection. This allows you to practice and enjoy self-care and healthy boundaries. You give love, support, and care to others with no strings attached—you know that your heart is already fully and safely tethered to Christ. Because of the overflow of love you receive from Him, you become secure and aware that in caring for others, you are actually participating with God in His care for those around you.

TYPE THREE

- When you are *misaligned* with the gospel, you become highly concerned with your image and performance. You do your job well and continually drive yourself to achieve goals as if your self-worth depends on it. You are terrified of failure and compare yourself with others as you search for status and recognition. You shape-shift to the expectations of others and cling to what you think is required both to be and appear successful. You are pragmatic and efficient but have lost touch with your feelings. At your worst, your fear of failure and humiliation leads you to become exploitative and opportunistic. You grow jealous of the success of others and become willing to do whatever it takes to preserve the illusion of your superiority. To avoid being exposed for wrongdoing or mistakes, you become devious and deceptive. Untrustworthy, malicious, and delusional, you begin to sabotage people to triumph over them.

- When you are *aligned* with the truth of the gospel, you can be your authentic self without fear. You know you are loved because of who you are in Christ, so His achievement is now your achievement. Because you no longer need to perform to earn love and admiration, you are more self-accepting, gentle, and authentic, and you allow your emotions to emerge. By experiencing your value in Christ, you can have healthy self-esteem and participate with God in both small and grand endeavors to improve yourself, others, and the world, finding your value not in the endeavor but in the God with whom you are participating.

Type Four

- When you are *misaligned* with the gospel, you begin to believe that your passionate feelings and imagination define your reality. You desire to stay in touch with your emotions, so you internalize everything and take things very personally. This leads to self-absorption, moodiness, hypersensitivity, shyness, and self-consciousness. You withdraw to protect your self-image and sort out your feelings. You believe you are different from others, thus exempt from living as everyone else does. Self-pity and envy of others lead you to self-indulgence, so you become increasingly impractical and unproductive. At your worst, regardless of what's really happening, your dreams appear to be failing, so you become self-inhibiting, angry at yourself, and depressed. You alienate yourself and face emotional paralysis, leading to personal shame, fatigue, and an inability to function. Tormented by your delusional self-contempt, guilt, self-hatred, and morbid thoughts, everything becomes a source of torment to you. You blame others and drive away anyone who tries to help.

- When you are *aligned* with the truth of the gospel, you are profoundly creative, expressing yourself with balanced emotions. You become deeply inspired and self-renewing. Your feelings are grounded in your higher reality in Christ, enabling you to internalize all your experiences, even the difficult ones, as beautiful and valuable in relation to His ultimate plans for your life. You see your significance through the eyes of your Creator, which renews your soul, allowing you to be true to yourself, self-revealing, emotionally honest, and humane. You participate with God to bring vulnerability and beauty to the world.

TYPE FIVE

- When you are *misaligned* with the gospel, you are remote, quiet, and withdrawn. You live mostly in your head and observe the world from a cerebral, outsider stance. You are objective and calm, analyzing the facts. Since you do not like surprises, intrusions, and too many emotions, if you are uncomfortable or overwhelmed, you detach from your feelings and from others. You minimize your needs and guard your inner resources by withdrawing and seeking as much privacy as you can. At your worst, you become frightened that your inner resources will deplete to the point of annihilation. You withdraw and become isolated, showing open hostility toward others who invade your rigid boundaries. You may even become suspicious of others and begin plotting ways to harm them. You become secretive, explosive, and relationally awkward. Because your mind is overactive and out of control, you have a hard time accessing the reliability of emotions that arise from yourself and others.

- When you are *aligned* with the truth of the gospel, you can experience and express your feelings in the moment. You begin to actively engage with life rather than merely observe it. You become more spontaneous, imaginative, and joyful. You go beyond the cerebral to engage in the fullness of life with enthusiasm for experiences, ideas, and emotions. You participate with God to share wisdom and insights that bless and enrich others.

TYPE SIX

- When you are *misaligned* with the gospel, you become overly busy, thinking that you must always be responsible. This can cause you to be reactive and short-tempered. You become highly perceptive, thinking thoroughly through the many possible outcomes. This can lead you to worry, self-doubt, and insecurity. You become suspicious and anxious about other people's motives, fearing harm or abandonment. You also become wary of authority, vacillating between trusting and not trusting authority figures. At your worst, you become extremely anxious; your mind is spinning out of control with worst-case scenarios about being hurt or in danger. You project negative motivations on others, which causes distance and feelings of abandonment, exacerbating your fears. You become paranoid, panicky, and judgmental of others based on your own internal perception of reality, often leading you to reject even the best advice. Suspicious of everyone, you isolate even further, which traps you even deeper into an unhealthy pattern of relating to the world.

- When you are *aligned* with the truth of the gospel, you can rest in the fact that you are safe, secure, resourced, and guided by Christ. You begin to recognize that because you are directed by the Holy Spirit, you can move forward more courageously and confidently. You no longer need or look for the same level of guidance and support from others as your sole sources of security. You have more of an inner calm, which in turn allows you to connect more deeply with others apart from skepticism or suspiciousness. You participate with God to bring courage and resilience to the world.

Type Seven

- When you are *misaligned* with the gospel, you avoid all pain, sadness, or disappointment. You redirect your energy toward creating new and exciting experiences to avoid feelings of discomfort. You are a master at reframing anything negative, and you convince yourself and others of silver linings. This strategy keeps you from living in the present reality and dealing with the situation at hand. You find it difficult to focus on projects, commit to relationships, and finish tasks. Even when others address these struggles, you still tend to escape into more exciting and fun experiences to avoid feeling trapped in emotional pain or negativity, but this still only intensifies the problem. At your worst, your entire focus becomes avoiding anything that causes you pain or boredom. You cannot tolerate restrictions or limitations placed on you, so you find ways to escape them. You may take more risks, become reckless, or develop an addiction. You also begin to feel that others are intentionally inhibiting you from a life of joy and happiness. You fail to see that your discontentment stems from your insatiable appetite that cannot be quenched with earthly pleasures.

- When you are *aligned* with the gospel, you recognize that the joy and satisfaction you long for will not come from exciting experiences and constant stimulation. You rest in knowing that it comes from being in the presence of God, who fills you up with real, radiant joy. You delight in simple wonders and savor your blessings. When you are resting in this deeply gratifying place, you can courageously address head-on the painful realities that come with living on earth because you know that your story ends in triumph. You participate with God to bring playfulness, fun, and creativity to the world.

TYPE EIGHT

- When you are *misaligned* with the gospel, you try to manage your anger and frustration, but it only leads you to become more controlling, authoritarian, and aggressive. You expect and even demand immediate responses and quick action from others. You can be highly impatient with others who are slower than you. You have strong opinions and are more than happy to share them without being asked. At your worst, you communicate in direct, hurtful, and cruel ways. You do not restrain your anger as you engage in punitive, destructive behaviors. You believe you must attack those who you perceive have harmed you. You refuse to open up or reveal any weaknesses or vulnerabilities. You become explosive with your anger and dominate your relationships.

- When you are *aligned* with the truth of the gospel, you trust that God will not betray you and will always protect you. This allows you to live more vulnerably and openhearted. You are still direct and honest but from a softer stance that acknowledges others' needs and your limitations. You become encouraging and open to others' opinions. You are compassionate, protective, warm, and confident in your abilities. You participate with God to plow a path for others.

TYPE NINE

- When you are *misaligned* with the gospel, you harbor incredibly strong needs and desires for peace and harmony in all your relationships, so you begin to accommodate and people-please, disregarding yourself in the process. If a conflict is directed toward you, you become anxious and completely withdraw. You can lose focus and live life as if you are in a thick fog. You don't know what you want or how to ask for it, so you *go along* to *get along*. At your worst, you completely forget yourself and focus only on others' agendas and desires. You trick yourself into believing that everything is okay when it is not. You become physically lazy and unmotivated. You can be passive-aggressive and, on rare occasions, burst into a rage that has been suppressed within you and building up pressure over time.

- When you are *aligned* with the truth of the gospel, you know and feel that your presence matters to God and others. You wake up, get up, and desire to live up to your full calling with confidence and strength. You realize that healthy conflict can be an effective way to grow and enhance relationships. You become intentionally involved, engaged, and alert, but with a peaceful, even serene presence. You participate with God to bring the world deeper grace and peace.

Regardless of your main type, as you become attuned to the alignment of your own feelings and behaviors, you can recognize when you're moving down the spectrum and begin to take actions before you reach rock bottom. The next step in this process is understanding some of the other significant parts that your type reveals.

Adding Connecting Types (Wings and Enneagram Paths) to Your EIP

As we have learned, even though each person has only one main type, we all use all nine types to varying degrees. However, we especially use the attributes from specific types to which we are more closely connected than others. Understanding these other parts is the final key to developing your EIP. These connecting types consist of your two wings and your two Enneagram paths. These are critical elements of your internal world that provide insight into where you are going, how fast or slow you are getting there, and whether you are doing so safely or with tires on the shoulder near the ditch.

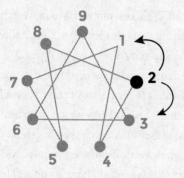

Example: Wings of Type Two

WINGS

Wings are the two numbers directly next to each main type on the Enneagram diagram. No other numbers can make up your wings but these two, so all Type Fives have the same two wings: a Four and a Six. For Type Nines, their wings are Eight and One. You can determine your wings in much the same way—and even though you may lean more heavily into one of your wings, you use and are affected by both of them in some way, depending on the differing circumstances.

We access the characteristics of our wings in our reactions and behaviors. Even so, we always remain our main type, complete with its core motivations. This means that even though our wings influence us in ways we need to be mindful of, they never actually replace our main type's core longing, core desire, core fear, and core weakness. Even if we begin to behave differently to accommodate the needs of a wing, we are still motivated by the same things from our main type's perspective. For some people who are struggling to determine their main type, they face confusion because they recognize behaviors of one of their wings. It is helpful to observe not just the behavior, but the motivation behind it—in the motivation lies the truth of the main type.

When we need to get back on track and become aligned with the gospel, we can choose to utilize the healthy attributes of our wings. By faith, we can access and use these attributes, knowing that God will show up and enable us to be transformed. We access our wings to move us back toward knowing, believing, and trusting that our identity in Christ allows us to express ourselves and see the complexity of who we really are. We can access either one of our wings depending on what we need in the moment—and how aligned or misaligned we are. It is beneficial to train yourself to become aware of your wings, including when and how we use them healthily. We will explore these wings and how they affect each type in greater detail in the later sections of the book where you will work on your individual EIP. For now, just know that growing in this area will benefit you and bless others.

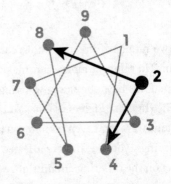

Example: Enneagram Paths of Type Two

ENNEAGRAM PATHS

The other two internal parts that make up our EIP's connecting types are our Enneagram paths (also sometimes commonly referred to simply as "lines" or "arrows" on the Enneagram symbol). Each main type is connected to two other types through these lines (paths) in the Enneagram symbol. At times, we travel down these paths and, like our wings, take on some of the aligned (healthy) or misaligned (less healthy) attributes of these two types, depending on our level of alignment with the gospel.

The paths (inner lines and arrows) that we see in the Enneagram diagram can bring great clarity to the internal shifts we often experience that differ from our main type's normal way of operating. This helps us understand why, at times, we can experience within ourselves competing thoughts, feelings, and reactions.

It's important to again remember that we always remain our main type with its core fear, desire, weakness, and longing. However, we do take on the qualities and attributes of our Enneagram paths in times of struggle and health, all depending on our heart's level of alignment with gospel truth. Just like wings, our paths are not random. For example, all Sixes have the same two Enneagram paths: Three and Nine. You can explore the Enneagram symbol to determine your own Enneagram paths.

Wings and Paths for Each Enneagram Type

Type One
Wings: Nine and Two
Enneagram Paths:
Four and Seven

Type Two
Wings: One and Three
Enneagram Paths:
Four and Eight

Type Three
Wings: Two and Four
Enneagram Paths:
Six and Nine

Type Four
Wings: Three and Five
Enneagram Paths:
One and Two

Type Five
Wings: Four and Six
Enneagram paths:
Seven and Eight

Type Six
Wings: Five and Seven
Enneagram Paths:
Three and Nine

Type Seven
Wings: Six and Eight
Enneagram Paths:
One and Five

Type Eight
Wings: Seven and Nine
Enneagram Paths:
Two and Five

Type Nine
Wings: Eight and One
Enneagram Paths:
Three and Six

We hope that this chapter has helped you to see that there is much more to your navigational processes than just your main type—many instruments are lit up by the Enneagram. Whether you realize it or not, we have just laid out all the necessary components for your EIP.

The fact that we all use all nine types to varying degrees is an important truth to remember as you use the Enneagram to work toward deeper understanding and better internal health. But for now, these six parts—your main type functioning as either the Beloved or Wounded child, two wings, and two Enneagram paths—make up the six main members of your internal team that all affect you negatively or positively, depending on whether you are operating out of your Wounded Child or Beloved Child parts. These are the parts by which the wisdom of the Enneagram will help you grow as you become aware of the patterns that cause each one to become negatively activated.

For your internal parts, each one can be known, welcomed, addressed, and led. A negatively activated part can be coached back into alignment with the gospel if you become aware of how each one interacts with your main type. In the next chapter, we're ready to begin putting it all together into your own EIP.

SIX

Beginning Your Enneagram Internal Profile

INTEGRATING AND APPLYING ENNEAGRAM
WISDOM TO YOUR INTERNAL WORLD

Now that you have a more solid foundation for understanding not only your main type but also the other connecting type parts that affect the composition and interaction of your internal world, we can define the EIP in even clearer terms. The concepts and the exercises to follow are not technically intended to help you "develop" an EIP. The truth is, these parts and their influences already exist within you as a result of your core motivations, along with the competing and sometimes overwhelmingly compelling strategies of your various parts. We want to help you "map out" your EIP so you can become aware of what already exists within you.

The more we get to know the internal parts of our EIP—with the goal of welcoming them with compassion so they can begin the journey of healing, growing, and maturing in alignment with the truth of Christ—the more we will understand how to lead them well. Understanding how your EIP functions daily in aligned and misaligned ways is foundational for a host of critical skills that will radically impact almost everything you say and do. In fact, becoming skilled at mapping out your EIP so you can navigate its parts in healthy ways, especially when life throws you curveballs, is the single biggest predictor of how healthy your personal and professional relationships will be.

These are huge statements, right? Could one's EIP really be so critical, especially since most of us have never even heard of such a thing? Again, we remind you that these parts are already functioning within you—and you are already interacting, leading, or being led by them. You already have coping strategies and familiar reactions to them—you have probably just never named these parts or used the Enneagram to understand why and how their core motivations and strategies are reflective of the state of health of your main type. Again, have you ever said, "There is a part of me that wants to do this, but there is another part of me that wants to do something else"? We commonly speak in these terms without even realizing it.

On this front, it bears repeating that if you are a Nine, a Peaceful Accommodator, and your Type Eight part, the Passionate Protector, becomes activated, the core motivations of the Eight are affecting you, but they are still governed by the core motivations of a Nine. In this specific scenario, a Type Nine being influenced by the wing Type Eight will speak up for the marginalized, but generally in a gentler way than someone whose primary type is an Eight. In moments of stress, distress, or elation, you do not become another type based on the part within you most activated by your current situation. It is important to study the core motivations of your EIP connecting type parts because it will help you understand *why* a part has become activated, which will help you know how to lead it back into healthy alignment.

EIP Example: Type Six

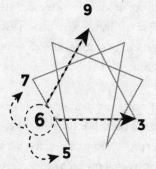

Example: Type Six Wounded Child

Dotted lines represent the broken strategies and strivings of our misaligned parts as they attempt to protect the Wounded Child.

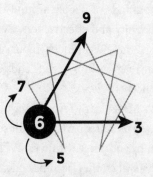

Example: Type Six Beloved Child

Solid lines represent the restored security and strengths of our aligned parts as they are being led by the Beloved Child.

You can take on the protective strategies of your parts.[1] For example, if you are a Six (a Faithful Guardian), you remain a Six with a Six's core motivations, but the varied negative strategies being employed by your Enneagram path Type Three part, Enneagram path Type Nine part, wing Type Seven part, or wing Type Five part can each feel familiar and even overwhelming. You are still running from the same core fear that all Sixes run from—you are merely being affected by the strategies of your internal connecting types. Your main type's core motivations reign supreme, like an umbrella with all your other connecting types' core motivations under it.

However, when we are in alignment with the gospel, we also borrow from the blessings of our wings and Enneagram paths. Remember that no type or part is good or bad—they can all be healthy and walk in redeemed spaces. When this happens, we adopt some of their giftedness, which brings life to our souls and relationships.

Understanding these elements will help you better utilize the EIP as a self-coaching strategy. We developed this strategy as we've coached thousands of people around the world, so we've already witnessed its necessity and effectiveness. Even more importantly, we have personally used these techniques in our own marriage and parenting, as well as in our relationships with friends and community. We have also used these concepts at work.

More clearly recognizing our internal profiles and their strategies has given us better paradigms for self-coaching our parts toward greater harmony and peace within us. We have also learned to recognize each other's parts when they become activated, allowing us to show each other more grace, kindness, and compassion in the foggy moments, which deepens trust and relationship connections.

Become attuned to your internal parts' reactions in foggy moments—along with the price you are paying for a lack of awareness and the benefits of doing otherwise—and you will have taken crucial first steps in not only understanding but implementing healthy EIP strategies.

What Cost Are You Already Paying and What Benefit Are You Experiencing?

I (Jeff) have an Amazon problem—and I don't mean that I'm addicted to swimming in the South American river.

There are times when I impulsively buy books from Amazon. When I hear in a casual conversation that someone enjoyed a book, I will have bought it on my phone before our conversation has ended, even when that person was not recommending I do so. It doesn't take much of anything to "motivate" me to log on and order another book. A passing statement. A reference on a podcast. The fact that it's a Tuesday (the day new books release).

My Amazon problem seems innocent enough. It even has upsides.

But there is also a cost to what I do. During the years of our life and marriage when Beth and I weren't as financially healthy, buying all those books was an extra (and extra expensive) stressor on our already literally overtaxed budget. "Why do you keep buying books?" she would ask as she anxiously pored over the bills. I had a hundred reasons, each one very sound in my own head. They were also mostly convincing to Beth because they seemed to be grounded in wisdom and reason. Truth is, I positioned my logical arguments in a way that made it difficult for her to disagree because the strategies I was implementing seemed real and legitimate. The bottom line was that I was unaware and just didn't see it as a problem, which kept me from listening to the fact that it was a problem for her, which soon began causing problems for us.

To be clear, book buying (or a host of other actions that you may take) can be either healthy or unhealthy. The action is merely a manifestation of something deeper—something aligned or misaligned with a heart functioning either as the Beloved Child or the Wounded Child. We must remember that most things are not good or bad—they are just things. A cheesecake is not evil or good. Rather, the motivations behind the patterns in which you approach that cheesecake in either moderation or excess—in either harmless moments of sharing a treat in community or in desperate moments of complete overindulgence—indicate alignment or misalignment. The same can be said of any other inanimate object or action.

A car is just a car, but if in moments of stress you choose to drive ninety miles per hour while screaming and cussing at every other person in your way on the highway, something within your use of the car has become misaligned with gospel truth. The most crucial first step in guiding our hearts into a healthier, aligned place is to become aware of why we are doing something. Is it from an overflow of our Wounded Child whose heart is misaligned or from our Beloved Child who is trusting in the security of an aligned heart based on gospel truth?

Books may have just been books, but there was something misaligned about the way I was buying them. In fact, Beth wasn't the only one a little bent out of shape over my obsession. I was a pastor at the time, and I was afforded a pretty healthy annual budget to buy books and resources—around a thousand dollars every year. I began surpassing that budget, which lets you know how many books I was buying. Of course, I always paid the church back for any amount over the budget, but a tension with the leadership arose over my actions. It was nothing immoral, illegal, or worth firing me over, but it was at least a strange curiosity that I would order quite so many books quite so often. I could chalk it up to my desire to learn or my dedication to becoming a better pastor and speaker, but the truth was, my book-buying patterns had become impulsive in nature. The "fog" of my anxiety was also blinding me to the feedback of others. It was hurting me and my relationships, but I wasn't aware of it.

As I grew in my knowledge of myself through the lens of the Enneagram, I began to learn about my core motivations as a Type Six, including my fears of being without support, security, or guidance. But from an EIP standpoint, there were even deeper layers of complexity. My Wounded Child was adopting the strategies of my Type Five part (gaining information and knowledge to feel capable and competent), looking for an alternate parent who would provide the guidance, support, and under-standing I needed. But why would I be looking for an alternate parent?

This goes back to my earliest memory as an adopted child. I was about five years old, and my parents were moving us from one suburb of Dallas to another so I could be in a better school district. On the day of the move, I stayed with a relative in a mobile home so my parents wouldn't have me underfoot.

At bedtime, they tucked me in, but as soon as they left the room, I got up and just sat there staring out the window—and I spent hours wondering if my parents were ever going to come back. Every time I'd see the headlights of a car approaching, I'd wonder if it was them—and I'd be devastated when the car would pass me by. I went through this cycle of hope and fear with each passing car. I didn't cry. I just sat there wondering if they would ever come back to get me.

This memory helps me understand that fear of abandonment is really what characterizes me as a Type Six. That Wounded Child at the window in Dallas still affects me today—I constantly look outside the window of myself just hoping that who and what I need will not pass me by. But when I am operating as the Wounded Child, different parts of me affect the process, each trying to drive the bus. When it comes to feeling ill-equipped and not having enough knowledge, it is my Five part that influences my main type the most.

When aligned, my Five part is such an asset. It is intelligent, introspective, and rational, helping me nail down the information I need to make decisions and move forward. This part loves to gather information, which is so helpful to my growth. That is why if you were to walk into my office, you would find an entire wall of more than three thousand books. There is nothing wrong with this, but there was a misalignment to my Five part. It was compelling me to buy these books, which would compel you to conclude within yourself (or even perhaps out loud): "Wow. This guy is a well-studied pastor." But truth is, it wasn't people's approval I was seeking. I wanted these sentiments—that I was a well-studied, well-prepared, well-adjusted pastor and knew what to do—to actually be true.

I was also invoking my Five part's defensive strategy in the process, a strategy based off the influence of its core motivations. Because my main type (Six) felt I did not have what it took to survive or be prepared enough to succeed, it saw the books I bought as my mentors. I falsely believed that they promised to guide me into becoming who I should be, either by their appearance on my shelves or by the content they contained to help me navigate through life safely so I could feel secure. They were books on fathering. Marriage. Pastoring. Anything. They were my attempts to find the security I so desperately felt in I needed in these areas.

But oh, the cost. I was willing to spend more money in search of this security—my Type Six's core desire. I was unknowingly willing to let my wife and my marriage suffer in search of this security. I was willing to endure tension at my church in search of this security. And since Christ and His work at the cross has established the true strength of my security, I was willing to betray what I knew to be true of Him in search of that security. And all for what?

A stack of books . . . well, actually to gain and hold on to my Type Six's core desire for safety, security, and guidance.

Ultimately, I was paying a high price in attempting to attain the security I was seeking in the act of buying books, which, oddly enough, was often just as powerful as the act of reading them. This was an illusion but felt so right and true related to what I thought I needed. Buying those books had become an idol to me, even though many of them were good, solid "Christian" books. Yet all idols denote an act of worship. Or, as it has sometimes been said, all worship demands a sacrifice. Ultimately, these idols don't work for us; they make us work for them. We go from enjoying freedom as God's adopted Beloved Children to the slavery of self-protection.

I was sacrificing far too much, including the health of other relationships, to seek this false security. After all, the books never made me feel truly secure. But the cost to my relationships was real, and it wasn't until I was willing to become aware of why I was doing it and what this process was really costing me that I was able to begin moving toward greater health.

The truth is, as a Six, my EIP reveals that other parts were attempting to help me address my Type Six's core motivations with their own type's misaligned strategies. This means that within me, it wasn't just the strategies of a Five but also those of a Seven, a Three, and a Nine that were all informing the process in different ways from their unique perspectives. When aligned and being led by the Beloved Child, each of these bring myriad gifts, strengths, and diverse abilities to the table. But misaligned, they each cost me something. This is why I must become attuned to what negatively activates them (their core motivations) and their strategies so I can see them in the moment and understand when they arise within me. This awareness will tell me I am no longer functioning as the Beloved Child in that circumstance, which allows me to come back to the Holy Spirit and ask for His guidance and help.

As we prepare to understand how the strategies of our parts play a role in our everyday interactions in life, the bottom line is that the misalignment of our parts feels natural, but it comes at a cost—and it's more than money for Amazon books. The good news, however, is that when we learn to pay attention to the fact that we're believing these misaligned parts and paying these costs, we can take intentional steps to realign our parts with the gospel. No matter how it may feel, every part within us can be aligned not simply because we will it or force it to, but ultimately because Christ's love and grace have made a divine-empowered way for gospel alignment to occur.

Remember the little lamb? *That* is the way Christ sees you not only in moments of strength but also in moments of weakness. You are safe. You are resourced. You are held. You are equipped. You are loved. When you are at your weakest, even when that weak part of you is displaying ugly, defiant, sinful attributes, Christ is not running away from you. In fact, He is not even *looking* away from you in avoidance or awkwardness. On the contrary, His heart—that is, the disposition of His very being—is divinely and eternally inclined to come closer to your brokenness, right down to your loudest inner part displaying the ugliest of sinful reactions (Romans 5:8). He does this so He can bear it all with you and bring healing to you through His gentle yet transformative work in it (Matthew 11:28–30).

Without this realization of the nature of your Shepherd who saves, preserves, and protects you, it can feel too painful or just too foreign to pay special attention to the negative reactions of various parts, especially when you've spent a lifetime dodging them, stuffing them, excusing them, or shaming them. My time in Texas looking out that window isn't the easiest memory to revisit. These things already affect us so much, so it is easy to keep trying to outrun them or ignore them. They don't deserve any more of our time or energy, right?

Yet it is all too common—and all too human—for us to continually suffer the same consequences of our negative patterns and never change course as a result. It seems counterintuitive, but we do it all the time. We pay a steep price for what we do. And we pay this price in many different ways. We may constantly harbor negative or shameful attitudes toward ourselves and others. We may constantly communicate in hurtful or unhealthy ways with family, friends, or coworkers. We may constantly return to an action or addiction that harms us and everyone around us. This is simply not what Jesus envisioned when He said, "I have come that [you] may have life, and have it to the full" (John 10:10).

Yet it can feel as if these patterns are just "the way it is" rather than a truer, fuller reality made up of many variables. These variables include things we can't control as well as actions and reactions that we most certainly can control, even if it feels like we can't. When you become aware and invite Christ into these parts, He grows the fruit of self-control within you, equipping you in ways you could never equip yourself. And even if you fail, which you will, He never stops pursuing His precious lamb—His Beloved Child. He wants you to be able to constantly recognize the cost of what is hurting you so you can be divinely equipped to lead all your parts back to the awareness of who you are and Whose you are.

His.

When we fully realize that we are His, we gain so much more than all we miss out on the other way. I have heard it said and believe it to be true that your greatest weakness is your greatest strength. In other words, we're not trying to eliminate a part of ourselves that always seems to cause us problems. In doing so, we would also eliminate the incredible value that part exudes. We only need to remind and reposition our parts in alignment with the truths believed and conveyed by the Beloved Child. When aligned with the Beloved Child, each of our parts brings fullness and strength to our lives.

In this case, my Five part has helped me quickly adapt to leading our business. If you are a professional, you have parts that do the same—when aligned, they can make all the difference in preparing a presentation, motivating a team, and securing a contract. In my case, my Five part helps me remain curious about new opportunities so I spend time reviewing all our key business metrics for our success. It remains observant and objective, helping me exercise the right amount of dispassionate engagement as I contemplate possible areas of passion to engage.

In much the same way, my aligned Three part is also a God-given asset. Instead of trying to find security through winning people, it can make a gathering of our team fun and affirming as the success of the team is elevated and celebrated. And no one is as fun as my Seven part; when it is aligned, it is able to light up the room, bringing everyone into a place of playful belonging with its seemingly endless energy, inspiring leadership, and creative flair.

Within me, these parts can either cost me or they can enrich me. The gospel offers me the path to understanding them better so I can reap their richness rather than suffer from their scarcity.

The Six Parts of Your EIP and Their Messages

We have many parts within us, and we use all nine types to some degree, but as we have already mentioned, there are six main connecting type parts that make up our basic EIP. The first two parts are simply expressions of our main type, and whether we are misaligned or aligned with gospel truth. We are beginning to know them well: the Wounded Child (misaligned part) and the Beloved Child (aligned part).

As we've learned, your connecting types are your two wings and two Enneagram paths. These are the other four parts that round out your EIP. The connecting types are there to assist your main type by bringing their own assets to the table. However, when our main type is functioning as the Wounded Child, these connecting type parts will also become misaligned and use their type's self-protective strategies to protect the Wounded Child. When operating in misalignment, they will become highly reactive and will do what they deem best for us from the perspective of their own type's core motivations.

But don't fret; there is good news! When our hearts know, believe, and trust in our secure identity in Christ, our main types are operating as the Beloved Child, which means our wings and Enneagram path types will follow suit and become aligned with gospel truth. This means that all the passengers riding in our internal bus will be safe. There will be inner peace and confidence not just in what each part brings to the table but more in the table itself. After all, it is the Shepherd's table that we are invited to regardless of our performance, which is why the shepherd psalmist famously declared: "You prepare a table before me in the presence of my enemies" (Psalm 23:5).

Our parts are not our enemies, but sometimes it can feel like it. Jesus welcomes all our parts to the table of His grace, where all His divine hospitality is graciously extended to all parts of ourselves. It is here that we begin to experience an internal reconciliation among our parts. A sense of wholeness and integration begins to set in. This is what it feels like to be who we really are in Christ—God's beloved. At this table, we become full and enabled by Christ to learn to shepherd our parts—even the ones we once despised.

In this state of awareness, each part knows, believes, and trusts who it is and Whose it is, which will result in each aligned part being able to bring its best attributes and qualities to benefit the whole of who we were created to be.

EIP Example: Type Four

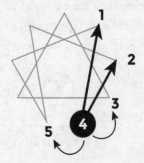

Example: Type Four Wounded Child

Dotted lines represent the broken strategies and strivings of our misaligned parts as they attempt to protect the Wounded Child.

Example: Type Four Beloved Child

Solid lines represent the restored security and strengths of our aligned parts as they are being led by the Beloved Child.

When you are not in a state of Beloved Child awareness, your main type is prone to believe the false messages not only of its own type but also of all its connecting type parts since they influence our thoughts, feelings, and gut reactions. All these false messages descend from the central false message that our Enemy began telling in the garden and continues to propagate in the hearts and minds of God's children today—that God can't be trusted. In essence, you will find that all the false messages we hear within us are merely energized and exaggerated versions of this same lie. After all, he is the father of lies (John 8:44), so the lies peddled to our parts are merely his deceptive offspring. As humans in a fallen state, the real issue is not that these false messages exist. The issue is whether we are actively believing them and living as if they are true in any given moment.

Once our main type begins to believe its primary false message, it moves on the continuum away from a Beloved Child toward the Wounded Child, which means that all the other EIP parts will begin to advance their own false messages as well, based on their respective types. The result is that many false messages bombard you at once.

Throughout life, you've believed many false messages about yourself—they replay over and over again in your heart, mind, and gut like a broken record. Here are examples of just one of the many false messages that bombard each type (more can be found in part 3 of this book).

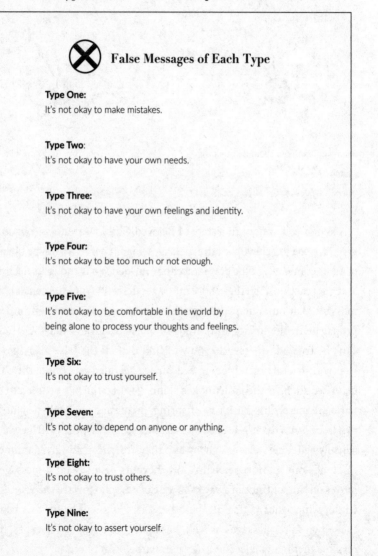

Type One:
It's not okay to make mistakes.

Type Two:
It's not okay to have your own needs.

Type Three:
It's not okay to have your own feelings and identity.

Type Four:
It's not okay to be too much or not enough.

Type Five:
It's not okay to be comfortable in the world by being alone to process your thoughts and feelings.

Type Six:
It's not okay to trust yourself.

Type Seven:
It's not okay to depend on anyone or anything.

Type Eight:
It's not okay to trust others.

Type Nine:
It's not okay to assert yourself.

It is likely that certain messages sound more familiar under specific circumstances. This is because when your main type operates as the Wounded Child, the situations in which this occurs may activate the false messages of different parts in different ways. As a Type Nine under various kinds of pressure, you may hear your Type Nine's false message that your voice doesn't matter. You may also hear the false message of your other connecting types, like your Type Eight part that says, "It's not okay to trust others with your voice." This is not the primary false message you are used to hearing, but it certainly affects the whole of your internal world's ongoing dialogue.

The main sting of these false messages is that something is "not okay," which leads you to believe that *you* are not okay. This is less logical and more a fundamental state of thinking, feeling, or reacting. These messages are aimed "under the hood" of our consciousness. This is why we feel the tension of *knowing* what is true according to the gospel yet *feeling* that these false messages are also true—perhaps even truer in our past or current experiences. You may technically know that you are okay, yet you sense you are not.

This tension is the human life—the tug-of-war between the false messages of this world and the higher, divinely true ethic by which your real life and identity already exists in Christ. Through Jesus' life, death, and resurrection, the truth is that your worth has already been fully revealed. Jesus loved and pursued you, died for you, and set you free from your striving. No matter what it may feel like, if you are in Christ, then in this moment, even if this moment is filled with confusion, anger, or despair, you are okay. Believing this is the first step to leading your internal world back into alignment.

Here are specific realities of what each type strives for and what Christ's completed work on our behalf already reveals through our lives right now.[2]

Each Type's Striving and What Christ's Completed Work Already Reveals

Type One: You strive to be good and right, but at this moment, by no effort of your own, you reflect God's virtue and integrity.

Type Two: You strive to be all loving and nurturing, but at this moment, by no effort of your own, you reflect God's compassion and care.

Type Three: You strive for hope and radiance, but at this moment, by no effort of your own, you reflect God's triumph and brilliance.

Type Four: You strive for depth and creativity, but at this moment, by no effort of your own, you reflect God's creativity and emotions.

Type Five: You strive for competency and intelligence, but at this moment, by no effort of your own, you reflect God's wisdom and innovation.

Type Six: You strive to be faithful and loyal, but at this moment, by no effort of your own, you reflect God's loyalty and bravery.

Type Seven: You strive for happiness and abundance, but at this moment, by no effort of your own, you reflect God's joy and playfulness.

Type Eight: You strive for intensity and invulnerability, but at this moment, by no effort of your own, you reflect God's protection and passion.

Type Nine: You strive for peace and oneness, but at this moment, by no effort of your own, you reflect God's tranquility and unity.

Given our high-paced, achieving society, is it difficult for you to believe that your value is already secured and displayed, not earned? Every day, we make mistakes and become misaligned with the truth of the gospel. We don't always reveal God in the way we want to, nor do we always feel like the *imago Dei*—the image of God (Romans 7:15). But the truth is, we can rest assured that God has redeemed us and is restoring us each day to become more like Christ (Philippians 1:16). We must learn to recognize the false messages that attempt to move us away from the truth and ask the Holy Spirit to renew our mind with his truth (Romans 12:2).

SEVEN

Understanding the Parts of Your Enneagram Internal Profile

PRIMARY STRATEGIES, DEFENSIVE MECHANISMS, AND NAMING YOUR PARTS

Each of us faces false messages and strivings that lead us to develop strategies for facing the hardships of this fallen world—and the fallen internal world within us. We discussed the core motivations for each type back in chapter 4, so it may be helpful to refer to these lists (pages 52–54) as you begin to tie those motivations to these strategies. The bottom line is that we all have a personality strategy to defend ourselves from our core fear and core weakness and to attempt to obtain our core desire and core longing.

Your strategy is the earthly theme of your life. It's always in the background, influencing all that you do. Think about the last big decision you had to make. How did your personality strategy play into that decision in positive and negative ways?

An example might be as follows. You are a Type Two and you are

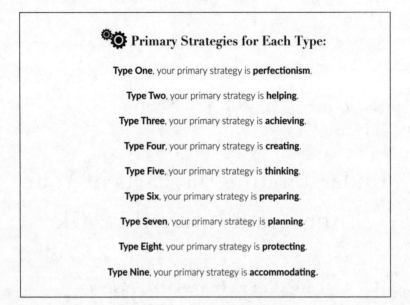

Primary Strategies for Each Type:

Type One, your primary strategy is **perfectionism**.

Type Two, your primary strategy is **helping**.

Type Three, your primary strategy is **achieving**.

Type Four, your primary strategy is **creating**.

Type Five, your primary strategy is **thinking**.

Type Six, your primary strategy is **preparing**.

Type Seven, your primary strategy is **planning**.

Type Eight, your primary strategy is **protecting**.

Type Nine, your primary strategy is **accommodating**.

contemplating leaving a toxic work situation. Your core desire is to be appreciated, loved, and wanted. This has already made this situation feel unbearable. Every time you are passed up for a promotion or your boss doesn't acknowledge your contributions, your core desire is not being met.

Your core fear is being rejected and unwanted, being thought worthless, needy, inconsequential, dispensable, or unworthy of love. This makes it hard to speak up for yourself in your situation. What if you are seen as a squeaky wheel? Or what if the team just throws you away because you really weren't that important to them in the first place? Your core fear is on full display.

Finally, your core weakness is pride. For you, this means denying your own needs and emotions, while using your strong intuition to discover and focus on the emotions and needs of others, confidently inserting your helpful support in hopes that others will say how grateful they are for your thoughtful care. At the job, you double down in making yourself completely indispensable, attempting to fix a situation far beyond your ability to fix, yet you strive to salvage it by helping everyone to win—except yourself.

Ultimately, can you see how your primary strategy of helping is the action you take in reaction to the situation at hand? So then, your core motivations are the driving force behind your thoughts, feelings, and actions, and they clearly reveal your personality strategy.

Of course, this will not be the only thing you feel. After all, you are more than one thing. The other connecting type parts of your EIP—your wing Type One, wing Type Three, Enneagram path to Type Four, and Enneagram path to Type Eight—may all be activated negatively or positively depending on whether you are operating out of your Wounded Child (misaligned heart) or your Beloved Child (aligned heart). Each of your connecting type parts will also approach the situation with their own type's primary strategies.

This is why understanding your EIP and the types and strategies of each part is so key. If you find yourself unhealthily responding in a certain way—perhaps, in this example, in an overly protective way—your Enneagram path Type Eight part may be negatively activated, meaning that somewhere on the spectrum, your main Type Two is operating from its Wounded Child part. One clues you in to the other.

Your primary strategy is not necessarily positive or negative. However, when the Wounded Child is behind the wheel, you will find yourself experiencing the negative sides of these strategies, also known as a type's defensive mechanism. It is very challenging to recognize your defensive mechanism in action and admit that it is harmful to you and others since your Wounded Child is convinced it is the best way to protect you in the moment.

When these defensive mechanisms are activated and can be recognized, we can awaken to the fact that our primary type is in the state of the Wounded Child in some form or fashion—and our parts have followed suit, which means we need to awaken our Beloved Child to guide our whole self back into alignment.

✝ Here Are the Defensive Mechanisms for Each Type:

Type One, your defense mechanism is **reaction formation**. When an unacceptable emotion arises, your Wounded Child conceals it and brings up the opposite emotion to contradict it. For example, you hide envious emotions by celebrating and praising others for their abilities.

Type Two, your defense mechanism is **repression**. To avoid your painful emotions, your Wounded Child represses—or hides—your feelings, desires, wishes, fears, and needs. For example, instead of expressing your own needs, you look for ways to help and love others.

Type Three, your defense mechanism is **identification**. Your Wounded Child fears being rejected for being yourself, so it embodies the admirable qualities of desirable people. For example, when you walk into a room, you shape-shift into an image that will be accepted and admired.

Type Four, your defense mechanism is **introjection**. Instead of blocking out negative information, your Wounded Child fully internalizes it into your sense of self, making it difficult for you to distinguish between reality and fantasy because it all feels real. For example, when you are given both positive and negative feedback, you discount the positive information. Instead of responding to the criticism, you fully absorb the negative information.

Type Five, your defense mechanism is **isolation**. Your Wounded Child retreats into your mind and isolates you from others so you can process your feelings privately. For example, you avoid events or people who are overwhelming and will hoard your resources so you're not depleted.

Type Six, your defense mechanism is **projection**. Your Wounded Child unconsciously attributes your own unwanted and unacceptable thoughts, feelings, and motives onto others. For example, when you can't accept and acknowledge your own issues, you will see those issues in others and believe that to be reality.

Type Seven, your defense mechanism is **rationalization**. Your Wounded Child is skilled at reframing any situation to justify your behaviors and avoid sadness, limitations, or the hurt you caused others. For example, you quickly turn on the charm and spin negatives into positives. Because you are so upbeat and likable, it's hard for anyone to stay mad at you.

Type Eight, your defense mechanism is **denial**. To present a strong exterior, your Wounded Child must deny that you are human and therefore vulnerable. For example, you deny, forget, or ignore that you caused someone harm because the vulnerability of seeing it and admitting it is too painful.

Type Nine, your defense mechanism is **narcotization** or **dissociation**. To maintain peace and harmony, your Wounded Child avoids conflict at all costs by numbing or checking out. For example, to avoid a difficult conversation, you might withdraw or turn to activities that are routine, familiar, require little effort, and give you comfort.

Positive Intent and Naming Your Parts

It is important to remember that each of your type's parts—or internal team members—has positive intent. This is not a validation of sin or its impact on our lives. It is an acceptance of our fallenness that has been redeemed—and is being redeemed—in Christ.

We are validating our Wounded Child, not overlooking or excusing it. As children, we did the best we could to survive. It is unhelpful to ignore this scared, wounded part of ourselves in adulthood. Acknowledging the positive intent of our parts validates their value, not their broken strategies or patterns.

Remembering this can feel counterintuitive because in the moment our parts are derailing us, we often resent them. But within the context of Christ's forgiveness and redemption for every part of our internal world, when we remember that these parts have not only positive intent for the whole of ourselves but, more importantly, redemptive grace from our Good Shepherd, we can also extend kindness and gratitude to them, even as we lead them to address their strategies in healthier ways.

From a biblical perspective, our Wounded Child doesn't know Jesus as well as we do. From a neuroscientific perspective, our Wounded Child also doesn't know how old we are. It struggles to grasp the concept of linear time—that is, that we have progressed and matured. It doesn't know what the Spirit and the Beloved Child know, which is why we have to patiently and gently lead it. Without the Beloved Child's wisdom, maturity, and understanding of the bigger picture of the Father's constant, loving intervention in all things, the Wounded Child can be reactive, impulsive, selfish, and destructive in seeking what it believes is best for us. But shaming yourself or reacting in frustration and condemnation will only cause more damage and ensure that the Wounded Child continues to react to life on autopilot. When you are in this cycle, it feels natural, so it must be broken by something steeped in the supernatural: grace.

To bring wisdom and healing to your Wounded Child, you need to see its good intent, have compassion for what it has gone through, and befriend it—something we will explore in the next chapter. For now, the first step in welcoming your Wounded Child is to name it. By naming it, you acknowledge its presence and history. Think about the power found in simply naming it. You are giving it the loving attention it needs and craves. You are opening the door to experiencing the Father's love simply by acknowledging that the Wounded Child exists, as opposed to keeping it buried and exiled. There's something powerful here because Jesus often called people out of exile, shame, and death (like Zacchaeus, Mary Magdalene, Peter, Lazarus, and many others) by using their actual names.

As I mentioned earlier in the book, I (Beth) call my Wounded Child "Little Bethy" because it represents my younger self who was vulnerable, hurting, scared, and trying to protect herself from getting hurt through her core fears. Again, since my Wounded Child is a misaligned version of my main type, Little Bethy is a Type Nine, but she exudes the less healthy and negative aspects of a Nine's core motivations.

When you begin naming your Wounded Child, think back to a particular moment in your childhood when you felt alone, hurt, vulnerable, or confused. Were you on your own to figure out a problem or work through difficult emotions? Did you blame yourself for the situation you were in? What false messages do you think your Wounded Child received from this event? You see, when you were younger, your Beloved Child was still developing and could not adequately guide you or combat the false messages you received from a fallen world. Therefore, your Wounded Child felt mostly alone to do the best it could to protect you with the resources and inadequate knowledge available to you.

Because of this, you are naturally more acquainted with your Wounded Child, more comfortable in allowing it to guide your inner world and interpret your circumstances. In many ways, your Wounded Child's perspective feels like reality. As you think about your Wounded Child, what name comes to mind? What is the significance or meaning behind that name? As we begin to name parts, we don't have to use negative associations, but this may be an easier place to begin the process because negative feelings can be the easiest to quickly identify.

The point of naming parts is so you can better understand them and know how to help them become aligned. When the Wounded Child trusts that you see it, hear it, and are there to help, it can then be guided by your true self—the Beloved Child. Your Beloved Child will bring the truth of the gospel to your Wounded Child. Wrapped in the arms of Jesus' love, redemptive work, compassion, and grace, the Wounded Child can leave behind its unhealthy and divisive strategies and begin to cooperate with the Beloved Child to bring about the greatest good for yourself and others, glorifying God in the process.

You've already met my Beloved Child in chapter three: "Coach Beth." How would you name your Beloved Child? When you think of who you really are in the eyes of an infinitely loving God who cherishes you, pursues you, and draws you close to Him, what comes to mind? Perhaps remember the moment you first came to trust in Christ or had a groundbreaking realization about His grace and love for you. This is the part that experiences radiance, joy, peace, unconditional love, and a sense of belonging. How would you name that part of yourself?

Naming parts can feel strange at first, but it is just an exercise to better recognize when they are activated, whether in alignment or misalignment. By quickly recognizing them, you can see when their defensive strategies arise so you can guide them back to health. If you remember the description of my parts in the fog in the second chapter, then you now realize that I described the connecting type parts of my EIP, but I didn't name them (I didn't want to overwhelm you too early).

Each of these names means something to me from my childhood, adulthood, relationships, or patterns of thought and action. It is also important to remember that while we might begin the naming process using negative examples, none of our parts are negative. We must be careful to not only create negative correlations, always remembering their positive intent and capabilities when aligned. For instance, I've named my Type Eight part

Regina. Regina can be "Raging Regina," attempting to wrestle control of the wheel of the bus away from the Beloved Child. Or she can be "Remarkable Regina." It all depends on if she is being coached or led by Coach Beth, or if she is trying to defend Little Bethy's interests, who consequently is curled up asleep on the backseat of the bus, fearing being hurt yet again.

My EIP looks like this:

Beth's EIP

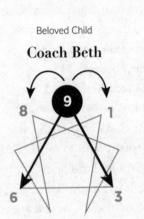

Beloved Child
Coach Beth

Wounded Child
Little Bethy

Type One (Wing):
Virtuous Victoria

Type One (Wing):
Vicious Victoria

Type Eight (Wing):
Remarkable Regina

Type Eight (Wing):
Raging Regina

Type Three (Enneagram Path):
Noble Natalie

Type Three (Enneagram Path):
Not Good Enough Natalie

Type Six (Enneagram Path):
Wonderful Wendy

Type Six (Enneagram Path):
Worrying Wendy

As you think through naming your parts, a negative memory or pattern may reveal a name that feels right, but always remember that each of these parts can be aligned or misaligned, so don't vilify them beyond redemption. They are each capable of positive or negative action or reaction. Our hope is that as we consistently surrender and depend on the Holy Spirit to remind our parts that we are redeemed, cherished, loved, and delighted in, we will more quickly move from a misaligned to aligned heart condition that will bless others, bless ourselves, and glorify God.

As we end this chapter, let's once again demonstrate more ways our parts show up.[1] This time, Jeff will share more about his parts, as well the way that parts have shown up in the lives of a few of the people who have walked with us through their own Enneagram path. You can learn more about this path at www.yourenneagramprofile.com.

Parts and Real People

Earlier in the book, you witnessed a part of me (Jeff) that pursued Beth when we were in an argument, trying to gain assurances from her that she would never leave me because of my core fear of being abandoned. Over time, I have also learned more about the parts of my EIP. My EIP looks like this.[2]

Jeff's EIP

Beloved Child
Pastor Jeff

Wounded Child
Jeffrey

Type Five (Wing):
Bob

Type Seven (Wing):
El McCordo

Type Three (Enneagram Path):
Charlie

Type Nine (Enneagram Path):
Phil

Naming all these parts has taken some time. In fact, I only recently began to notice a particular pattern in my life—that is, a different part that is activated within me. It usually begins soon after Beth and I have spun out again. It feels as if a cloud has covered my mind and heart, but something is different—my typical Type Six patterns of frenetic thinking and fearful panic begin to subside.

At first glance, this might appear to be a sign of maturity, but it is actually very sobering. As a Six, much of my interior world revolves around finding security. In recent years, I have begun to face my coping strategies related to finding security, such as buying books and trying to counsel Beth into my way of thinking when I feel that I am losing her in conflict. I have begun to see that when I don't know how to find Beth in that cloud of discord, I shut down instead. I lose affect. I deaden emotion. I stop thinking. I go numb.

When I am facing powerlessness, shutting down is becoming my new norm.

I call this part Phil—and he has been a longtime acquaintance. Now that I recognize him and have named him, I can remember Phil showing up when I was a kid. He was there during times my mom was in the hospital and I would wake up at someone else's home before school, my dad having taken me there so he could get to work on time. I remember sometimes being alone during summer days when my mom was sick and bedridden. I remember Phil showing up when an important relationship was in turmoil during my eighth grade and freshman years of school. During some of these times, Phil really protected me. Other times, he isolated me.

Phil is my Enneagram path Type Nine part who shows up when I cannot find connection or security. Like all parts, he can be aligned or misaligned: Fantastic Phil or Fail-safe Phil. When being led by my aligned main Type Six—that is, the Beloved Child I have named Pastor Jeff—Fantastic Phil lives in the security of the gospel and can see the value in conflicting opinions and difficult, seemingly impossible scenarios. This aligned Phil can listen with confidence and respond without burying his head in the sand or losing his head in anger—he trusts that the Father is in charge, so he can rest in this sovereignty, even as he continues searching for the right steps to take, usually which have not yet presented themselves.

However, the misaligned Fail-safe Phil finds that it is too difficult to face unmet longings, so instead, he tries to deaden it all by influencing Jeffrey (my Wounded Child) with his defense mechanism of narcotization (numbing out or shutting down). Phil tries to help Jeffrey by *calming* everything down. But in doing so, he also *shuts* everything down. Honestly, when the misaligned Phil persists, I can slip into complete numbness—a deep internal fog of disassociation, and, in some seasons, depression. When I recognize Phil's negative strategies, it is a sign that Jeffrey needs Pastor Jeff's (Beloved Child) presence—to be led back to a strong, faithful, loving, pursuing Father who is not powerless. Phil gives me a kind and gentle reminder that I am not alone but that I belong.

All my parts need this alignment. My Three part is named Charlie, and, as we explored earlier (though we didn't name him), he can also be aligned or misaligned with gospel truth. When aligned, he can use his drive to achieve in a healthy way, allowing his strengths to serve the greater good and create an affirming environment for those around me. However, when Charlie is trying to protect Jeffrey, as I previously mentioned, he attempts to gain others' approval and find security through winning people. He is the part who incessantly buys gifts for others for the wrong reasons. Charlie in alignment can buy gifts for the right reasons, but misaligned Charlie may do the same good thing, but not out of a place of rest and security that flows from being led by the Beloved Child.

My Seven part can also function in either a misaligned or aligned state. I lovingly call him El McCordo. Being half-Mexican and adopted, this expression of this part of me taps into the fun-loving, positive-seeing, joke-telling side of my personality. When I was a pastor, El McCordo was often in action, emerging as the life of the many parties we would throw—or in our case, they were called "community groups." When El McCordo is aligned with the gospel, he can produce the kind of environment in which everyone present feels welcomed, valued, and positively engaged in fun times. When misaligned, El McCordo can become crude and attempt to show off his fun-loving, seemingly secure self amid a brash, loud bravado.

The bottom line is that all my parts are a gift from God—and like every good thing affected by the fall, they face a brokenness that must be brought before Christ in order to be reconciled to the gospel and ultimately redeemed. While their negative aspects may be more easily recognizable, the good news is that the Father constantly invites me to once again listen and believe as I really am: His Beloved Child. In this lies the key to seeing all my parts grow into the versions of themselves God has creatively crafted them to be.

JOHN (TYPE FOUR, INTROSPECTIVE INDIVIDUALIST)

John is a dear friend and a Type Four. He and I have traveled together to the deepest recesses of one another's hearts, seeing Jesus bring clarity and hope to our deepest pains.

John was previously a member of a certain denomination. He has discovered that his involvement in that community was at least partly a result of his love for their life-changing theological perspective about the grace of God revealed in Christ. But in another way, the community inadvertently served to increase his guilt and shame.

Since John's main type is Type Four, his connecting type parts (or EIP) are wing Type Three, wing Type Five, Enneagram path Type One, and Enneagram path Type Two. John has named his Type One part Larry and his Wounded Child Little John. Little John found security in a theologically robust community. It gave him a sense of belonging and foundation. He felt "okay" because he shared the same beliefs as everyone else in the community.

For Little John, he internalized a false message he believed his denomination was saying to him: "If you believe these things, you will be seen and loved." John's Type One part, Larry, would become activated and strive to make sure that all his theological beliefs were in line with the denomination—that he was always on the correct side. On vacations, he would seek out and attend another church in the same denomination because Larry would say it was the right thing to do. He felt there were certain authors he could read, along with other authors he should never have on his bookshelf. He aligned himself with what seemed right, and that rightness was very much framed within the denomination to which he belonged.

Larry was always there to help Little John know when he was doing it right and to scold him when he wasn't. Why was Larry such a strong part of John's interior world? Because he was the Wounded Child in this area of his life, which is why he was being influenced by the defensive strategies of one of his connecting type parts. Little John needed the Spirit-filled John, the Beloved Child, to compassionately guide Little John's attention away from finding acceptance in a restrictively harsh view of God, the Bible, and his people. He needed to coach Little John into seeing that the grace he believed was available was already accessible to him, even if all his theological ducks were not always in a perfect row. He needed to know that he was allowed to grow in Christ, not just in one group of people who loved Christ.

ARIANA (TYPE SIX, FAITHFUL GUARDIAN)

Ariana grew up in a tragic setting. Her sister had a rare epileptic condition—so rare, in fact, that she was a patient of world-renowned neurosurgeon Dr. Ben Carson.

Using EIP, one of the ways Ariana has begun to understand the impact of growing up with a very ill sister is in her present-day relationship to her four-year-old daughter. Ariana's daughter can become very sad, very quickly. If she is emotionally hurt in a particular way, her sadness can be expressed with yelling and screaming. As a child, Ariana was well accustomed to screaming because during seizures, her sister would often fall to the ground, sometimes bloodying herself in the process, then wake up screaming. Her family would also respond often to her sister's situation with loud voices and commanding actions in trying to help.

Through looking back at her past and looking up at her present, Ariana has seen two parts become more evident to her: her Type Nine and Type Six parts. They actually show up in conflict with one another. She hasn't named them, which is perfectly fine, but her Type Nine part shows up with a desire to hide from the chaos. She is overwhelmed and wants to avoid the pain. Her Type Six part, on the other hand, shows up wanting to demonstrate extreme loyalty and responsibility for her family. Despite being the youngest, when she looks back, this responsible part would show up to move her into the very situation that another part of her desperately wanted to avoid.

Now as a parent, loud noises and demands for attention can overwhelm her—so much that she and her husband have agreed that at certain times, he is better equipped to attend to their daughter. One day when he wasn't home, her daughter needed her attention and affection, which took the form of screaming in sadness. Recognizing her own responses to her daughter's situation, she was able to invite Christ to bring peace to her Nine and Six parts in the moment, which allowed her to let her daughter experience sadness while she, her mother, also remained emotionally present in what would otherwise be a very foggy situation. Rather than avoiding or trying to fix the situation, her Type Nine part created space for her daughter to feel in a safe environment. All the while, her Type Six part remained loyal and present with her daughter.

On to AWARE

You may not be ready to recognize or name your parts, but in the next chapter, we want to offer you an exercise that has allowed me, Beth, John, and Ariana to apply the principles of EIP in real-time circumstances. The consequences of remaining unaware are too steep. We can begin to awaken to various parts within us, understanding the strategies they employ based on their types, so we can always be moving on the spectrum toward the health and security offered to us as Beloved Children.

EIGHT

Unpacking AWARE

By now we hope you have a framework for understanding the concept of the parts within you and how they relate to one another based on the core motivations of your main type and its interaction with the motivations and strategies of your four connecting types. Now you are ready to begin applying these principles to your actual life. In the sections that follow, we will show you how all this can play out for each type.

In this chapter, we want to introduce you to a process that can be adopted both as a daily discipline as well as an exercise that can be applied to almost any situation: AWARE. This chapter is a culmination of everything we've learned up to now, so don't be surprised when we repeat or reference some of the other points, scriptures, or takeaways from earlier chapters. Think of it as if we have been showing you the building blocks, and now we're going to show you the significance of how they can be stacked together to create something that can stand.

We created AWARE as a spiritual exercise to help apply the gospel to the various parts of our heart, especially when they become misaligned and feel the need to protect our Wounded Child. In regular times of silence and solitude coupled with the Scriptures, we can break free of these unhealthy patterns so we can lead, mentor, and shepherd our heart in partnership with the Holy Spirit. AWARE helps us be present and grounded in the moment, walk in step with the Holy Spirit, and understand ourselves with greater clarity and deeper grace.

The acronym AWARE stands for:

AWAKEN to your thoughts, feelings, body sensations, and inclinations.
WELCOME these experiences without judgment.
ASK your internal parts what they are feeling and the Holy Spirit for guidance.
RECEIVE what is true.
ENGAGE with yourself and your relationships in a new way.

As we map out EIPs for each type in the sections to follow, we will end with the AWARE exercise in each section. Though you will soon see the AWARE exercise for your own type, here are some examples of how we use this exercise as a Type Nine (Beth) and a Type Six (Jeff).

Example of AWARE for Type Nines

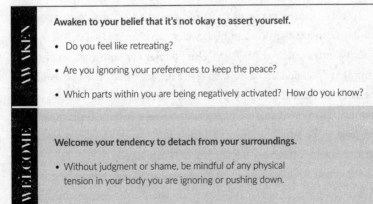

AWAKEN

Awaken to your belief that it's not okay to assert yourself.

- Do you feel like retreating?

- Are you ignoring your preferences to keep the peace?

- Which parts within you are being negatively activated? How do you know?

WELCOME

Welcome your tendency to detach from your surroundings.

- Without judgment or shame, be mindful of any physical tension in your body you are ignoring or pushing down.

ASK

Ask the Holy Spirit what is going on inside you so you can engage with it and not avoid it.

- What are you afraid of?
- Why do you lose yourself in others?

RECEIVE

Receive the truth that your voice and dignity matter to God.

- Reflect on this verse: "For God gave us a spirit not of fear but of power and love and self-control" (2 Timothy 1:7 ESV).

ENGAGE

Engage in life by taking the next right step even though the resolution and outcome are unknown.

- Walking in step with the Holy Spirit, asserting yourself, and being grounded in Christ will lead you in the right direction.

Example of AWARE for Type Sixes

AWAKEN

Awaken to your belief that it's not okay to trust yourself.

- Name one of your racing thoughts—you can't address everything. (To focus, it may help to write in a journal.)
- Which parts within you are being negatively activated? How do you know?

WELCOME

Welcome the thought with kindness and curiosity, paying attention to the way it makes your body feel.

- Name the thought(s) or part(s) within you that you are perceiving as negative.
- How can you hear this concern apart from self-judgment or condemnation?

ASK

Ask the Holy Spirit to reveal the anxiety and motivation behind your thought.

- Resist the urge to look for a solution from an outside source.
- Listen to the wisdom and discernment the Holy Spirit has already promised to put within you.

RECEIVE

Receive the felt presence of Jesus—His guidance and loving counsel.

- Spend time in this verse: "So do not fear, for I am with you; do not be dismayed, for I am your God. I will strengthen you and help you; I will uphold you with my righteous right hand" (Isaiah 41:10).

ENGAGE

Engage in life with gratitude, self-leading your inner committee with the assurance and security you have found in Christ.

- With wisdom and self-control, speak or act courageously in this current situation according to the truth and guidance you have now become aware of.

Now that we've glimpsed where we are going, let's circle back and explore the goal and the process of learning to use AWARE. The purpose of this exercise is not to analyze every feeling or thought. It is to truly experience what we already know to be true about the gospel. As author and pastor Tim Keller says, "The gospel is this: We are more sinful and flawed in ourselves than we ever dared believe, yet at the very same time we are more loved and accepted in Jesus Christ than we ever dared hope."[1] To that end, AWARE is a tool to help ourselves wake up and recognize in any given moment the truth that keeps getting lost in our fog: that we are God's "workmanship, created in Christ Jesus for good works, which God prepared beforehand, that we should walk in them" (Ephesians 2:10 ESV).

Workmanship is not a word we use very often in our modern English vernacular. It might sound fairly transactional and sterile, but in the Greek version of the early manuscripts, readers would have recognized the term as something much more special, relational, and significant. The original word is *poiēma*, related to our English word *poem*.

In other words, being God's workmanship is a deeply personal expression of God's unique affection and handiwork in our lives. In his eyes, we are beautiful works of art designed in very specific ways to glorify Him and to bless others. And He intends for us to have joy in the working—that is, the daily living—He has prepared for us to navigate.

Even when you feel that your canvas has become torn beyond repair or that the paint has become mixed, dried, or splattered beyond usefulness, God promises that "he who began a good work in you will carry it on to completion until the day of Christ Jesus" (Philippians 1:6). You are not merely the sum of your parts behaving well or behaving badly. You are a work of art that Christ Himself is perpetually tending to because He delights in doing so for His own good pleasure (Philippians 2:13). And you are being carried by Him in both safety and purpose toward an ultimate, joyful completion.

The divine Artist-in-residence within our hearts directs the attention of our transformative process not solely *at* us, nor completely away *from* us, but rather *through* us. Our lives become illuminated as painted lines and colors drawn from the endless store of resurrection life that flows from the One who is personally crafting our beauty, even amid the dry ashes we bring to the easel.

In the end, this is for His glory, yet by grace, we are invited to share in it as the objects of His purpose, not the originators of it. This frees us from the constant obsession of seeking purpose for or in ourselves. As Dane Ortlund says, "We are pieces of art, designed to be beautiful and thus draw attention to our artist. We are simply made for nothing else."[2]

The goal of this book has been to help you navigate the parts of your inner world that become misaligned from this energizing, joyful state of living. But to be clear, this realignment doesn't happen *only* when you do everything right—it can happen smack-dab in the middle of both the right and the wrong of your life. You don't have to be fully aware to experience the Artist's gentle, loving, and corrective brushstrokes. In fact, He longs to bring His brush closer to your canvas when it needs more attention. He never throws you out; after all, you can't paint yourself, and He delights in painting who you are becoming.

Or to call back our primary metaphor, a Good Shepherd is most attentive to the needs of a sheep when the sheep is lost, sick, or most likely to be attacked by a predator. Ortlund expounds on the truth of the Shepherd's increasing nearness in our increasing neediness: "Christians intuitively know that it pleases Christ when we listen to him and obey him. But what if his very heart and joy is engaged in a new way in our foibles and failures?"[3] Theologian Thomas Goodwin answers his question like this: Christ's "own joy, comfort, happiness, and glory are increased and enlarged by his showing grace and mercy, in pardoning, relieving, and comforting his members here on earth."[4]

In other words, your Shepherd isn't waiting for you to become unstuck before He helps. He is the only One who can help you become truly unstuck in the first place—and it is not just something He does because He's God and He has to. No, it is His very nature to delight in forgiving, healing, and restoring you over and over again.

As we begin to engage in this spiritual exercise, remember that the most important goal is to first rest in who you are in Christ. You can't successfully implement AWARE if you don't ultimately believe that Jesus Christ is for you and not against you. You might awaken to where you are, but without His grace and love as a central anchor for your soul's paradigm of seeing yourself and the world, you won't be able to healthily welcome your internal parts. And even if you could, without the Holy Spirit's guidance, your parts cannot experience healing and alignment back into living as the Beloved Child.

The reality is that since you are still a human on this side of the fall, you will still get stuck. You won't always be able to notice it as it is happening, and you certainly won't be able to implement your own internal discipline that instantly causes you to be completely at rest with yourself. Striving to become unstuck without the Good Shepherd's help is like struggling to get out of quicksand: the more you move, the deeper you will sink into a desperate situation. But if you invite Him to help, you will find that the Holy Spirit is the One changing you *through* these experiences, not *apart* from them.

The negative moments in your life have a special usefulness in the hands of Christ to lead you to greater awareness of your deep need for daily redemption and Spirit intervention. In other words, the goal is not to *never* get stuck—it is to become aware of when you are doing so and to learn to invite the Holy Spirit's work into your misaligned brokenness as a way of living. It will not be aligned perfection but rather an aligned brokenness that will become your new way of living. And yes, along the way, you will get stuck less, but even when you still do, you will not run from the Shepherd. Rather, you will run to Him as your familiar Source of strength, comfort, and rescue.

Begin with Silence and Solitude

This journey through EIP that leads to AWARE is one that we have been walking ourselves for multiple years. Before we dive into AWARE itself, we'd like to share with you a bit more of the story that led us to create this exercise.

In our own experience, we have found that when our hearts are aligned with the truth of the gospel, we can live in the reality that so often gets lost in the fog: that God is not done with us and that He is intimately involved in our spiritual growth, even when we have misaligned and ugly parts. This constant realignment translates into peace in our relationships (including our marriage), peace in our relationship to the work that the Lord has given us to do, and peace in relationship to ourselves. We don't always stay in this peace. Rather, we expect to have to return to it every day—and when we face familiar circumstances that tend to leave us in the fog.

As we've referenced so many times, Romans 12:2 describes a process about which most Christians make assumptions. "Do not conform to the pattern of this world, but be transformed by the renewing of your mind. Then you will be able to test and approve what God's will is—his good, pleasing and perfect will." Many people assume that this transformation is a thing God does to us in a single moment at conversion rather than a continual process we experience as we keep walking toward His ways through the fog of this world. The truth is that it is both, but it is the second kind we tend to overlook the most. We miss the present-tense reality: "Be transformed by the renewing of your mind," not just "you *were* transformed when your mind *was* renewed." Paul is clear: this is something that is supposed *to be happening* to you, not just something that *has once happened* to you. If you have no need to be transformed, you can't experience a present-tense transformation.

This means that as we apply the AWARE exercise to our EIP, it is supposed to be a dynamic process. We're not simply trying to expose the problems as they relate to who we should be because of our salvation. An "I should be" way of thinking leaves us with a shameful sense of scarcity and a nagging assumption that God must be disappointed with us. No, the goal is to repeatedly bring all of who we are today back into a perpetual, life-changing relationship with God that happens in our real life, even the disappointing parts.

We tend to assume that the guilt and shame that result from a static viewpoint of God's transformation will somehow prove effective in rendering us changed. But guilt and shame never get the job done. Shaking this assumption is a key to becoming aware—and we can't shake it while we're still humming along at full speed through our preexisting patterns and strategies. We have to learn to push pause and remind ourselves of the truth our souls seem to run from the fastest.

In our journey, the writings of Jerry Bridges introduced us to the idea of reminding ourselves by "preaching the gospel" to ourselves.[5] Depending on past experiences or perspectives, we can get hung up on terms like *preach*, so we just call this "gospel self-talk." In the EIP sections to follow, we will give examples of what this gospel self-talk might look like for each type. But for now, the idea is that the gospel isn't merely something to be believed for conversion alone but is also something to be reminded of daily so our spiritual life can be grounded in the truth of what Christ has done for us and what He is still doing for us. Then we can face whatever may come our way each day. This means the gospel has a central place in both our failures and our successes.

This gospel self-talk reminds us of what our parts often lose sight of, awakening the Beloved Child within us again each day afresh. As Jerry Bridges explains:

> Preaching the gospel to ourselves every day gives us hope, joy, and courage. The good news that our sins are forgiven because of Christ's death fills our hearts with joy, gives us courage to face the day, and offers us hope that God's favor will rest upon us, not because we are good, but because we are in Christ. . . .
>
> To preach the gospel to yourself, then, means that you continually face up to your own sinfulness and then flee to Jesus [because] . . . God's holy wrath is no longer directed toward you.[6]

A few years after we were introduced to this concept of gospel self-talk, we began reading Brennan Manning's book *Abba's Child,* which impacted us deeply. In this book, Manning includes a letter he wrote to what he calls his "false self." The elements within his own internal world felt strangely familiar to us, even though we had yet to study or name our own parts. In part, Manning wrote:

> Good morning, Impostor. Surely you are surprised by the cordial greeting. You probably expected, "Hello, you little jerk," since I have hammered you from day one of this retreat. Let me begin by admitting that I have been unreasonable, ungrateful, and unbalanced in my appraisal of you. (Of course, you are aware, puff of smoke, that in addressing you, I am talking to myself. You are not some isolated, impersonal entity living on an asteroid, but a real part of me.) I come to you today not with rod in hand but with an olive branch. When I was

a little boy and first knew that no one was there for me, you intervened and showed me where to hide. (In those Depression days of the thirties, you recall, my parents were doing the best they could with what they had just to provide food and shelter.) At that moment in time, you were invaluable. Without your intervention, I would have been overwhelmed by dread and paralyzed by fear. You were there for me and played a crucial, protective role in my development. Thank you.[7]

This was a similar concept to Bridges', but as Manning preached the gospel to himself via a letter, he directed it toward a specific part of himself—and he began to show God's grace to this part in ways he never had before. This was before we had really explored the concepts of parts, but it resonated. We began to sense that there was more than one thing going on inside us.

The next piece of the puzzle was that Manning had engaged in the process of addressing at least one of his internal parts while he was on a silent retreat. This concept of a silent retreat was very intriguing. Around the same time, we were introduced to the book *Invitation to Solitude and Silence* by Ruth Haley Barton. This book challenged the way many Christians approach their spiritual growth, and specifically their times of interaction with Jesus.

In modern culture, we have been trained by well-meaning mentors and disciplers to focus on certain self-imposed agendas during our devotional times. We have reading plans, scriptures to memorize, and a list of people and circumstances to "pray through" (a term indicating the importance of getting the process done). The idea of pausing to simply allow our minds and our hearts to be attuned to the Spirit can seem touchy-feely or mystical in our modern age of metric-based, time-efficient pursuits.

We (Beth and Jeff) often laugh remembering a certain men's Bible study group in which moments of silence and solitude produced mixed results for those present. The Sixes and Sevens would sit there with their minds racing, mentally arguing back and forth with their inner committees about what they should be focusing on. The Nines and Fives would just disassociate and drift off into some other mental universe. The Twos and Threes would sometimes fall asleep because it was the first time during their day that they had slowed down enough to be present in their exhausting lives. It became apparent that silence and solitude were not easily accessible disciplines in the modern Christian context as it relates to times of devotion.

For both of us who have Type Six parts in our EIP (though we hadn't named them yet), we began to recognize patterns in our thoughts and feelings. We saw that sometimes we tended to default to an anxious state of ruminating over circumstances or feeling certain ways that rendered us upended rather than upright in our confidence in Christ. When misaligned, our Six parts tended to get out of bed in the morning and face the day through the strategy of embodying anxiety. This had been the case for our entire lives—we were just unaware of it. But as we learned to practice silence and solitude, we were able to observe that this was happening.

As we know, observation isn't transformation, so just realizing what was happening didn't change it. In some cases, we noticed that in these awkward internal moments of overactive thinking, we would choose to fixate even further in an attempt to escape the terrifying silence. We doubled down on our anxious thoughts. Dr. Dan Zink, a professor of counseling at Covenant Theological Seminary, calls this filling, numbing, and blinding.[8] The idea is that we find additional idols to serve to avoid dealing with our true selves that are exposed in moments of solitude— things we don't want to recognize or acknowledge in our own hearts.

Finally, the concept of Internal Family Systems (IFS) as introduced to us through Dr. Alison Cook in her and Kimberly Miller's book *Boundaries for Your Soul* and through other IFS resources really began to tie all these concepts together and lead us to a unique conclusion. As we observed that parts of us were fighting harder against the silence and solitude than others, we wondered why. We noticed many places in Scripture where Paul, David, and others acknowledged their own confusion over the dissonance of the parts within their hearts.

We concluded that the fog was universal, even though it surfaced in different ways for different people. This is where the Enneagram turned on the lights within us as we realized we could know our parts via Enneagram wisdom (types, wings, and paths), thus inviting them all to be heard, known, and led into healthier spaces.

All this began with the invitation to solitude and silence. Most of us would rather create a list of activities to try harder at fixing ourselves, but it is the kindness, patience, and mercy of our Savior that changes us. We must have a process to enter a daily renewal of the mind toward these truths to bring the various parts of ourselves in alignment with them. Real change doesn't happen in isolated disciplines but in union with God's Spirit.

As we have learned, we too often approach change from the perspective of an orphaned heart—the Wounded Child—where we feel abandoned to the task of being solely responsible for our own transformation. As Christians, we may feel forgiven of our past sins but also somehow still responsible for the continual change still needed each day within our souls. It is a pattern of insanity where we keep doing the same things but expecting different results. But in slowing down long enough to really look at ourselves, we can come to know ourselves in a way that helps us stop hiding our misaligned parts from the only One who can receive them in grace and bring them into the beloved security of gospel alignment.

As we enter the AWARE process, we encourage you to first begin learning to sit in moments of solitude and silence as a precursor to this daily exercise. Otherwise, it's all too easy for this to become yet another checklist of items you use to try to fix yourself. The Enneagram and your EIP have hopefully helped you identify the areas where only Jesus can heal your brokenness.

For us, this begins in the morning. We try to do it most mornings, and when we are at our best, we might string together a number of consecutive days. To remind us of what this daily return is all about, we each have three sets of framed drawings hanging on the walls of our respective sides of the bedroom. We chose them independently of each other, though we used the same artist. Amazingly, we chose the same sequence of concepts.

We each chose different animals, an elephant for Beth and a lion for Jeff. In both drawings, the characters face the morning fog by welcoming their counterparts—the lion and the elephant, each representing various parts of each of us that struggle with alignment amid myriad issues. Strength. Community. Leadership. Danger. Appetite. Conflict. Communication. Confidence. Fear. Faith. And more. As the drawing shows, our Beloved Child attempts to begin our day seeing the fog for what it is, not denying it or trying to outrun it through overworking and busyness.

In the second drawing, there is an attunement to the reality of these parts. As one boy bows to the tree in one drawing and as the other bows to the elephant in the second, there is a humility in acknowledging that this is all bigger than ourselves. We can't control the growth of a tree, the hunting of a lion, or the strength of an elephant. But we can attune ourselves to these realities, acknowledging our smallness and limitations in relation to the world around us and within us—limitations this day will require us to face.

In the final drawing, attunement has led to engagement. The boy is riding atop both the lion and the elephant, one in a leap of power into motion for grand causes (which represents the aligned parts, gifts, and disposition of Jeff), and the other in a confident, unbreakable stride into whatever waters may arise (which represents the aligned parts, gifts, and disposition of Beth).

In silence and solitude, we are learning to position ourselves for daily awareness. When we are willing to sit in quietness with ourselves and with our Shepherd, the process of becoming AWARE is less daunting and more natural—not because we are good at it but because we are honest about ourselves and more attuned to the loving nature of our Father.

Everything we have explored up to now points to this truth: transformation happens through relationships. It is a relational reality. Ultimately, the gospel tells us that transformation happens through our relationship with Jesus. It is our connection to Christ (being seen, welcomed, and loved by Him) that brings true healing, freedom, and wholeness. This is what Jesus is getting at with His metaphor of branches "abiding" in the vine (John 15 ESV).

What does this have to do with EIP? As we abide in Jesus, He calls us to love our neighbors as we love ourselves (Matthew 22:37–39). We are called to show others—and ourselves—the same transforming love God shows us in the gospel. This is how we are to treat the various parts of the self that make up our EIP. The way Jesus brings transformation is through love, relationship, and healthy connection.

Many Enneagram paradigms terminate on self-awareness as the means of transformation. EIP takes it one step further to say that true and lasting transformation happens not by merely knowing about ourselves but by also actually getting to know ourselves, and more specifically the various parts of ourselves. EIP equips us to build a relationship with our parts, get to know them, welcome them, connect with them, empathize with them, earn their trust, build a healthy relationship with them, and lead them. This seems revolutionary, yet it is keeping with God's design for how humans grow and change—through loving relationships.

Once we have prepared our hearts, we can begin to engage in the AWARE exercise and start building these better relationships. Remember that this is so much more than an exercise. It is not life-giving, but rather, it reminds us Who is life-giving so we can navigate through whatever fog has set in. When we become aware of where we are, Whose we are, and who needs to be behind the wheel of the bus, we can move toward the abundance of life our Good Shepherd desires for us, leaving the fog behind.

NINE

Walking Through AWARE

Implementing the AWARE Exercise

for Your Enneagram Type

Once we understand the concepts of AWARE on a deeper level, we can be free to implement them in various situations, knowing they are meant to help wake up the Beloved Child within. As a reminder, here are the steps for the exercise:

A	**Awaken** to your internal parts through thoughts, feelings, and body sensations.
W	**Welcome** these experiences without judgment or shame.
A	**Ask** the Holy Spirit for guidance.
R	**Receive** what is true.
E	**Engage** with yourself and your relationships in a new way.

Awaken to Your Internal Parts Through Thoughts, Feelings, and Body Sensations

The concept of AWARE begins with *awakening*. Much of this book has focused on this concept. Awakening is a complex thing because it is something you should do daily, but it is also something that you must do over and over again based on your circumstances. It is hard to recognize that you're asleep while you're asleep. By definition, you are unconscious. This is why we have offered you the rumble strip of the Enneagram to help you realize you may be not completely awake to your current state of thinking, reaction, or feeling.

Even in the midst of an argument, if you know what to look for, you can awaken to feelings, thoughts, and inclinations. The goal is to observe what's actually happening inside us—sadness, anger, a certain thought or process, or the like. Then we can begin to ask ourselves why we are feeling so upset, frustrated, or hurt by another person or a certain circumstance.

This is the moment to ask our Wounded Child or other misaligned parts what they are feeling, taking note of what comes to mind. We can also attempt to identify which specific parts of us are feeling what so we can understand why they are activated and using certain strategies to influence us. Again, this is why the Enneagram is such a helpful tool; in recognizing the strategies of our parts, we can more easily identify which parts are negatively activated, which will also help us address the Wounded Child these parts are trying to protect.

We can also tailor-make connections between what we are observing and the core motivations of our type. As a Nine, we might ask, "In what situations am I feeling the inclination to shut down?" Over time, we have noticed in our marriage that when certain passions or a level of intensity arises, both of our Nine parts may begin to disassociate. We have also noticed the same thing when there are stressors in our company, meaning that these principles apply as much to the professional sphere as the personal. Regardless of when you begin the exercise to awaken, the first goal is to notice that this is happening rather than pretending that it isn't happening (or doesn't happen all the time).

This is not just an emotional process—it will also bleed over into physical reactions as well. These patterns might lead one of us to say, "I really want to be present in this conversation, but my body is trying to keep me from it right now." For each of us, the physical signs are different, but they are determinate signals that something is going on in our internal worlds to which we need to awaken. It can be a sense of uneasiness, headaches, upset stomachs, or neck and back pain, but our bodies will offer signs that we need to awaken to something that is becoming misaligned.

For example, Elizabeth is a Type Two who is helping to plan an event for her team. When functioning out of her Wounded Child part, she is still overly helpful, but her body begins to respond to the whole situation with anxiety. This response, if noticed, can help her awaken to areas of misalignment. She takes note that the anxiety is at least partly resulting from her wing Type Three part, which desires to be adaptable and to charm people, but feels that this isn't going so well. In addition, Elizabeth's Type Four part, one of her Enneagram paths, really wants the experiences to be beautiful so everyone present can open up and go deep with vulnerability. But when these goals seemingly aren't being met (even if it is actually going better than she realizes), her wing Type One shows up with even more anxiety in tow. Feeling responsible, it reminds her that she can't do this job well enough. Along the way, her Eight part notices that someone at the event is being overbearing, hindering someone else's growth, nurture, or care. This part steps up to protect the one being hindered, plowing a path for them. When aligned, it is a champion who handles the issue with tact; when misaligned, it is a bully who hurts even more feelings in the process. All these feelings and reactions in a situation like this can help Elizabeth awaken to what's occurring within her, even finding out what parts are responding in what ways.

The goal here is not to analyze, but to notice and observe. Many people move straight from observation to judgment, shame, or guilt. But awareness begins by simply awakening to what is happening in the moment it is happening. If you can at least start there, the gospel applied through your EIP and the Enneagram can help you welcome what is happening rather than reject, shame, or shut down the parts of you that need to be heard and led, not dismissed.

Welcome These Experiences Without Judgment

Once you have *awakened* to the fact that something significant is indeed happening within your internal parts, the next step is to implement what we have already explained in the previous chapters: *welcome* these parts without judgment.

James 1:2–4 in the Phillips version expresses this concept in beautiful language: "When all kinds of trials and temptations crowd into your lives my brothers, don't resent them as intruders, but welcome them as friends! Realise that they come to test your faith and to produce in you the quality of endurance." This creates context for us to extend *invitations* instead of *citations* to our troubled parts within so we can hear them and help them become aligned with the gospel.

In mindfulness, compassion, and empathy toward those who have experienced significant trauma, this is not meant to dismiss or trivialize the deep pain of your experiences. Horrific experiences are not our friends in this manner, and no one should feel obligated to accept them as such. Rather, we are speaking of the parts within you that experienced the trauma. These parts have value apart from what has wounded them, so let's remain mindful of the differences between our parts and their trauma. We can rightly address trauma amid appropriate boundaries while also welcoming the parts that have been traumatized.

As we learn more about ourselves, welcoming should become our normal response. Usually, certain feelings we believe to be negative or certain bodily sensations that make us uncomfortable are things we want to shut out. We either blind ourselves to them or fill our souls with other things to numb them. We errantly think this will keep us from experiencing these negative things, but they actually lead to more negative experiences, namely a feeling of shame or a sense of being accused, judged, or caught in the act. We don't welcome these parts because, like Adam and Eve, we don't want to be exposed. Adam and Eve hid themselves to try to keep their misaligned patterns of relating from being seen by God (Genesis 3:8).

Whatever we're feeling or experiencing, we must learn to welcome it without judgment and without running away. We could potentially be running away from something God's Spirit is trying to teach us. We could be missing out on invitations to pivot away from our fleshly self and turn instead toward living in the Spirit-led self that can connect with God and with others.

It might be easy to misunderstand and wonder if we are suggesting to welcome sin, or perhaps that sin somehow has positive intent. We are not saying this at all. We simply mean that our sin can become the trailhead to understanding something about who we are and who Christ is toward us. When our parts feel like our enemies because of their sinful ways, the Shepherd prepares a table (Psalm 23) for the whole of us—parts included—to come and be restored. Also pay attention to the fact that Jesus invited Himself to Zacchaeus's table, the table of a despised sinner at which no one wanted to eat (Luke 19). Yet Jesus desired to go there. He welcomed the sinner but also welcomed Himself to the sinner's table.

By welcoming our experiences and feelings, whatever they may be, we step into transparency, vulnerability, and honesty. In this recognition we can not only awaken to but also welcome an understanding of the strategies by which we keep trying to live apart from God's ways. By welcoming, we can ask for forgiveness so we can move by faith in the direction God is calling us to walk.

A paraphrased quote by Joseph Campbell relates to our fear and reticence to look at the negatives in our lives: "The cave you fear to enter holds the treasure you seek."[1] Our inclination to pursue certain behaviors that lead us away from Christ or avoid certain healthy paths that lead us closer to Him can tell us a lot about what's happening in our hearts and what we're seeking to satisfy. For me (Beth), as a Nine, the cave I fear to enter is promoting myself or asserting myself with courage and boldness for others to see. I would rather just hide in the background, even though this is not what God has called me to. The cave leads me to want to withdraw, shut down, or check out. And for me (Jeff), as a Six, the cave I fear to enter is trusting God and the wisdom and discernment He has granted me to exercise for myself, which means my inclination to be anxious, ruminating, or afraid. It is my ongoing sense of insecurity about what could happen, even though God has promised to direct my path and guide me in the sovereignty of His final and ultimate redemption of all things. The cave leads me to overeat or numb out by binging Netflix.

But for both of us, the treasure lies in asking: Why are we withdrawing, checked out, overeating, or the like? Why do we feel overwhelmed or anxious? For both of us, the answer is revealed in different ways, but in those misaligned parts we both feel like we're alone and we're not enough.

If we can't welcome these thoughts, feelings, and reactions without judgment, shame, or self-condemnation, then we can't bring them to Christ in the next step of becoming AWARE: asking for guidance.

Ask the Holy Spirit for Guidance

If we can genuinely welcome what is happening in our various parts, we can ask for a deeper understanding of where to invite the Spirit to be present and active. Again, since transformation is the ultimate goal and we are powerless to transform ourselves, this is the step where awareness crosses from our vulnerable willingness into Christ's transformative nearness. The reality is that if He doesn't show up, we can't survive, much less change.

As we read in Psalm 40:12, David knew that his sins were beyond his ability to understand or fix: "For troubles without number surround me; my sins have overtaken me, and I cannot see." He had become aware that he was in a fog, he had named his fog as sin (in this case), and then in the next verse, he reached out for help beyond himself: "Be pleased to save me, LORD; come quickly, LORD, to help me" (v. 13).

We see things happening, but we often interpret them through the wrong lenses. We need help from outside ourselves to understand our own hearts, as David admitted in Psalm 139. This step moves beyond self-realization and into divine interaction with God on a very intimate level. By connecting to our Source, we begin to move from observation to transformation, just not by our own means.

This step involves bringing to Christ all the realization and vulnerability from the first two steps in a very intentional way. Sometimes we bring what people consider overtly sinful things—addiction, lust, rage, or violent thoughts or actions. Other times, we bring seemingly less-harmful patterns or thoughts related to things not necessarily sinful. In the end, it's all just fallenness, and it all needs a Savior.

For example, the overeating while numbing out to Netflix is not a sin found in the Bible. But in this step, we begin to ask the Holy Spirit to help us see what we are really trying to accomplish apart from Him. He will also show us if it is working—are we truly satisfied, seen, refreshed, or released from anxiety? He will reveal the true realities behind the self-protective actions we are taking in response to our activated parts.

Even if we don't feel or hear anything in the moment of asking, we can trust that we are heard and that He will respond. This means that sometimes we will need to keep asking, trusting not in our feelings, but in God's promises to hear us and help us—always. To that end, Jesus is emphatic that "the one who comes to Me I will *by no means* cast out" (John 6:37 NKJV, emphasis added). James 4:8 reminds us: "draw near to

God, and he will draw near to you" (ESV). And even when we can't hear an answer or feel a change, Scripture promises that His Spirit is more active than we are in praying for us and advocating on our behalf: "The Spirit helps us in our weakness. For we do not know what to pray for as we ought, but the Spirit himself intercedes for us with groanings too deep for words" (Romans 8:26 ESV).

When we come as we truly are and present ourselves, a dynamic and relational event happens in that moment by God's Spirit. His truth comes alive again within us because He is with us, regardless of how we feel. His Spirit, which is already in us, longs to come closer alongside our parts that are suffering from misalignment—He is supporting us and rooting for the whole of us to live. We are not alone. He is right there with us, helping us not only name what's happening, but also understand its true source and motivations.

The next step sounds short and simple, but it is crucial to the process: *receive*.

Receive What Is True

This is the moment we begin to *receive* gospel truth in new ways, relaying it to whatever parts within us need to hear it the most. This is when the Wounded Child sits at the feet of Jesus and is again reminded that she is not an abandoned orphan, but rather an adopted Beloved Child. To receive, we must unfold our guarded arms, unclench our defensive fists, and open our closed hands to the good news and truth of Christ's love. We return from our orphaned self to our true self as we take in afresh the Father's pure delight in us.

This can be more difficult than it sounds because receiving what is true entails abandoning the false messages that your main type or your connecting types are hearing and repeating with such deafening volume inside your head, heart, and gut. This is not just some mind-over-matter or positive confession mumbo jumbo. This is alignment with what your Beloved Child already knows to be true. People love to talk about "being true to yourself," but this can inadvertently lead to self-serving and unsatisfying places. This is how to really be true to yourself in a way that gives life rather than diminishes it: endeavor to keep bringing truth to the part of yourself that already is the Beloved Child and who may just need a reminder.

This means believing the theological concept called "the double cure," which attests that not only does Christ remove all our sins, past, present, and future, but He also grants us His perfect righteousness right where we are today. We may not live perfect lives, but because He lived a perfect life, if we are "in Him" (Acts 17:28), we take on His perfect righteousness. This is why we can live as Beloved Children—not because we are worthy of being the beloved, but because He has already secured perfect affection from the Father on our behalf. This is what Paul is referring to when he says, "I have been crucified with Christ and I no longer live, but Christ lives in me. The life I now live in the body, I live by faith in the Son of God, who loved me and gave himself for me" (Galatians 2:20).

If our real lives are the life of Christ, we can receive every single one of His promises with perfect confidence, regardless of the misalignment of our parts. It is by returning to this truth that our Wounded Child finds healing over and over again and our Beloved Child begins to lead our internal parts closer to health by drawing closer to Christ. The center of our being moves from an orphaned disposition to an adopted disposition—and the source of life and motivation again becomes Christ in us, not the loneliness in us.

As the Holy Spirit reveals our need, we are reminded of our true state, and we are able to receive the truth of the gospel not as something to only show us where we're lost, but to remind us where we are gloriously found. Like the father running to the prodigal, there is no space for condemnation, even if the son tries to condemn himself. Before he can even fully express his unworthiness, the father is kissing his cheek, clothing him, adorning him with treasure, throwing a feast for him, and above all, speaking gospel truth over him: "'For this my son of mine was dead and is alive again; he was lost and is found.' So they began to celebrate" (Luke 15:24).

Every time we are willing to again receive gospel truth into the prodigal parts of our internal world, our Father celebrates and receives us, morphing our perceived state of abandonment into alignment with our true state of adoption.

Engage with Yourself and Your Relationships in a New Way

The final step of the AWARE exercise is to *engage*. When we recognize and apply what has already been accomplished through the love of Christ, remembering that He already is the fulfillment of our every need, we can rest fully in what He has done for us and enter into different, healthier actions toward ourselves and others around us. "We love because he first loved us" (1 John 4:19).

Once our Beloved Child has regained confidence in Christ and has regained Spirit-empowered leadership toward our other parts, we will not only begin engaging again in the good things we once did, but through the process of transformation we just went through, we will also be catapulted into even better things beyond where we were before the latest fog set in. In other words, we will have experienced transformation that changes the way we think and act.

Galatians 5:6 says, "In Christ Jesus neither circumcision nor uncircumcision has any value. The only thing that counts is faith expressing itself through love." Don't get tripped up on the concept of circumcision in this passage. Paul was speaking to Christians who were struggling to avoid becoming enslaved to their own efforts as the source of their confidence in Christ—and for the Jews around them, being circumcised was an essential part of being qualified.

Paul's point here is an organizing principle for the Christian life. If you live within the life that Christ provides, getting it right doesn't count for anything. We do not just *do* the works that display God's glory—we *are* the works that display God's glory. It is our trust in Him—our faith—being expressed in a daily life reflecting His love that now defines our existence.

By faith, we know God has adopted us as sons and daughters since before the foundations of the world (Ephesians 1:5). By faith, we know He has set the times and places in which we live (Acts 17:26). By faith, we know He has knit us together in our mothers' wombs (Psalm 139:13). By faith, we know He has prepared good works in advance for us to do (Ephesians 2:10). Furthermore, out of these realities, He has gifted us with gifts to serve His body and our world (Ephesians 4:7–13).

This faith leads us to trust in the ongoing process of what He is faithfully, joyfully enacting in our lives by His grace. After all,

> We know that in all things God works for the good of those who love him, who have been called according to his purpose. For those God foreknew he also predestined to be conformed to the image of his Son, that he might be the firstborn among many brothers and sisters. And those he predestined, he also called; those he called, he also justified; those he justified, he also glorified. (Romans 8:28–30)

We may not feel like we're winning, but as the Good Shepherd continues His work in our lives, our identities are being irreversibly, eternally transformed from "conquered" to "conquerors."

> In all these things we are more than conquerors through him who loved us. For I am convinced that neither death nor life, neither angels nor demons, neither the present nor the future, nor any powers, neither height

nor depth, nor anything else in all creation, will be able to separate us from the love of God that is in Christ Jesus our Lord. (Romans 8:37–39)

These truths are already true, but they drift away from us amid the fallen currents, which is why we must lead our parts back to them every day so we can engage the world as we are in Christ, not as we are in this world: Beloved Children of grace. Jerry Bridges explains,

> So an all-out, unreserved, nothing-held-back commitment to the pursuit of holiness may be exhausting, but it will not be oppressive if it is grounded in grace. But to be grounded in grace, it must be continually referred back to the gospel. So don't just preach the gospel to yourself every day merely to experience the cleansing of your conscience. You certainly need to do so for that reason. But as you do so, reaffirm, as a response of love and gratitude to God, your commitment to Him. And do so in reliance on His Spirit that by His grace He will enable you to carry out your commitment.[2]

If all this is true "in the faith," what would it look like for us to not only to love and cherish who God has uniquely made us to be but also love others just as well? God has distinctively created and positioned us to do both. He did not make us to be uniformed robots, each with the same personalities, gifts, and attributes. He created us to glorify Him in very specific ways through our individuality, while also benefiting and blessing one another through it.

The Enneagram helps us understand others so we might have compassion, grace, and mercy on them. In knowing our own limitations that are being used and transformed by Christ, we are then able to encourage one another (1 Thessalonians 5:11) as we "consider how we may spur one another on toward love and good deeds" (Hebrews 10:24). We spur others along toward these "good deeds" according to the specific ways God has made and called them, not in the ways He has made and called us. We help them pursue Christ's plan for their lives as He thinks they should do it, not as we think they should do it.

We often spend so much of our time trying to "do better" in our relationships instead of spending our time becoming aware so we can invite and engage with the truths of the gospel. If we become aware, we can live higher than mere good intentions of becoming better friends to others. Rather, we can experience renewal in the gospel on a regular basis, going through a process that leads us back to a transformative reengagement in our relationships with ourselves, our spouse, our children, our work, our teams, and our friends. All of this is available to us so Christ might be honored in all that we do. This is faith working itself out through love.

For us, this is the representation of the third picture on each of our walls in our bedroom—both of us riding into our lives atop the strengths of our parts that have been revealed, redeemed, and aligned through the regenerating work of the gospel. We enter the day not as perfect riders, but as Beloved Children reminded of Christ's work at the cross and of an infinitely affectionate Father who desires for us to experience the fullness of His love now and forever.

As you prepare to map out your own EIP in the sections to follow, may your heart also find clarity that leads from awakening to engagement. May you remember the little sheep and its relationship to the Shepherd. May you begin to become awakened to the various parts within you that are responding to your Wounded Child or your Beloved Child.

And when you think you've learned a lot about your internal world, may you have the humility and wisdom to keep starting over again every day—being made as new as the morning mercies your Father re-creates with every sunrise, dissipating the fog with His grace.

And along the way, may you truly live to become aware that you are so much more than a number—you are His Beloved Child.

PART THREE

Mapping Out Your Enneagram Internal Profile (EIP)

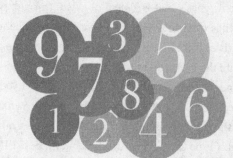

EIP and AWARE Exercises
for Each Main Type

As you map out your own EIP, try thinking of the nine types as if the people around you are all wearing different-colored lenses. If they have blue lenses, they will see the world in a shade of blue, but if they have red lenses, they will see the same world in red. The elements of the world they are examining are seemingly definitive things, yet they couldn't see them any more differently. Life may feature objective facts, but people see and interpret these facts in vastly, sometimes fiercely divergent ways.

We have already learned that Enneagram wisdom contends that there are nine different types—that is, colors of lenses through which people see and experience the world. And as we've explored, there are infinite hues of each of these colors, even if they fall under the same color palette. So as you explore the EIP process to follow, we pray you will continue to deepen your understanding of the kaleidoscope within you that affects the way you see, interpret, and react to reality in your own unique ways.

NOTE: In the first two sections of the book, Enneagram types were written as words (Type One, Type Two, etc.) but in these EIP application sections, types are written as numerals (Type 1, Type 2, etc.). We made this adjustment simply to make the content more visually accessible in repetitive exercises.

Special thanks to Lydia Craig for her excellent work as a collaborative developer on these EIP profiles and creative writer in this key section of the book.

---- T E N ----

Type 1: Principled Reformer

CONSCIENTIOUS | ORDERLY | APPROPRIATE | ETHICAL | JUDGMENTAL

Core Motivations

CORE FEAR

Being wrong, bad, evil, inappropriate, unredeemable, or corruptible.

CORE DESIRE

Having integrity; being good, ethical, balanced, accurate, virtuous, and right.

CORE WEAKNESS

Resentment: repressing anger leads to continual frustration and dissatisfaction with yourself, others, and the world for not being perfect.

CORE LONGING

To hear and believe, "You are good."

Primary Perspective

To achieve your core motivations, your primary focus of attention is seeing errors, mistakes, and problems that need fixing. You are not seeking out these imperfections; they leap out at you and assault you. You believe everything can and should be done right, perfectly, and in an orderly and systematic way. You follow particular procedures to complete each task with precision and accuracy.

Summary Overview

God created you to reveal His goodness and wisdom and to participate with Him in stewarding His creation. Unfortunately, sin disrupted God's perfect creation. You see how things should be and take on a personal obligation to improve these errors in yourself, others, or the world. This overwhelming burden leaves you with chronic dissatisfaction, as the work of fixing things is never finished.

You struggle with resentment because you can't control life and make everything right, but you won't admit you're angry because that would be "bad," and your core longing is to be seen as "good." Because of this, you can become perfectionistic and controlling of yourself and others, harming your relationships when others experience your "helpful advice" as criticism or perceive you as demanding perfection. The reality is that your heart truly longs to help.

Internally, you struggle to believe you are good or worthy enough because your inner critic constantly finds fault with everything you do. To silence this berating voice, you strive never to make mistakes, which is exhausting and impossible. The good news is, Jesus lived a perfect life on your behalf. Because of His life, death, and resurrection, His righteousness is credited to you. He says you are good based on His righteousness applied to you.

Jesus came to restore His creation, and He invites you into that process. When your heart is aligned with the gospel and you learn to take your longing to Christ and rest in Him, you can begin to let go of the unrealistically high standards you hold for yourself and others. Then your moral and purposeful nature can bring out the best in yourself and others, truly making the world a better place.

Type 1 Enneagram Internal Profile (EIP)

THE WOUNDED CHILD (MISALIGNED TYPE 1)

Summary

As a child, you longed to hear that "you are good" from your authority figures. You made every effort not to be wrong or bad, and you avoided condemnation and punishment by obeying all the rules.

Your inner critic felt that the authority over you did not provide sufficient rules, so it created more rigorous rules for you to follow. It was (and remains) exhausting to try to please your inner critic, who is constantly criticizing you and the world. The resentment within you is actually deep sorrow for thinking you needed to be the "responsible adult" instead of a playful child.

Your Wounded Child part falsely believes that it is not good and needs to be more responsible, be more accurate, and strive harder for what is right. It longs to experience childlike joy, rest, and acceptance, yet the inner critic always points out that there is more to correct and improve. As an adult, your core longing remains the same: to hear and believe that "you are good."

False Messages the Wounded Child Believes Are True

- "It's not okay for me to make mistakes."

- "I must always strive for balance, integrity, and being right in order to be seen as good."
- "I must listen and follow what my inner critic tells me is true."

NOTE: Every type has an "inner critic" and any of our internal parts can function in this role. For Type 1s, this critic can be particularly judgmental, critical, and cruel.

Misaligned Attributes

- Your Wounded Child fears and believes it is corrupt, bad, and unredeemable.
- The loud and berating inner critic shows up as a judge and jury, constantly pointing out and assaulting you with your mistakes and the detailed awareness of all the errors and imperfections around you. The Wounded Child reacts and does its best to adhere to the inner critic's direction in hopes that when things are fixed and corrected, the inner critic will finally quiet down and stop criticizing you. But the more you try to appease the inner critic by striving for perfection, the more you see mistakes and shortcomings.
- Your Wounded Child struggles to accept that imperfection is an inevitable part of human life. This causes it to be obsessed with micromanaging and asserting its control to bring relief to the tyranny of the inner critic. Unfortunately, not only does this not work, but it only compounds your problems.

THE BELOVED CHILD (ALIGNED TYPE 1)

Summary

Only when your Beloved Child part is leading your heart can your misaligned parts loosen their grip on the need to be perfect. Your Beloved Child reminds them that when God looks at you, He sees

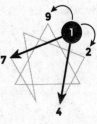

1

His perfect Son, Jesus Christ, and not a sinner (Romans 8:1). You are His child who is loved, cherished, and cared for right where you are, in all your imperfections (Romans 5:8).

Your Beloved Child knows it is free from accusation, condemnation, and the burden to be correct. Under its leadership, you can now rest and safely admit when you make mistakes, and you can extend the same grace, kindness, and compassion to others when they make mistakes.

When your heart is aligned with the gospel, you are free to embody true wisdom and can discern the most compassionate and appropriate action to take. You will radiate nobility, generosity, and gentleness and experience a profound connection with others. This inspires people to join you as you steward and restore God's perfect creation.

True Messages the Beloved Child Believes

- "I can experience joy and a restful childlike heart because all of my past, present, and future sins and mistakes are forgiven and replaced with Christ's perfect righteousness."
- "God shows His love for me in that while I was and still am sinning, Christ died for me." (Romans 5:8)
- "God is able to bring about the change He seeks in me, others, and the world."
- "When I hear the harsh judgments of the inner critic, I can remind myself that the Holy Spirit is kind, gentle, tender, patient, and reassuring of His love and care for me."

Aligned Attributes of the Beloved Child

- You recognize when your inner critic is assaulting and criticizing you and remind yourself that there is no more condemnation in Christ and that this is the opposite of how the Holy Spirit treats you.
- You remind yourself that God alone is responsible for changing or perfecting others, which leads you to ask clarifying questions

instead of making judgment statements as you assume most people are trying their best in life.

- When you receive feedback, you do not feel overly criticized or defensive because your heart is resting in Christ's provision for you.
- You mirror Christlikeness by being patient, gracious, merciful, and forgiving, and you offer affirmation and encouragement to yourself and others instead of criticism or condemnation.

CONNECTING TYPES

EIP Reminder: We all use all nine types to some degree. Therefore, the descriptions to follow reflect a combination of your main type's characteristics and your connecting types' characteristics. Out of their own core motivations, our four connecting types (wings and Enneagram paths either aligned or misaligned) use their respective strategies to attempt to meet our main type's core motivations, which still reign supreme.[1]

Wing Type 9

Summary

Do you sometimes avoid conflicts or tense situations? Can you see, understand, and have compassion for differing perspectives, even though you are confident in what you believe is right? These are characteristics of your wing Type 9 part.

This part is nonjudgmental and does not want to have disagreements with loved ones or feel angry. It supports your main type by encouraging you to be kind, patient, and peaceful toward yourself (counteracting your inner critic) and bestow that same grace on others.

How to Recognize Misaligned Traits of Wing Type 9

- Do you ever withdraw, over-accommodate, or people-please to avoid conflict or tension?

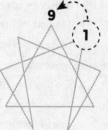

- Are you sometimes less aware of how you feel or what you're passionate about because you are so focused on what is right and wrong?
- Do you ignore or suppress feelings of irritation so you can keep a peaceful connection with others and be seen as good?
- Do you ever quietly dig in your heels and become stubborn until the other person gives in to your correct way of doing things?

How to Recognize Aligned Traits of Wing Type 9

- Do you know your presence, thoughts, wisdom, and feelings matter?
- Are you more kind, compassionate, understanding, and gracious to yourself (unlike your inner critic) and toward others?
- Are you more adaptable, accommodating, and easygoing when stating what you want or need?
- Do you have the ability to mediate and harmonize groups by bringing people together and actively seeking ways to bring peace and healing to the world?

Wing Type 2

Summary

Do you sometimes sense the needs of others? Do you exhaust yourself trying to help others in difficult situations? These are characteristics of your wing Type 2 part.

This part is highly relational and can sense the needs of others. It brings you more relational warmth with a desire to connect with and help people. It supports your main type by encouraging you to roll up your sleeves to serve and bring wisdom to others lovingly and practically.

How to Recognize Misaligned Traits of Wing Type 2

- Do you feel rejected and hurt when your helpful advice is not well received or is ignored?
- Do you sometimes fixate on others' needs, feelings, and imperfections without adequately addressing your own?
- Do you exhaust yourself trying to help others by taking on too much responsibility, causing you to feel like a "martyr"?
- Do you wish people would return the favor and be equally responsible, helpful, and loving toward you?

How to Recognize Aligned Traits of Wing Type 2

- Do people go to you for advice and support because they find you sincere, wise, warm-hearted, caring, loving, and generous?
- Do you put a charitable interpretation on the behavior of others, emphasizing that people are trying their best?
- Do you maintain appropriate boundaries by saying no to helping and caring for others when it is not your responsibility?
- Do you give support, advice, and unconditional love with no strings attached?

Enneagram Path Type 4

Summary

Do you sometimes feel misunderstood by others or feel like you don't belong? Can you tap into a side of you that is profoundly creative and sees beauty in the ordinary? These are characteristics of your Enneagram path Type 4 part.

1

This part lives primarily in imagination and feelings. Deep down, it has an idealized vision of the person it desires to become, but it feels like it is tragically flawed and lacks qualities that others possess. It supports your main type by giving you profound depth and authenticity, a necessary component of integrity.

How to Recognize Misaligned Traits of Enneagram Path Type 4

- Do you ever feel resentful or angry that others are not fulfilling expectations in a specific or ideal way, causing you to get stuck in your feelings and take everything personally?
- Do you withdraw when you feel moody, melancholy, or misunderstood to protect your reputation and work out your emotions alone?
- Do you daydream about becoming free of your responsibilities, of being your authentic self and not living under the tyranny of rules?
- Does self-pity and envy of others lead you to secretive self-indulgences, making you increasingly impractical and unproductive?

How to Recognize Aligned Traits of Enneagram Path Type 4

- Do you enjoy resting in the beauty of nature or quiet, allowing your feelings, emotional inspirations, creativity, and unique passions to surface and be experienced?
- Can you withhold judgment, making room for raw, unprocessed emotions and authenticity from yourself and others?
- Can you set aside your to-do list, temporarily slow down, and experience the beauty of the present moment?
- Can you sit with others in their difficult emotions, providing support without offering advice?

Enneagram Path Type 7

Summary

Is there a side to you that feels more relaxed, playful, and optimistic? Do you sometimes feel overpowered by life's demands and then distract yourself with fun self-indulgences? These are characteristics of your Enneagram path Type 7 part.

This part is upbeat, fun, and happy. It sees life as cotton candy, super sweet to the taste but disappearing quickly, leaving it unsatisfied and wanting more. It supports your main type by giving you opportunities to break free from your responsibilities and the demands of your inner critic so you can enjoy all life has to offer.

How to Recognize Misaligned Traits of Enneagram Path Type 7

- Do you ever demand that others meet your needs, criticisms, and desires?
- Do you find "escape hatches" (unhealthy indulgences) from your inner critic (and other responsibilities) to distract yourself from the ongoing pressures you face?
- Have you ever experienced an irrational, childish urge to do something that isn't right, especially if you believe you can secretly get away with it?
- Do you ever avoid feelings of pain, sadness, or disappointment or find yourself reframing a negative situation to sound more positive?

How to Recognize Aligned Traits of Enneagram Path Type 7

- Do you experience moments of grace and joy, which creates a more self-accepting and others-accepting heart?
- Are you more enthusiastic, spontaneous, playful, joyful, and fun, seeing the world and your circumstances through an optimistic lens?

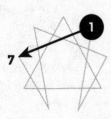

- Do you see that life is not all serious and daunting but rich with life-giving experiences and emotions, including happiness, abundance, and freedom?
- Are there times you relax more, become less rigid, and take great delight in the present moment?

Type 1: AWARE Exercise

AWAKEN

Awaken to your belief that it's not okay to make mistakes and that you need to fix things. When does your inner critic show up, and what does it say? What other misaligned parts are influencing you right now? Have you asked them what they are feeling?

WELCOME

Welcome and extend kindness to your inner critic expressed through your misaligned part without guilt or shame. Recognize that the parts of your heart are both a gift and a burden. Remain curious, not critical.

ASK

Ask the Holy Spirit to help you interpret what your inner critic and your misaligned parts are trying to communicate and the motives behind them. How are they trying to protect your Wounded Child part? Resist any urge to fix your situation.

RECEIVE

Receive the forgiveness and compassion Christ offers you, allowing the Beloved Child part to lead your misaligned parts back to the truth of the gospel. Spend time reading verses about God's compassion, freedom, and grace.

ENGAGE

Engage yourself, your relationships, and your circumstances in a new way, with love, grace, and mercy—the same way Christ engages with you. From this aligned place, others will experience Christ's wisdom and insights through you.[2]

Gospel Self-Talk

"Because of Christ's work on my behalf, I am now righteous and free. I can loosen my grip on needing to be perfect because when God looks at me, He sees His Beloved Child, who is loved and cherished right now in all my imperfections. Jesus says that I am good because of His work, and this message brings me comfort and relief from my inner critic. I am not responsible for perfecting the world around me. I'm invited to cocreate with God, stewarding and restoring His perfect creation in a way that brings me fulfillment, peace, and joy. I bring God's wisdom and integrity to the world. And because of the overflow of grace I've received, I can bestow grace to others."[3]

Type 1 EIP

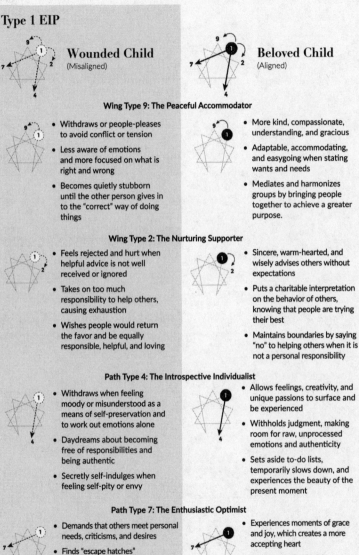

Wounded Child
(Misaligned)

Beloved Child
(Aligned)

Wing Type 9: The Peaceful Accommodator

- Withdraws or people-pleases to avoid conflict or tension
- Less aware of emotions and more focused on what is right and wrong
- Becomes quietly stubborn until the other person gives in to the "correct" way of doing things

- More kind, compassionate, understanding, and gracious
- Adaptable, accommodating, and easygoing when stating wants and needs
- Mediates and harmonizes groups by bringing people together to achieve a greater purpose.

Wing Type 2: The Nurturing Supporter

- Feels rejected and hurt when helpful advice is not well received or ignored
- Takes on too much responsibility to help others, causing exhaustion
- Wishes people would return the favor and be equally responsible, helpful, and loving

- Sincere, warm-hearted, and wisely advises others without expectations
- Puts a charitable interpretation on the behavior of others, knowing that people are trying their best
- Maintains boundaries by saying "no" to helping others when it is not a personal responsibility

Path Type 4: The Introspective Individualist

- Withdraws when feeling moody or misunderstood as a means of self-preservation and to work out emotions alone
- Daydreams about becoming free of responsibilities and being authentic
- Secretly self-indulges when feeling self-pity or envy

- Allows feelings, creativity, and unique passions to surface and be experienced
- Withholds judgment, making room for raw, unprocessed emotions and authenticity
- Sets aside to-do lists, temporarily slows down, and experiences the beauty of the present moment

Path Type 7: The Enthusiastic Optimist

- Demands that others meet personal needs, criticisms, and desires
- Finds "escape hatches" (unhealthy indulgences) to distract from life's ongoing pressures
- Avoids feelings of pain, sadness, or disappointment, or reframes negative situations to sound more positive

- Experiences moments of grace and joy, which creates a more accepting heart
- Enthusiastically playful, spontaneously joyful, and optimistic in life and relationships
- Is relaxed and less rigid, taking great delight in the present moment

2

E L E V E N ———————

Type 2: Nurturing Supporter

THOUGHTFUL | GENEROUS | DEMONSTRATIVE
| PEOPLE-PLEASING | POSSESSIVE

Core Motivations

CORE FEAR
Being rejected and unwanted; being thought worthless, needy, inconsequential, dispensable, or unworthy of love.

CORE DESIRE
Being appreciated, loved, and wanted.

CORE WEAKNESS
Pride: denying your own needs and emotions while using your strong intuition to discover and focus on the emotions and needs of others, confidently inserting your helpful support in hopes that others will say how grateful they are for your thoughtful care.

Core Longing

To hear and believe, "You are wanted and loved."

Primary Perspective

To achieve your core motivations, your primary focus of attention is winning the approval of others by feeling their emotions and fulfilling their needs. You project an image of being a completely selfless, loving, and supportive person to earn love and affirmation. You are convinced that if you acknowledge and take care of your own needs, others might view you as "selfish" and reject you.

Summary Overview

God created you to reveal His compassion and care. You prioritize relationships, taking a genuine interest in others, and come alongside anyone in need through acts of service, helpful advice, and nurturing. Unfortunately, sin disrupted our relationships, and the depth of need and suffering in our world is especially burdensome to you. You feel like it is your job to alleviate people's pain, which is an unending responsibility.

You struggle to believe that you are loved and wanted for who you are outside of the support you offer. In your attempt to fulfill your longing for love and appreciation, you become people-pleasing and possessive, inserting yourself into the lives of others and violating boundaries. In your pride, you may believe that you know what's best for everyone while also denying the care you require. When others feel crowded by your efforts to help, you feel hurt and insecure. The good news is, Jesus came to earth to save you and care for you. He says that you are wanted and loved.

Jesus came to restore our relationships, and He invites you into that process. When your heart is aligned with the gospel and you learn to take your longing to Christ and rest in Him, you can begin to tend to your own needs, knowing that you are wanted and loved apart from what you can do for others. Then your selfless generosity and kindness can bring out the best in yourself and others, truly making the world a better place.

Type 2: Enneagram Internal Profile (EIP)

THE WOUNDED CHILD (MISALIGNED TYPE 2)

Summary

As a child, you longed to hear that "you are wanted and loved" from your authority figures. You feared being rejected, unwanted, and unloved, so you became a "little helper" who selflessly loved and cared for others to gain their love, appreciation, and approval.

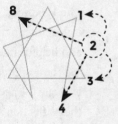

You constantly measured people's response to your helpfulness to assess if you'd earned the love and approval you believed you needed. If you didn't receive it, you became more intrusive with your "helpful" strategies to get the responses you craved.

Your Wounded Child part falsely believes that it is not okay to have your own needs and that it is selfish to care for yourself. It longs to be loved unconditionally and be free from the pursuit of approval. As an adult, your core longing remains the same: to hear from others that "you are wanted and loved."

False Messages the Wounded Child Believes Are True
- "It's not okay to have my own needs or say no to fulfilling the needs of others."

- "If I am close to others, loved by them, and appreciated for all I do for them, then I will be okay."
- "I must help, serve, and extend myself for others no matter what it costs me."

Misaligned Attributes

- Your Wounded Child fears and believes it is unwanted, rejected, worthless, needy, and unworthy of being loved.
- The Wounded Child reacts and does its best to become the selfless caretaker of others in hopes of gaining their appreciation, love, and approval. The problem is that the more you insert your people-pleasing help and support, the more others push away or avoid being overtaken by your care.
- The Wounded Child part of your heart struggles to accept that it is doing anything wrong and can only believe that it has good and helpful intentions. This causes it to be obsessed with receiving some appreciation for its efforts. Therefore, it will continually evaluate the needs and emotions of others so it can continue to win their affection through inserting advice and care. Unfortunately, not only does this not work, but it only compounds your problems.

THE BELOVED CHILD (ALIGNED TYPE 2)

Summary

Only when your Beloved Child part is leading your heart can your misaligned parts loosen their grip on needing to be needed and wanted. Your Beloved Child reminds them that when God looks at you, He sees His Beloved Child whom He pursued for a 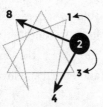 perfect loving relationship with Himself. You are loved, cherished, and cared for right where you are, and this is never dependent on what you do or don't do for others.

Your Beloved Child knows it is free from feeling rejected, shamed, and selfish. Under its leadership, you can now rest in the delight and care of your Good Shepherd, which enables you to extend the same care and love to others without needing any affirmation or appreciation in return.

When your heart is aligned with the gospel, you are able to express and address your feelings and needs to others in a healthy way. You demonstrate God's unconditional love by caring for others with warm-hearted tenderness that does not need to be reciprocated.

True Messages the Beloved Child Believes

- "Jesus Christ demonstrated through His perfect life, death, and resurrection that He wants me and loves me unconditionally, and I no longer need to do anything to receive His love and care."
- "Christ delights in providing for all my needs and tenderly caring for my emotions."
- "Because I know that Christ loved me first based on His pursuit of me, I can extend the same love, grace, and tenderheartedness to others."
- "I can follow Jesus' example of taking care of my physical, emotional, and spiritual needs so I can care for others from an overflow of God's replenishment."

Aligned Attributes of the Beloved Child

- You maintain a generous approach to life because you're taking care of your needs and being kind to yourself, just as Christ did for Himself.
- You base your value on being Christ's Beloved Child instead of on others' appreciation, and you point others to Christ instead of needing others to depend on you.
- You are sincere, humble, warmhearted, caring, and generous as you interpret the behavior of others charitably, emphasizing the good in people.

- You maintain appropriate relationship boundaries by saying no to what is not your responsibility and don't insert your help when it is not wanted.

CONNECTING TYPES

EIP Reminder: We all use all nine types to some degree. Therefore, the descriptions to follow reflect a combination of your main type's characteristics and your connecting types' characteristics. Out of their own core motivations, our four connecting types (wings and Enneagram paths either aligned or misaligned) use their respective strategies to attempt to meet our main type's core motivations, which still reign supreme.[1]

Wing Type 1

Summary

Do you sometimes have a strong sense of responsibility and obligation to do the proper, ideal, and right thing for others? Do you have the drive to help people see a more ethical, moral, and appropriate way of doing life? These are characteristics of your wing Type 1 part.

This part is objective, detail-oriented, impersonal, serious, and more emotionally self-controlled. It focuses on improving the world and the lives of others by serving them more quietly from behind the scenes versus desiring to stand out for praise.

How to Recognize Misaligned Traits of Wing Type 1

- Are you quick to judge and condemn others while justifying yourself based on your high standards, principles, and morals?
- Do people feel controlled by your moral intensity, impatience, and demands to follow through with your advice?

- Do you struggle with self-condemnation, guilt, and negative self-talk, particularly if you are proved wrong or selfish?
- Are you internally conflicted between your moral principles and your heart for people in need?

How to Recognize Aligned Traits of Wing Type 1

- Do you strive to give the most ideal and best service to others without needing praise and recognition?
- Are you an excellent teacher who focuses on improving the lives of others by combining your principles, values, encouragement, and relational warmth?
- Do you use your wisdom and discernment to establish healthy boundaries and not overstretch yourself?
- Are you more principled and intentional with your self-care?

Wing Type 3

Summary

Do you try to gain love and bless others by being charming, likable, and adaptable, and creating valuable intimate relationships? Do you strive for acceptance, validation, and admiration from others both relationally and professionally? These are characteristics of your wing Type 3 part.

This part is outgoing, affirming, friendly, and self-assured and does not want to be exposed as a failure or worthless. It supports your main type by creating connections with others through accomplishments and winning affection by meeting the needs of others.

How to Recognize Misaligned Traits of Wing Type 3

- Do you ever project an image of incredible personal warmth and friendliness to win connection and admiration from others?

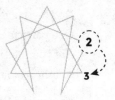

- Are you less aware of how you name-drop, flatter, charm, and draw attention to yourself to people-please and win admiration?
- Do you ignore or suppress your feelings so you can focus on your self-worth in the eyes of others?
- When someone exposes your weaknesses or failures, do you become hostile, vicious, and manipulate others into seeing and appreciating your accomplishments and relational value?

How to Recognize Aligned Traits of Wing Type 3

- Do you easily connect with others through nurturing warmth, likability, and social graces, bringing a sense of modesty and generosity to your relationships?
- Do you offer the fullness of your abilities, talents, and gifts to others as an overflow of your heart with no need for recognition?
- Are you more self-assured and energetic, seeing the value God has given you?
- Do you see your limitations and live within them, all the while still knowing that you are valuable to others?

Enneagram Path Type 4

Summary

Do you sometimes feel misunderstood by others or feel like you don't belong? Can you tap into a side of you that is profoundly creative and sees beauty in the ordinary? These are characteristics of your Enneagram path Type 4 part.

This part lives primarily in imagination and feelings. Deep down, it has an idealized vision of the person it desires to become, but it feels like it is tragically flawed and lacks qualities that others possess. It supports your main type by giving you profound depth and authenticity, a necessary component for developing healthy connections and relationships with others.

How to Recognize Misaligned Traits of Enneagram Path Type 4

- Do you withdraw when you feel moody, melancholy, or misunderstood to protect your reputation and work out your emotions alone?
- Do you daydream about becoming free of always needing to be helpful and selfless, being your authentic and ideal self, and focusing on your own emotions and needs?
- Do you feel that others do not listen to or understand you and how difficult it is to be constantly others-focused, helpful, and self-sacrificial?
- Do self-pity and envy of others make you increasingly self-focused and cause you to exhibit martyr-like tendencies?

How to Recognize Aligned Traits of Enneagram Path Type 4

- Do you enjoy resting in the beauty of nature, allowing your creativity, feelings, and needs to surface and be experienced?
- Can you temporarily set aside helping others and practice self-care?
- Do you intentionally schedule a time to process your feelings and intuitive insights so you can bring truth and healing to any feelings of rejection or pride?
- Can you sit with others in their difficult emotions, providing support without offering unsolicited help?

Enneagram Path Type 8

Summary

Is there a side to you that feels more self-assertive, protective, and passionate? Do you find yourself more self-confident in knowing and caring for your emotions and needs while doing the same for others? These are characteristics of your Enneagram path Type 8 part.

This part is resourceful, driven, decisive, and a natural leader. It is a champion of others by leading the way, providing protection, and plowing a path for others. It supports your main type by giving you opportunities to truly see the needs of others and provide for them with your relational warmth and care.

How to Recognize Misaligned Traits of Enneagram Path Type 8

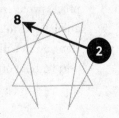

- Do you ever become confrontational, irritable, angry, or defensive if you feel your love and support are ignored, unappreciated, or rejected?
- Are there times you are more controlling, demanding, and dominating in your relationships and in your efforts to help and serve others?
- Do you become overly protective and aggressive when you think someone you care about is being harmed in some way?
- Do you ever avoid being vulnerable, fearing that others will take advantage of you or reject you?

How to Recognize Aligned Traits of Enneagram Path Type 8

- Knowing you are loved, provided for, and safe in God's care, can you humbly help others with God's strength and tenderness?
- Do you have the ability to vulnerably share your emotions and needs with directness and emotional balance?

- Do you see that you are shifting your focus from people-pleasing to doing what is best for everyone, including yourself?
- Do you find yourself feeling courageous, strong, self-affirming, and self-confident in all the abilities God gave you?

2

Type 2: AWARE Exercise

AWAKEN

Awaken to your belief that you will be rejected by others or seen as selfish if you care for yourself. What misaligned part of your heart is telling you this false message right now? Have you asked this part what it is feeling? What needs and emotions do you have that deserve your attention? Do you feel any tension or pain in your body? Are your thoughts being pulled away from yourself and toward a relationship status or others' emotions and needs?

WELCOME

Welcome and extend kindness to yourself and your misaligned parts without guilt or shame, knowing that Jesus unconditionally loves and wants you for who you are, not because of how well you serve others. Recognize that this part of your heart is both a gift and a burden. Remain curious and nonjudgmental; release any feelings of shame to Christ.

ASK

Ask the Holy Spirit to help you interpret what your misaligned part is trying to communicate and the motives behind it. How is it trying to protect your Wounded Child part? Resist any urge to fix your situation. Then ask the Holy Spirit to help you care for yourself in the same ways Christ took care of Himself.

RECEIVE

Receive Christ's unconditional love and unending pursuit of you, resting in the truth that it is not dependent on your service to others. Allow the Holy Spirit to remind you of Jesus' perfect example of caring for Himself so He could then serve and bless others from a filled and satisfied heart.

ENGAGE

Engage yourself, your relationships, and your circumstances in a new way, from a heart resting in the truth that you are loved and wanted for being you. From this aligned place, you can voice your needs and emotions, asking for help when needed and caring kindly for yourself. Then others will experience your love and care in a healthy, life-giving way, free from any strings or expectations.[2]

Gospel Self-Talk

"Because of Christ's work on my behalf, I am loved and wanted. Jesus says that His love is never dependent on what I do for others but solely on His desire to and care for me, and this message brings me comfort and relief. I can loosen my grip on needing to be needed because when God looks at me, He sees His Beloved Child, who is loved and cherished just as I am. I'm invited to rest in His care and be completely filled with His love. I bring God's compassion and care to the world. And because He gives me more than I could ever ask for in His loving pursuit of me, I am free to bestow this same abundance to others without needing anything in return."[3]

Type 2 EIP

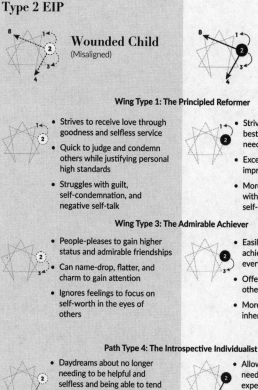

Wounded Child
(Misaligned)

Beloved Child
(Aligned)

2

Wing Type 1: The Principled Reformer

- Strives to receive love through goodness and selfless service
- Quick to judge and condemn others while justifying personal high standards
- Struggles with guilt, self-condemnation, and negative self-talk

- Strives to give the most ideal and best service to others without needing praise and recognition
- Excellent teacher who focuses on improving the lives of others
- More principled and intentional with healthy boundaries and self-care

Wing Type 3: The Admirable Achiever

- People-pleases to gain higher status and admirable friendships
- Can name-drop, flatter, and charm to gain attention
- Ignores feelings to focus on self-worth in the eyes of others

- Easily connects with others by achieving what is good for everyone, including oneself
- Offers abilities and talents to others with no strings attached
- More self-assured, recognizing inherent value

Path Type 4: The Introspective Individualist

- Daydreams about no longer needing to be helpful and selfless and being able to tend to personal needs
- Feels that others do not understand how difficult it is to be constantly others-focused
- Can be moody, temperamental, and exhibit martyr-like tendencies, especially when disappointed by others

- Allows creativity, feelings, and needs to surface and be experienced
- Processes emotions and brings truth and healing to any feelings of rejection or pride
- Sits with others in their difficult emotions, providing support without offering unsolicited help

Path Type 8: The Passionate Protector

- Becomes confrontational or defensive if love and support are ignored or unappreciated
- More controlling, demanding, and dominating in relationships
- Avoids being vulnerable, fearing the rejection and manipulation of others

- Shares emotions and needs with assertiveness and emotional balance
- Shifts focus from people-pleasing to doing what is best for everyone, including oneself
- More courageous, strong, and self-confident

173

3

Type 3: Admirable Achiever

**Efficient | Accomplished | Motivating
| Driven | Image-Conscious**

Core Motivations

Core Fear
Being exposed as or thought incompetent, inefficient, or worthless; failing to be or appear successful.

Core Desire
Having high status and respect; being admired, successful, and valuable.

Core Weakness
Deceit: deceiving yourself into believing you are only the image you present to others; embellishing the truth by putting on a polished persona for everyone (including yourself) to see and admire.

Core Longing
To hear and believe, "You are loved and valued for simply being you."

Primary Perspective

To achieve your core motivations, your primary focus of attention is to be or appear successful. You believe receiving love is tied to your achievements; therefore, you avoid failure at all costs and shape-shift into someone with a more appealing image. You tend to embellish the truth and dress to impress, hoping others will see you as accomplished, admirable, efficient, and valuable.

Summary Overview

God created you to reveal His triumph and brilliance and participate with Him to reveal His radiant creation. Unfortunately, sin disrupted God's perfect creation. Our society is fast-paced and comparison-driven, and you believe that you must be successful in every area of life. Being competitive, self-promoting, and constantly comparing yourself to others, you struggle with burnout and believing you are only as good as your last accomplishment.

You live under constant pressure to measure your worth by external achievement and confidence. This causes you to struggle with deceit, hiding parts of yourself that you don't want others to see and only portraying a successful exterior. In doing so, you become unaware of who you authentically are in your own heart, which affects you and those around you.

The good news is that Jesus saves you through grace, a gift you cannot earn. He says you are loved and valued for who you really are, not through your success and productivity. You are free to be your true self.

Jesus came to restore His radiant creation, and He invites you into that process. When your heart is aligned with the gospel and you learn to take your longing to Christ and rest in Him, you can become a humble team player and champion of others. Your confidence, enthusiasm, and determination inspire people to reach ambitious goals for the greater good, truly making the world a better place.

Type 3: Enneagram Internal Profile (EIP)

THE WOUNDED CHILD (MISALIGNED TYPE 3)

Summary

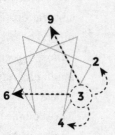

As a child, you longed to hear that "you are loved for simply being you." You grew up believing others would only love you if you were successful, valuable, and admirable. To you, second place was losing, which was unacceptable.

Because you always had to be the best, you put aside your own feelings and true identity and shape-shifted into any image or persona your parents, teachers, coaches, and peers accepted and admired. To determine your worth, you constantly measured their responses to assess if you had earned their love or admiration. This pursuit was and still is exhausting.

Your Wounded Child part falsely believes that receiving love is dependent on your success and image management. It longs to be its authentic self and finally rest from the constant pursuit of winning. As an adult, your core longing remains the same: to hear and believe that "you are loved for simply being you."

False Messages the Wounded Child Believes Are True

- "It's not okay to have my own identity and feelings since they get in the way of being successful and accomplished."
- "I must not be average and inefficient, so I must do something valuable and admirable, or else I will be seen as a failure and worthless."

- "I must appear victorious and accomplished and never show my fear of failing or being incompetent."

Misaligned Attributes

- When your Wounded Child part is activated, it fears and believes it is seen as incapable, unimpressive, worthless, a failure, or exposed for being a fraud.
- The Wounded Child reacts and does its best to become the most successful person to gain others' recognition, applause, and admiration. The problem is that the more it confidently shows off and boasts of your accomplishments, the more others become annoyed or envious of you, causing them to look for and expose any faults, failures, and shortcomings you have to bring your image down.
- The Wounded Child part of your heart struggles to accept that it is unsustainable for you to keep raising the bar of success and striving to reach it. This causes it to be obsessed with setting more goals, plans, and tasks to achieve the next great accomplishment and win the status and adoration it craves. Unfortunately, not only does this not work, but it only compounds your problems.

The Beloved Child (Aligned Type 3)

Summary

Only when your Beloved Child part is leading your heart can your misaligned parts loosen their grip on needing to be admired and successful. Your Beloved Child reminds them that when God looks at you, He already sees the perfect status you are striving for. Christ's status is your status, and it is no longer dependent on what you achieve.

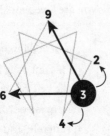

Your Beloved Child knows it is free from feeling shame, worthlessness, and failure. Under its leadership, you can now rest in knowing that you do not need to earn love, for you are loved for simply being you.

When your heart is aligned with the gospel, you feel Christ's warm embrace and allow your authentic self and emotions to come out. You inspire people to accomplish goals for the greater good, revealing God's restoration and triumph over sin.

True Messages the Beloved Child Believes

- "Jesus Christ demonstrated through His life, death, and resurrection that He values all of me, and I don't need to accomplish anything to receive His love. I am loved unconditionally for simply being me."
- "Christ credits to me His successes and righteousness so I can rest in His provision and merit, which brings great relief and delight to my exhausted heart."
- "I am not what I do. I am God's Beloved Child. Therefore, I am free to put down my 'achieving masks' and be my true self."
- "Because of my position in Christ, I can continue to excel and bless others with my abilities, talents, and gifts."

Aligned Attributes of the Beloved Child

- You enjoy working with others toward shared goals and helping them become the best version of themselves. You do not need to outshine your peers.
- You have a healthy work–life balance because you can take off your "achieving masks" and reveal your authentic self without fear.
- Knowing that Christ rescued you from your shortcomings and that His achievement is now your own, you can feel, name, embrace, and sit with your emotions versus pushing them aside to achieve more.
- You use your incredible gifts, talents, and abilities to bless others and glorify God by being gracious, modest, and charitable.

CONNECTING TYPES

EIP Reminder: We all use all nine types to some degree. Therefore, the descriptions to follow reflect a combination of your main type's characteristics and your connecting types' characteristics. Out of their own core motivations, our four connecting types (wings and Enneagram paths either aligned or misaligned) use their respective strategies to attempt to meet our main type's core motivations, which still reign supreme.[1]

Wing Type 2

Summary

Do you pride yourself on having excellent social skills, a warm and nurturing touch, and a likable charm that wins the affection of others? Are you more outwardly emotional, friendly, affectionate, and generous? These are characteristics of your wing Type 2 part.

This part is highly relational, friendly, cheerful, energetic, talkative, and engaging in the lives of others. It focuses on successfully connecting with others through its abilities, compassion, and generous support in hopes of winning attention and love.

How to Recognize Misaligned Traits of Wing Type 2

- Do you quickly "turn on" the relational warmth and charm to flatter and connect with others and receive the affirmation, adoration, and attention you long for?
- Do you feel hurt and insecure when you are not needed and double down on your efforts to win people over by "people-pleasing," flattery, and looking for more ways to make people like you?
- Are you constantly hiding your own needs and emotions and focusing on how to win appreciation, praise, applause, and admiration through energetically performing in the spotlight?

- Do you manipulate, feel entitled, or demand others see your good intentions and give you the attention, recognition, and praise you seek because you believe you need to earn love and affection by helping, supporting, and advising others?

How to Recognize Aligned Traits of Wing Type 2

- Do you instinctively know how to make others feel special, seen, cared for, and supported by extending emotional friendship, compassion, and support, and expressing your care and affection toward others?

- Knowing that Christ is caring for your emotional, relational, and physical needs, are you able to extend love, care, and support to yourself first and then to others selflessly without constantly needing love and affection from others?

- After first filling yourself up with Christ's love and closeness to you, and after taking care of your emotions and needs, are you able to be warmly responsive and generous to others with your time, talents, abilities, and social connections?

- When you are resting in God's love for you, do you bless others by maintaining appropriate boundaries and saying no to helping or caring for someone who is not your responsibility?

Wing Type 4

Summary

Do you have a deeper, more creative, and emotional part of yourself? Are you torn between turning on the charm to be what others desire (Type 3) versus being your unique and authentic self (Type 4)? These are characteristics of your wing Type 4 part.

This part is more withdrawn, private, quiet, less energetic, and primarily focused on achieving recognition and praise for your unique accomplishments and special status. It supports your main type by drawing out your sensitivity, emotional vulnerability, creativity, and desire for beauty and the ideal.

How to Recognize Misaligned Traits of Wing Type 4

- Do you struggle with the tension of putting on a likable persona to charm and win others' admiration (Type 3) but also demand authenticity and realness from them and yourself (Type 4)?
- Do you find yourself struggling with being moody, temperamental, withdrawn, and doubting your ability to succeed?
- Do you demand that others see, praise, and admire your unique contributions, notable accomplishments, and profound creativity?
- Do you feel that you are different from others and exempt from the same rules others must follow and thus find yourself self-indulging and going after what you want?

How to Recognize Aligned Traits of Wing Type 4

- Do you master and excel at your craft or skill with introspection and creativity?
- Can you observe your emotional world and develop more depth, balance, vulnerability, and genuine authenticity?
- Are you self-assured, highly accomplished, introspective, intuitive, sensitive, and self-aware at work and home?
- Do you want to bless others by taking an average piece of work and transforming it into something uniquely valuable, redemptive, and reflective of your creative touch?

Enneagram Path Type 6

Summary

Do you have a cooperative, loyal spirit that strives to work hard and troubleshoot problems? Do you sometimes doubt yourself and seek out support from those you trust? These are characteristics of your Enneagram path Type 6 part.

This part anticipates how circumstances could go wrong. It believes it needs to constantly be on the lookout, plan, and prepare for possible threats to you and those you are loyal to. It supports your main type by encouraging you to be reliable, faithful, and courageous.

3

How to Recognize Misaligned Traits of Enneagram Path Type 6

- Do you express your frustration, dissatisfaction, self-doubt, and dread when your anxiety rises?
- Do you struggle with self-doubt and confusion, leading you to seek guidance and support from others?
- Do you strongly react when blamed or accused of something?
- Do you become suspicious of others and test their loyalty?
- Do you avoid trying things you think you might fail?

How to Recognize Aligned Traits of Enneagram Path Type 6

- Do you take your anxieties and insecurities to God, trusting that He will care for you and give you the clarity, courage, and strength you need to handle life's many challenges?
- Are you less competitive and more loyal, cooperative, committed, and focused on the well-being of others?
- Do you have more of a team-player mindset, ask for help and advice, and use your talents to help and promote others?

- Are you more warm, vulnerable, faithful, committed, witty, engaging, trusting, and reveal who you are behind any "achieving masks"?

Enneagram Path Type 9

Summary

During conflicts, can you see both sides to an issue and help bridge the gap between people? When you are feeling overwhelmed, do you check out and find comfort in familiar routines? These are characteristics of your Enneagram path Type 9 part.

This part is warm, loving, caring, and focused on affirming, encouraging, and supporting others. To keep the peace and not disrupt your relationships, it merges and accommodates others' agendas, losing itself in the process. It supports your main type by encouraging rest, experiencing serenity, and helping you see everyone's perspective to maintain harmony.

How to Recognize Misaligned Traits of Enneagram Path Type 9

- Do you appear busy to avoid looking lazy, even when you're not able to focus?
- Do you ever withdraw because you have lost interest in accomplishing and want to be left alone and not bothered?
- When you are overwhelmed and stressed, do you numb out by watching TV, playing video games, shopping, eating, or some other outlet to escape?
- Do you stubbornly resist help from others or even hearing that you need help?

How to Recognize Aligned Traits of Enneagram Path Type 9

- Have you learned how to slow down and be present in each moment instead of constantly doing, achieving, and performing?

- Do you value the viewpoints of others and appreciate their contributions?
- Do you seek to collaborate and support others in their success instead of needing to be the main person who stands out?
- Are you able to relax and rest, knowing your identity isn't tied to what you accomplish or what others think of you but is found in being loved for simply being you?

Type 3: AWARE Exercise

Awaken

Awaken to your belief that you are only the image you present to others. What misaligned part of your heart is telling you this false message right now? Have you asked it what it is feeling and why? Do you fear being exposed as a failure, incompetent and worthless? Do you feel any tension or pain in your body? Are your thoughts being pulled away from your emotions and toward your list of goals?

Welcome

Welcome and extend kindness to yourself and your misaligned part without guilt or shame, knowing that Jesus loves you for simply being you and not for your accomplishments. Recognize that this part of your heart is both a gift and a burden. Remain curious and nonjudgmental; release any feelings of shame.

Ask

Ask the Holy Spirit to help you interpret what your misaligned part is trying to communicate and the motive behind it. How is it trying to protect your Wounded Child part? Resist any urge to go and do. Then ask the Holy Spirit to help you rest in Christ's accomplishments on your behalf and trust that you are valued and loved based solely on His achievements for you.

Receive

Receive Christ's perfect example. He did not look for man's admiration; He rested in His Father's unconditional love. Allow the Holy Spirit to remind you of who you are in Christ—His Beloved Child, loved for who you are and not what you do. Your status is complete because of Christ's accomplishment on your behalf.

Engage

Engage yourself, your relationships, and your circumstances in a new way, from a heart resting in the truth that you are loved for simply being you. From this aligned place, you can put away your "achieving masks," find rest from your pursuit of status, and be your authentic self. Then you can be an inspiring team player who accomplishes goals for the greater good.[2]

Gospel Self-Talk

"Because of Christ's work on my behalf, I am loved for simply being me. I can loosen my grip on needing to be praised and admired by others because when God looks at me, He sees His Beloved Child, loved and cherished just as I am and not for what I accomplish. His love for me is never dependent on my achievements, image, or status in the eyes of others but based solely on His desire to love me and credit me with His perfect accomplishments. I'm invited to be filled with His love and affirmation and allow His love to overflow from me into others without needing adoration from them. He frees me from an exhausting life of striving for success. I can now rest in His accomplishments and provision and freely be my authentic self with no fear or shame."[3]

Type 3 EIP

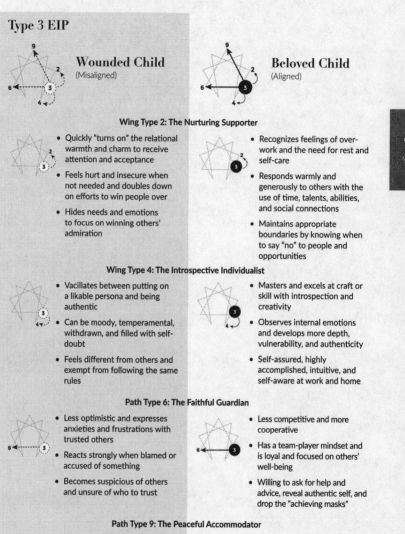

Wounded Child
(Misaligned)

Beloved Child
(Aligned)

3

Wing Type 2: The Nurturing Supporter

- Quickly "turns on" the relational warmth and charm to receive attention and acceptance
- Feels hurt and insecure when not needed and doubles down on efforts to win people over
- Hides needs and emotions to focus on winning others' admiration

- Recognizes feelings of over-work and the need for rest and self-care
- Responds warmly and generously to others with the use of time, talents, abilities, and social connections
- Maintains appropriate boundaries by knowing when to say "no" to people and opportunities

Wing Type 4: The Introspective Individualist

- Vacillates between putting on a likable persona and being authentic
- Can be moody, temperamental, withdrawn, and filled with self-doubt
- Feels different from others and exempt from following the same rules

- Masters and excels at craft or skill with introspection and creativity
- Observes internal emotions and develops more depth, vulnerability, and authenticity
- Self-assured, highly accomplished, intuitive, and self-aware at work and home

Path Type 6: The Faithful Guardian

- Less optimistic and expresses anxieties and frustrations with trusted others
- Reacts strongly when blamed or accused of something
- Becomes suspicious of others and unsure of who to trust

- Less competitive and more cooperative
- Has a team-player mindset and is loyal and focused on others' well-being
- Willing to ask for help and advice, reveal authentic self, and drop the "achieving masks"

Path Type 9: The Peaceful Accommodator

- Withdraws and loses interest in accomplishing or remains unproductively busy to avoid looking lazy
- Wants to be left alone and not bothered in order to numb out with unhealthy habits
- Stubbornly resists help from others or even hearing advice that help may be needed

- Slows down to rest and be present in each moment instead of constantly doing and performing
- Values the viewpoints and contributions of others
- Excels out of joy and not desperation or fear, knowing how to separate actions from identity

Type 4: Introspective Individualist

4

AUTHENTIC | CREATIVE | EXPRESSIVE | DEEP | TEMPERAMENTAL

Core Motivations

CORE FEAR

Being inadequate, emotionally cut off, plain, mundane, defective, flawed, or insignificant.

CORE DESIRE

Being unique, special, and authentic.

CORE WEAKNESS

Envy: feeling that you're tragically flawed, something foundational is missing inside you, and others possess qualities you lack.

CORE LONGING

To hear and believe, "You are seen and loved for exactly who you are—special and unique."

Primary Perspective

To achieve your core motivations, your primary focus of attention is believing you are tragically flawed and lacking qualities others have. This false belief leads to feelings of inferiority and envy and isolates you because you feel like an outsider. You are on a never-ending journey to find what you are missing inside, be understood by others, and be loved for your authentic and unique self.

Summary Overview

God created you to reveal His creativity and emotions and bring beauty and deep understanding to the world around you. Unfortunately, sin disrupted God's perfect creation, and you feel that you alone are missing something important. You compare yourself to others and envy those who possess the things you long for. Because you feel disconnected and fundamentally flawed, you can become self-absorbed, temperamental, and appear disinterested in others, which causes relational conflicts and confirms the lies you believe about yourself. You always wonder what people think about you, perpetually seeing your weakness and never your glory.

You eagerly explore your inner world, looking for meaning, significance, and pathways to authentic connection. The good news is Jesus sees and loves you for exactly who you are—special and unique. Because of His work on your behalf, you are complete and truly belong.

Jesus came to restore humanity, and you are invited into that process.

By taking your longing to Christ, you can step out of your waterfall of emotions and bring forth your gifts. You are uniquely attuned to despair and suffering and bravely press into those depths to discover rich meaning in all of life. You can shoulder others' deep pains and emotions without becoming overwhelmed. It brings you great joy to connect and support others in their distress and bring attention to all that is beautiful, which is an amazing gift to the world.

Type 4: Enneagram Internal Profile (EIP)

THE WOUNDED CHILD (MISALIGNED TYPE 4)

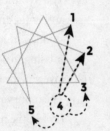

Summary

As a child, you longed to hear that "you are seen and loved for exactly who you are—special and unique." Longings, feelings, and passions ran deep within you. You used your emotions as the primary source to build your unique identity.

To some degree, you felt disconnected and misunderstood by those who took care of you. Feeling misunderstood led you to assume there was something fundamentally missing or tragically flawed within you. So you believed you needed to find something different and unique about you to stand out so others would see you and have a reason to love you. Discovering your authentic and distinctive self became your primary focus in life.

Your Wounded Child part falsely believes that it's not okay to be too functional or happy. It longs for others to see your unique abilities and to finally feel whole and accepted. As an adult, your core longing remains the same: to hear from others that "you are loved and seen for who you truly are."

False Messages the Wounded Child Believes Are True

- "It's not okay to be too much and not enough."
- "If I am authentic and true to myself, then I am okay, so sometimes I have to exaggerate my uniqueness to get the attention and affection that I crave."
- "No one understands me because I am tragically flawed and something foundational is missing inside me that others possess, which is why I am so different and defective that I do not belong."

Misaligned Attributes

- When your Wounded Child part is activated, it fears and believes it is tragically flawed, something foundational is missing inside you, and others possess the qualities you lack.
- The Wounded Child reacts and does its best to become a unique, authentic, and idealized version of you in hopes of being seen, understood, and loved. You walk a never-ending journey to find what is missing inside you, hoping that people will finally understand and love you for being unique.
- The more your Wounded Child part searches for your most authentic self, the more you compare yourself against an idealized version of yourself that you can never obtain. This leaves you feeling hopeless, flawed, envious, and moody, causing you to withdraw from the relationships you long for. Unfortunately, not only does this not work, but it only compounds your problems.

THE BELOVED CHILD (ALIGNED TYPE 4)

Summary

Only when your Beloved Child part is leading your heart can your misaligned parts loosen their grip on needing to be special and unique. Your Beloved Child reminds them that God's love for you is not based on an idealized version of yourself. When God looks at you, He already sees you as His unique, redeemed creation, and He delights in all He sees.

Your Beloved Child knows it is free from feeling shame, rejection, or thinking you are defective. Under its leadership, you can now rest in knowing that you are seen and loved for exactly who you are— set apart and seen in the eyes of the One who created you.

When your heart is aligned with the gospel, you can let go of envy, comparison, and feeling incomplete. You have all of Christ's spiritual blessings, forgiveness, and righteousness. You feel secure in His love, knowing He will never abandon or reject you, which brings your emotions into balance. You belong to Him!

True Messages the Beloved Child Believes

- "I no longer need to feel shame or defectiveness, because Christ has made me into a new beautiful creation." (2 Corinthians 5:17)
- "Christ pursued me, saved me, and brought me in so I could forever sit at His glorious banquet table. He sees me, understands me, values me, and loves me deeply."
- "Like Christ, I can feel deep emotions, find beauty where others can't, bestow compassion, and extend emotional care to those who are in pain."
- "I am not too much or less than others. I am part of a bigger story, a beautiful tapestry that God is weaving together. I *belong*!"

Aligned Attributes of the Beloved Child

- You believe God fully knows you, loves you unconditionally, and created you special and unique to bless the world.
- Knowing you have all of Christ's spiritual blessings, forgiveness, and righteousness and, therefore, lack nothing, you let go of envy and comparison.

- Your heart finds rest in the truth that you are not alone and will never be rejected because you belong to Christ.
- With your vast emotions being both experienced and balanced, you place your focus on others and take the time to create, inspire, listen, and extend compassion and care to those who are in greater need.

Connecting Types

EIP Reminder: We all use all nine types to some degree. Therefore, the descriptions to follow reflect a combination of your main type's characteristics and your connecting types' characteristics. Out of their own core motivations, our four connecting types (wings and Enneagram paths either aligned or misaligned) use their respective strategies to attempt to meet our main type's core motivations, which still reign supreme.[1]

Wing Type 3

Summary

Are you self-confident and driven to create beautiful and meaningful things? Do you enjoy the finer things and see yourself as more refined and sophisticated than others? These are characteristics of your wing Type 3 part.

This part is optimistic, accomplished, adaptable, and driven to excel in all areas of life. It focuses on what needs to happen and how to adapt to appear successful and prestigious.

How to Recognize Misaligned Traits of Wing Type 3

- Do you try to earn love and admiration by becoming a successful and unique individual?
- Do you sometimes forgo authenticity and shapeshift into a particular image to gain praise from others since you envy what they have and feel you're lacking?
- Do you express a surplus of confidence in your unique qualities,

work, and accomplishments, refusing to admit when you are wrong or to reveal anything that diminishes your image?

- Do your relationships suffer when you become self-focused in reaching a goal or when you embellish and boast about your accomplishments?

How to Recognize Aligned Traits of Wing Type 3

- Do you make your unique mark on the world by mastering your craft or skill with your creativity, originality, and ambition?
- Do you have healthy self-confidence in who God created you to be and find satisfaction in the image you now have in Christ, that you no longer strive to perform to earn love and admiration from others but thrive in creating something meaningful that expresses your authentic self?
- Can you recover more quickly from emotional setbacks and continue to make substantial progress in personal development?
- Are you an optimistic, friendly, and upbeat person who is hardworking, competent, efficient, and able to accomplish a great deal?

Wing Type 5

Summary

Do you bring profound creativity to the world by combining your intuition with intellectual insights? Do you procrastinate on projects because you fear you don't have all the information and resources you need? These are characteristics of your wing Type 5 part.

This part is withdrawn, wise, and an innovative observer who lives with curiosity and a craving to learn more. It fears it lacks inner resources and that too much interaction with others will lead to catastrophic depletion of its energy and emotional reserves. Therefore, it withdraws from others and tends to its own needs.

How to Recognize Misaligned Traits of Wing Type 5

- Do you first need to sort out your feelings by using your intellect before moving forward in life?
- Do your thoughts and emotions feel true, causing you to react to life and people from a false reality?
- Do you find yourself becoming secretive and isolating from others to protect and focus on your inner world?
- Do you feel that others do not understand your fierce independence and your need for privacy, thus not appreciating how you process information and emotions?

How to Recognize Aligned Traits of Wing Type 5

- Are you remarkably creative and able to combine intellectual insights with emotional intuition to produce stunning original works?
- Do you generously give others helpful insights and information you have gathered over time, connecting on both intellectual and emotional levels?
- Do you have the ability to intellectually pull things apart and then conceptualize new ways to look at them from a creative viewpoint?
- Do you value wisdom and facts and use them to help stabilize your fluctuating emotions?

Enneagram Path Type 1

Summary

Do you complete what needs to be done before moving to other creative interests? Do you feel resentful that others are not doing their part to make things right and ideal? These are characteristics of your Enneagram path Type 1 part.

This part is sensible, ethical, responsible, serious, and self-disciplined, and feels personally obligated to improve you and the world. It supports your main type by giving you self-discipline and balanced emotions.

How to Recognize Misaligned Traits of Enneagram Path Type 1

- Do you focus on flaws, becoming more judgmental and critical of others and the world?
- Are you vocal about your frustrations and disappointments, and do you visibly display your disappointment in your body language?
- Are you impatient, picky, and controlling when you feel others are incorrect, irresponsible, or not being their authentic selves?
- Are you self-critical and hyperaware of your imperfections, and do you feel the need to improve yourself to reach what is ideal?

How to Recognize Aligned Traits of Enneagram Path Type 1

- Are you more emotionally balanced, objective, and grounded in your relationships?
- Do you embrace mundane tasks as opportunities to be a good steward and be responsible, disciplined, and organized?
- Do you recognize that your feelings are not always the reality and focus more on doing what is best for the good of all?
- Are you more reliable, completing what needs to be done before moving to other creative interests?

Enneagram Path Type 2

Summary

Do you pride yourself on having excellent social skills, a warm and nurturing touch, and a likable charm? Do you become overinvolved and clingy to win the affection of others? These are characteristics of your Enneagram path Type 2 part.

This part is highly relational, friendly, cheerful, energetic, talkative, and engaging in the lives of others. It supports your main type by pulling from your inner well of emotions and connecting you with others through compassion and generous support.

How to Recognize Misaligned Traits of Enneagram Path Type 2

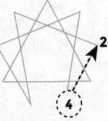

- Do you defend your hurt feelings by describing how your intrusive helpful advice or care was from a good place and others should accept it, or do you remove your affection to manipulate others to tend to your hurt emotions?
- Do you discuss the current condition of your relationship and how you're special and unique so others will see their need for you?
- Do you manipulate and create dependency through helping, giving attention, and doing favors for others?
- Do you use flattery and act possessive in your social groups because you secretly fear you don't belong or will be rejected and left out?

How to Recognize Aligned Traits of Enneagram Path Type 2

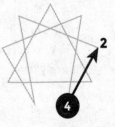

- Have you learned to recognize your full value in Christ and feel the unconditional love He lavishes onto you constantly, which enables you to put the needs of others ahead of your own with no strings attached?
- Do you acknowledge the positive qualities in others and generously affirm, encourage, and support them?
- Do you instinctively know how to make others feel special, seen,

cared for, and supported by extending emotional friendship, compassion, support, and expressing your care and affection toward others?

- Knowing that Christ is caring for your emotional, relational, and physical needs, are you able to extend love, care, and support to yourself first and then to others selflessly without constantly needing love and affection from others?

Type 4: AWARE Exercise

AWAKEN

Awaken to your belief that you are only your emotions and that you are defective and flawed. What misaligned part of your heart is telling you this false message right now? Have you asked this part what it is feeling? Do you feel the need to withdraw because a tsunami of emotions is sweeping over you? Do you feel any tension or pain in your body? Are your thoughts focused on what you lack and how you don't belong?

WELCOME

Welcome and extend kindness to yourself and your misaligned parts without guilt or shame, knowing that Jesus fully sees you for who you truly are and celebrates your uniqueness as a special and cherished child. Recognize that this part of your heart is both a gift and a burden. Remain curious and nonjudgmental; release any feelings of isolation or shame.

ASK

Ask the Holy Spirit to help you hear and trust His loving voice so your rich emotions can become balanced with insight, wisdom, and beauty rather than washed out with a tsunami of feelings that pushes away others. Then ask the Holy Spirit to help you believe and trust that you are seen, valued, and loved based solely on Christ's deep love and desire for you.

RECEIVE

Receive Christ's delight and acceptance of you, resting in the truth that you reflect His deep and passionate emotions, and with His help, you can balance your emotions so they do not overcome you and others. Ask the Holy Spirit to remind you that you are God's unique and Beloved Child who He delighted to create uniquely, and you belong to Him and His kingdom.

ENGAGE

Engage yourself, your relationships, and your circumstances in a new way, from a heart resting in the truth that you are complete, delighted in, and accepted by Christ. From this aligned place, you can move toward others without needing them to understand you. Then you can sit with and support those who are struggling and bring awareness to the overlooked beauty in all of creation.[2]

Gospel Self-Talk

"Because of Christ's work on my behalf, I am seen and loved for exactly who I am—special and unique. I can loosen my grip on needing to be different from others because when God looks at me, He sees His Beloved Child, who is uniquely created, loved, and cherished just as I am. His love for me is never dependent on me feeling whole or becoming an idealized version of myself. He sees, values, cherishes, and delights in me, and I fully belong to Him. This truth balances my many emotions and allows my heart to rest and find joy in who I am. I am free and uniquely able to support others in sorrow, and I can bring attention to all that is beautiful in the world."[3]

Type 4 EIP

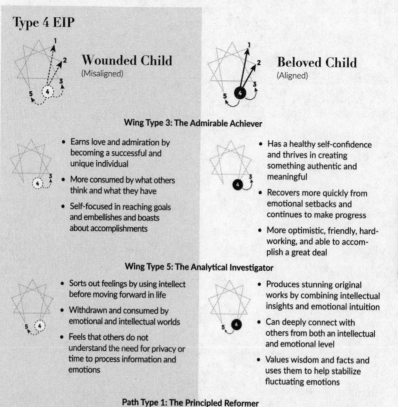

Wounded Child
(Misaligned)

Beloved Child
(Aligned)

Wing Type 3: The Admirable Achiever

- Earns love and admiration by becoming a successful and unique individual
- More consumed by what others think and what they have
- Self-focused in reaching goals and embellishes and boasts about accomplishments

- Has a healthy self-confidence and thrives in creating something authentic and meaningful
- Recovers more quickly from emotional setbacks and continues to make progress
- More optimistic, friendly, hard-working, and able to accomplish a great deal

Wing Type 5: The Analytical Investigator

- Sorts out feelings by using intellect before moving forward in life
- Withdrawn and consumed by emotional and intellectual worlds
- Feels that others do not understand the need for privacy or time to process information and emotions

- Produces stunning original works by combining intellectual insights and emotional intuition
- Can deeply connect with others from both an intellectual and emotional level
- Values wisdom and facts and uses them to help stabilize fluctuating emotions

Path Type 1: The Principled Reformer

- Vocal about frustrations and disappointments and visibly display them with body language
- Impatient, picky, and controlling when perceiving that others are incorrect or not being their authentic selves
- More self-critical and feels the need to improve to reach an ideal

- More emotionally balanced, objective, and principled
- Embraces mundane tasks as an opportunity to be a good steward
- Completes what needs to be done before moving on to other interests

Path Type 2: The Nurturing Supporter

- Defends hurt feelings by withdrawing your affection
- Manipulates and creates dependencies through helping, giving attention, and doing favors for others
- Uses flattery in your social groups due to a fear of not belonging, rejection, or exclusion

- Puts the needs of others first with no strings attached
- Can experience others' emotions and support them
- Feels gratitude instead of longing for what is missing

4

FOURTEEN

Type 5: Analytical Investigator

PERCEPTIVE | INSIGHTFUL | INTELLIGENT | DETACHED | ISOLATED

5

Core Motivations

CORE FEAR

Being annihilated, invaded, or not existing; being thought incapable or ignorant; having obligations placed on you or your energy depleted.

CORE DESIRE

Being knowledgeable, capable, and competent.

CORE WEAKNESS

Avarice: feeling you lack inner resources and that too much interaction with others will lead to catastrophic depletion; withholding yourself from contact with the world; holding on to your resources and minimizing your needs.

CORE LONGING
Hearing and believing, "Your needs are not a problem."

Primary Perspective

To achieve your core motivations, your primary focus of attention is obtaining more knowledge, believing it will bring you security and independence. You perceive the world and people as intrusive, overwhelming, and draining on your limited energy reserves. You withdraw from others and detach from your emotions to recharge alone. Without solitude, you fear you will experience catastrophic depletion, so establishing and maintaining boundaries feels essential to your well-being.

Summary Overview

God created you to reveal His intelligence and innovation. You are a perceptive and curious observer who walks through life craving to learn new things. Your objective and practical nature enables you to make wise decisions based on reason and knowledge. Unfortunately, sin disrupted the world, and you experience it as an intrusive and overwhelming place. Feeling that life demands too much of you, you focus your attention on conserving your energy and resources to avoid a sense of catastrophic depletion. This intense desire to hoard and control your environment makes you private and emotionally distant, which can damage your relationships.

You often feel that you must know everything before sharing your insights so you do not look incompetent, which overwhelms you and causes you to retreat. Seeing the demands of living in relationships, you distance yourself because you feel ill-equipped to meet them, but emotions and vulnerability are natural components to a healthy partnership.

You believe the confidence to engage will eventually come. Still, you feel like you do not have enough knowledge or resources to enter into the mysterious and complex world of another person.

The good news is, Jesus came to meet all your needs and fully replenish you. When your heart is aligned with the gospel, you discover that your needs are not a problem for Christ. Resting in His replenishment, you can begin to be more generous to others. You live not just from your head but your heart and the whole of who you are. That gift, coupled with your great vision and perspective, reflects the true wisdom of God.

Type 5: Enneagram Internal Profile (EIP)

THE WOUNDED CHILD (MISALIGNED TYPE 5)

Summary

As a child, you longed to hear that "your needs are not a problem" from your authority figures. You felt that the world and other people were overwhelming and energy depleting, so you kept a safe distance from them.

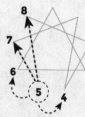

You preferred observing the world versus actively participating in it, and you enjoyed retreating into the comfort and safety of the fortress of your mind. It felt safer and wiser to keep your thoughts and feelings to yourself, so you remained more private and isolated than other kids. Others saw this as socially unacceptable and forced you to interact with life and people more, which felt harmful and uncomfortable.

Your Wounded Child part falsely believes the world says, "It's not okay to be comfortable and process your thoughts and feelings privately." To be comfortable, it needs time alone to recharge, and it longs for others to understand and accept this need. As an adult, your core longing remains the same: to hear from others that "your needs are not a problem."

False Messages the Wounded Child Believes Are True

- "It's not okay to be too comfortable and process my thoughts and feelings privately."
- "I must conserve my energy and resources to avoid a sense of catastrophic depletion."
- "To find security, I must withdraw from others by detaching from my emotions and retreating into the safety of my mind."
- "I must master a body of knowledge so I appear knowledgeable, insightful, and competent when I do interact with the world."

Misaligned Attributes

- When your Wounded Child part is activated, it fears being seen as incapable, incompetent, unknowledgeable, and ignorant.
- The Wounded Child reacts and does its best to become the most intelligent and informed person so you can confidently move forward with great insight and competence. The problem is that the more you believe you do not have enough knowledge, the more you will withdraw and detach from others and the world to try to gain the insights you feel you are missing, which becomes a never-ending search for knowledge.
- The Wounded Child part of your heart struggles to accept that learning all there is to learn is unsustainable since the depths of knowledge and information are infinite. This causes it to feel desperate and dive deeper into learning, hoping to reach the secure foundation of being fully intelligent and competent one day. Unfortunately, not only does this not work, but it only compounds your problems.

THE BELOVED CHILD (ALIGNED TYPE 5)

Summary

Only when your Beloved Child part is leading your heart can your misaligned parts loosen their grip on needing to be knowledgeable, capable, and competent in all areas. Your Beloved Child reminds them that they are secure in Christ, and nothing can take that away from them. They cannot earn this security through more knowledge or capability. Christ saw their need and fully met it with His finished work on the cross.

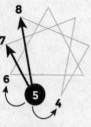

Your Beloved Child knows it is deeply loved and provided for and has all of Christ's blessings. Under its leadership, you can confidently enter the world and bless it with your wisdom. You no longer need to hold on to your resources and energy since you know God gives you all you need.

When you know, believe, and trust in who you are in Christ and that your core longing is fully satisfied in Him, your Beloved Child part will lead and guide all the misaligned parts of your heart back into alignment with the gospel truth. Here, you experience the satisfaction and joy of being part of a community where you can collaborate and give generously to others while also having a healthy balance of alone time.

True Messages the Beloved Child Believes

- "Jesus Christ demonstrated through His life, death, and resurrection that He values all of me, generously shares His wisdom with me, and replenishes me when I feel depleted."
- "The world may not always understand my need, but Christ understands me and gives me the freedom to rest and recharge."
- "I am not what I know. I am God's Beloved Child. Therefore, I am free to try new things even if I am not an expert or fully competent in an area."
- "Because Jesus meets all my needs, I can generously give others my time, knowledge, and emotions from the overflow of His good gifts."

Aligned Attributes of the Beloved Child

- You find yourself more freely engaging with others and expressing your feelings and needs to them, knowing God put them in your life as a gift to care for you.
- You see your great value and worth, knowing that Christ rescued you from your shortcomings and delights in meeting all your needs.
- You observe and generously share incredible things—knowledge, insights, and resources that most people cannot see or notice—with others, trusting that God will replenish them.
- You assert yourself with confidence, knowing you already have tremendous insights and understanding that will benefit the world.

CONNECTING TYPES

EIP Reminder: We all use all nine types to some degree. Therefore, the descriptions to follow reflect a combination of your main type's characteristics and your connecting types' characteristics. Out of their own core motivations, our four connecting types (wings and Enneagram paths either aligned or misaligned) use their respective strategies to attempt to meet our main type's core motivations, which still reign supreme.[1]

Wing Type 4

Summary

Do you express your authentic self in an eccentric and unique way? Do you find yourself withdrawing to analyze and process your emotions? These are characteristics of your wing Type 4 part.

This part is highly creative, expressive, emotional, self-focused, and deep. It helps you move from living primarily in your head to accessing your heart and emotions. It supports your main type in helping you connect deeper with others by being authentic and balancing your intellectual and emotional world.

How to Recognize Misaligned Traits of Wing Type 4

- Do you struggle with intense feelings that you need to withdraw and figure out what you're missing before you can engage and move forward?
- Do you find yourself holding everything at arm's length due to moodiness and self-doubt in your ability to do something competently?
- Do you ignore the real world and dive deeply into your imagination, emotions, creativity, and intellectual pursuits?
- Do you feel you are different from others and exempt from following social rules, giving yourself permission to detach and be self-absorbed with your unique interests?

How to Recognize Aligned Traits of Wing Type 4

- Do you excel at combining your creativity and intellectual achievement to create something truly innovative?
- Do you want to bless others by taking an average piece of work and transforming it into something valuable, redemptive, and reflective of your creative touch?
- Are you attuned to your intellectual and emotional world, and do you connect more deeply with others because of your relational authenticity?
- Do you unify your aesthetic appreciation and high intelligence to create unique atmospheres at home and work that others find inspiring?

Wing Type 6

Summary

Do you have a problem-solving part of you that is loyal and committed to a group or field of study? Do you seek the advice and insights of others to feel safe, assured, and secure in what you should do? These are characteristics of your wing Type 6 part.

This part is reliable, trustworthy, responsible, and a natural trouble-shooter. It supports your main type by helping you persevere through difficulties and engage with others to gain the support, guidance, and security you need to face life's challenges.

How to Recognize Misaligned Traits of Wing Type 6

- Do you express your insecurity, dissatisfaction, self-doubt, and dread when your anxiety rises?
- Do you struggle with self-doubt and confusion, leading you to seek guidance and support from people or books?
- Are you more committed and loyal to your beliefs, viewpoints, and relationships than to your emotions?
- Do you become suspicious of others and either test their loyalty or avoid them?

How to Recognize Aligned Traits of Wing Type 6

- Do you take your anxieties and insecurities to God, trusting that He will care for you and give you the clarity, courage, and strength you need to be in the world?
- Can you see your circumstances with immense clarity and make accurate predictions to solve an issue?
- Do you have more of a team-player mindset, ask for help and advice, and use your talents to bless others?
- Do you balance your data-driven mind with warmth, vulnerability, faithfulness, commitment, and humor?

Enneagram Path Type 7

Summary

Is a part of you excitable, resilient, spontaneous, energetic, and optimistic? Do you sometimes take on too many exciting projects, become scattered, and struggle to complete them? These are characteristics of your Enneagram path Type 7 part.

This part has a hard time denying what it desires. It fears being bored, limited, and deprived, so it does whatever necessary to gain more resources. It supports your main type by creatively seeking out new ways to achieve exciting stimulation and experiences.

How to Recognize Misaligned Traits of Enneagram Path Type 7

- Do you sometimes have a racing mind and become scattered, restless, and hyperactive?
- Do you overbook your schedule with fascinating experiences and interests or impulsively take on too many projects?
- Are you more talkative with others, sharing all the new possibilities you see and information you've absorbed?
- Do you become erratically focused on learning everything at a feverish pace, causing you to be less patient with people?

How to Recognize Aligned Traits of Enneagram Path Type 7

- Do you enjoy life more, trusting God is benevolent and kind and will provide for your needs?
- Are you more fun, spontaneous, and physically active?
- Do you enjoy a more exciting and abundant life shared with others?

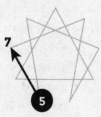

- Are you more hopeful, optimistic, and joyful, seeing that life is full of purpose and meaning?

Enneagram Path Type 8

Summary

Is part of you decisive, assertive, and protective of others? When you feel your space or energy is being intruded on, do you challenge anyone breaching your boundaries? These are characteristics of your Enneagram path Type 8 part.

This part is protective, self-confident, intense, confrontational, and big-hearted. To ensure you are not blindsided or betrayed, it will fortify boundaries to remain in control of all circumstances. It supports your main type by increasing your confidence and helping you trust your instincts.

How to Recognize Misaligned Traits of Enneagram Path Type 8

- Do you assert your boundaries forcefully and confront anyone who displeases you?
- Do you become aggressive and vengeful if you are blindsided or betrayed?
- Do you question others' competence while asserting your knowledge with strength and intellectual arrogance?
- Do you interrupt conversations with your thoughts and opinions, placing your voice and expertise over others?

How to Recognize Aligned Traits of Enneagram Path Type 8

- Are you more self-confident, assertive, and decisive—willing to take on more responsibility and demonstrate courage and confidence?
- Do you trust your instincts, becoming bolder and quicker to take action?

- Are you more active with your body, connecting your head with your heart and gut?
- Do you isolate yourself less often because you want to share your wisdom and resources to plow a path for others?

Type 5: AWARE Exercise

AWAKEN

Awaken to your belief that you must gain more information or resources before moving forward. What misaligned part of your heart is telling you this false message right now? Have you asked this part what it is feeling? Do you feel a need to withdraw and protect yourself from depletion? What is happening in your body? Do you feel any tension or pain? Are your thoughts fixating on information or resources you don't have that you believe you need to feel competent and capable?

WELCOME

Welcome and extend kindness to yourself and your misaligned part without guilt or shame, knowing that Jesus sees your need and wants to be generous with you. Recognize that this part of your heart is both a gift and a burden. Remain curious about not only your thoughts but also your body and emotions.

ASK

Ask the Holy Spirit to help you interpret what your misaligned part is trying to communicate and the motives behind it. How is it trying to protect your Wounded Child part? Resist any urge to fix your situation by seeking out more information. Then ask the Holy Spirit to help you trust that He has given you enough insights to take action.

RECEIVE

Receive Jesus as your perfect example. He balanced alone time with bold action and never hoarded His wisdom or resources. Rest in the truth that your needs are never a problem for Him, and you will not experience catastrophic depletion, because He will gladly renew your energy and care for your needs.

ENGAGE

Engage yourself, your relationships, and your circumstances in a new way, from a heart resting in the truth that Christ sees, understands, and takes care of all your needs. From this aligned place, you can generously share the overflow of your wisdom and resources, blessing others and the world.[2]

Gospel Self-Talk

"Because of Christ's work on my behalf, my needs are taken care of. I can loosen my grip on needing to be fully competent to feel secure. I will not experience catastrophic depletion because Christ knows what I need and provides for me out of His immense love. I can come to Him in solitude, and He will recharge and replenish me with more satisfying energy than I could have ever found for myself! It is not a burden for Him but a delight to pour out blessings onto me, His cherished and redeemed child. Therefore, I receive His knowledge, insights, energy, and resources, allowing me to connect with others in deeply profound ways. Because I've been given so much, I can generously give to others from a place of abundance and joy."[3]

Type 5 EIP

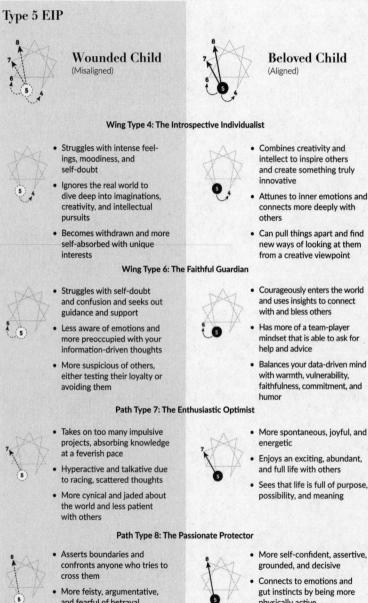

Wounded Child
(Misaligned)

Beloved Child
(Aligned)

Wing Type 4: The Introspective Individualist

- Struggles with intense feelings, moodiness, and self-doubt
- Ignores the real world to dive deep into imaginations, creativity, and intellectual pursuits
- Becomes withdrawn and more self-absorbed with unique interests

- Combines creativity and intellect to inspire others and create something truly innovative
- Attunes to inner emotions and connects more deeply with others
- Can pull things apart and find new ways of looking at them from a creative viewpoint

Wing Type 6: The Faithful Guardian

- Struggles with self-doubt and confusion and seeks out guidance and support
- Less aware of emotions and more preoccupied with your information-driven thoughts
- More suspicious of others, either testing their loyalty or avoiding them

- Courageously enters the world and uses insights to connect with and bless others
- Has more of a team-player mindset that is able to ask for help and advice
- Balances your data-driven mind with warmth, vulnerability, faithfulness, commitment, and humor

Path Type 7: The Enthusiastic Optimist

- Takes on too many impulsive projects, absorbing knowledge at a feverish pace
- Hyperactive and talkative due to racing, scattered thoughts
- More cynical and jaded about the world and less patient with others

- More spontaneous, joyful, and energetic
- Enjoys an exciting, abundant, and full life with others
- Sees that life is full of purpose, possibility, and meaning

Path Type 8: The Passionate Protector

- Asserts boundaries and confronts anyone who tries to cross them
- More feisty, argumentative, and fearful of betrayal
- Questions others' competence with intellectual arrogance

- More self-confident, assertive, grounded, and decisive
- Connects to emotions and gut instincts by being more physically active
- Less isolated and willing to take on responsibility

5

FIFTEEN

Type 6: Faithful Guardian

COMMITTED | RESPONSIBLE | FAITHFUL
| SUSPICIOUS | ANXIOUS

Core Motivations

CORE FEAR

Feeling fear itself; being without support, security, or guidance; being blamed, targeted, alone, or physically abandoned.

CORE DESIRE

Having security, guidance, and support.

CORE WEAKNESS

Anxiety: scanning the horizon of life and trying to predict and prevent negative outcomes (especially worst-case scenarios); remaining in a constant state of apprehension and worry.

CORE LONGING

To hear and believe, "You are safe and secure."

6

Primary Perspective

To achieve your core motivations, your primary focus of attention is scanning the horizon, looking for worst-case scenarios so you can predict and prevent potential harm. Because you struggle with self-doubt, you look outside yourself for guidance, support, and security. You believe that if you rehearse in your mind what might happen and develop strategies to stop negative circumstances, you can keep yourself and others safe.

Summary Overview

God created you to reveal His loyalty and bravery. You are reliable, hardworking, dutiful, and steady. Your dependability, sense of humor, ability to foresee problems, and fierce loyalty make you an incredible team player who can hold groups together to benefit the common good. Unfortunately, sin entered our world and made it a dangerous place, leaving you plagued with constant fears and uncertainty. You hypervigilantly look for things that could threaten your safety, security, and relationships so you can avoid the danger or challenge it head-on. Inside your mind is a nagging inner committee constantly asking, "But what about this?"

You struggle with self-doubt, feel anxious, and are unable to relax or trust yourself and others. In relationships, you can project your own fears, doubts, and insecurities onto people as a way to protect yourself, which erodes your trust in others and even in God. Your mind becomes cluttered with all possible worst-case scenarios, making you skeptical and hesitant to make decisions. By planning for and trying to control catastrophes, you hope to live in a trouble-free and predictable world, which is an impossible goal.

The good news is, Jesus came to earth to save you from sin and destruction and give you eternal security. If you take your fears and anxieties to Christ, He can transform them into great courage. When your heart is aligned with the gospel and you learn to rest in Christ's protective arms, you will experience a peace that surpasses the fear and danger you see around you. Then your loyalty and bravery will bring out the best in yourself and others, making the world a better place.

Type 6: Enneagram Internal Profile (EIP)

THE WOUNDED CHILD (MISALIGNED TYPE 6)

Summary

As a child, you saw the world as a dangerous and unreliable place and longed to hear that "you are safe and secure." You feared being blamed or getting into trouble, so you learned to forecast and strategize for what could go wrong.

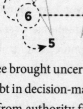

Your "inner committee" started early, informing you of every possible outcome to ensure your safety. Instead of helping you, your inner committee brought uncertainty and confusion by creating a great degree of self-doubt in decision-making. This caused you to seek clear and reliable advice from authority figures you trusted to help you feel secure.

Your Wounded Child part falsely believes that it's not okay to trust and depend on yourself. It longs to be free from your fear, your inner committee, and your constant pursuit of security. As an adult, your core longing remains the same: to hear and believe that "you are safe and secure."

False Messages the Wounded Child Believes Are True

- "It's not okay to trust myself, so I must seek out wisdom, feedback, and guidance from others to ensure I am on the right path."
- "If I am completely prepared, have covered all the bases, and have done all that is expected of me, I will be okay."

- "I cannot trust anyone until they prove their loyalty and commitment to me or to those I am loyal to."
- "To maintain my relationships, I must always be responsible, hardworking, trustworthy, and warm."

Misaligned Attributes

- When your Wounded Child part is activated, it fears and believes it is abandoned and without support, guidance, and security.
- The Wounded Child reacts and does its best to be responsible, prepared, hardworking, and diligent in hopes of gaining security, safety, and loyalty from others. The problem is that the more you believe you cannot trust yourself, the more you ignore the incredible discernment God has gifted you with and seek input from others that is potentially harmful.
- The Wounded Child part of your heart struggles to accept that you have courage and insight on what to do next. This causes it to desperately seek guidance and support from anyone who appears more insightful than you. Unfortunately, not only does this not work, but it only compounds your problems.

THE BELOVED CHILD (ALIGNED TYPE 6)

Summary

Only when your Beloved Child part is leading your heart can your misaligned parts loosen their grip on needing to find guidance, security, and support apart from Christ. Your Beloved Child reminds them that they cannot find security through any other person or belief system outside of Christ, who freely offers you safety and peace.

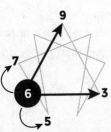

Your Beloved Child knows it is loved and provided for and has all of Christ's blessings, which allows your heart and mind to rest. You no longer need to seek safety and security from anyone or anything since God gives you enough resources and the courage to face reality.

When your heart is aligned with the gospel, you experience a peace that surpasses understanding. It is here that you feel the strong yet loving embrace of your heavenly Father, who secures your permanent place with Him.

True Messages the Beloved Child Believes

- "Jesus Christ demonstrated through His life, death, and resurrection that He values me and will go to any length to keep me safe and secure with Him for eternity."
- "I can be courageous, committed, warm, playful, and treat everyone as an equal because of the secure foundation I have in Christ."
- "I am not alone or abandoned. I am God's Beloved Child, and I can fully trust Him to free me from my insecurities, fears, and doubts."
- "Because of the Holy Spirit's discernment, guidance, and support, I can confidently and courageously face life's trials with the assurance that I will be okay."

Aligned Attributes of the Beloved Child

- After taking your anxieties and insecurities to God, you find peace in the knowledge that He is able, willing, and faithful to care for you.
- Trusting that you are safe and secure as God's Beloved Child, you are more trusting, warm, fun, engaging, and playful with others.
- Even though there is still uncertainty on earth, you trust that God will always be there to love, protect, and provide for you.
- You trust that God will give you the clarity, courage, strength, and confidence you need to make decisions and handle life's challenges.

CONNECTING TYPES

EIP Reminder: We all use all nine types to some degree. Therefore, the descriptions to follow reflect a combination of your main type's characteristics and your connecting types' characteristics. Out of their own core motivations, our four connecting types (wings and Enneagram paths either aligned or misaligned) use their respective strategies to attempt to meet our main type's core motivations, which still reign supreme.[1]

Wing Type 5

Summary

Do you find yourself withdrawing to analyze and process circumstances and relationships? Do you seek out information and data to help you solve issues and prepare more effectively? These are characteristics of your wing Type 5 part.

This part is observant, wise, curious, analytical, intellectual, emotionally distant, and independent. It feels it does not have enough knowledge to move forward competently. Therefore, it will withdraw to gain the information it needs to feel guided and secure.

How to Recognize Misaligned Traits of Wing Type 5

- Do you build boundaries so you can privately process your racing thoughts and anxieties and escape people who drain your energy?
- Do you first need to sort out your thoughts using your intellect and research skills before you can move forward in life?
- Do you become fiercely independent, secretive, and isolated to protect yourself from potential harm or disloyalty?
- Do you look to books or a belief system for guidance and security more than your committed relationships?

How to Recognize Aligned Traits of Wing Type 5

- Are you insightful, well researched, and willing to courageously engage with life's uncertainties knowing you are highly resourceful and prepared?

- Do you generously give others the wisdom and information you have gathered over time, connecting both intellectually and emotionally?

- Can you intellectually pull things apart and then conceptualize new ways to look at them for the good of society?

- Do you champion and support the disadvantaged with your insights and information?

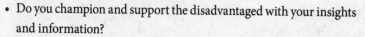

Wing Type 7

Summary

Do you lean on connecting with others for stimulation, adventure, and companionship? Are you more gregarious, talkative, and ready to have fun? These are characteristics of your wing Type 7 part.

This part is outgoing, spontaneous, distracted, impatient, friendly, and likes to have fun. It supports your main type by helping you establish a larger support system through loyal friendships and broader connections so you can immediately seek guidance from others when you feel uncertain about what to do.

How to Recognize Misaligned Traits of Wing Type 7

- Do you demand that others meet your need for excitement and fun to distract you from your anxieties?

- Do you use "escape hatches" (unhealthy indulgences) to avoid your anxieties, self-doubt, and contradictory thoughts from your inner committee?

- Have you ever experienced a spontaneous and excitable urge to do something that isn't responsible or appropriate, especially if you believe you can get away with it and not get blamed?

- Do you avoid feelings of pain, sadness, or disappointment by looking on the bright side or seeking out new adventures or friendships?

How to Recognize Aligned Traits of Wing Type 7

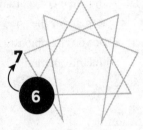

- Do you experience moments of grace and joy that enable your heart to be more trusting of others and confident in your abilities?
- Are you more enthusiastic, spontaneous, playful, joyful, and fun, seeing the world and your circumstances through a more optimistic lens?
- Do you believe that life is not all serious and daunting but rich with life-giving experiences and emotions, including happiness, abundance, and freedom?
- Are there times you relax from your role of always being responsible and instead delight in life's present, abundant joys?

Enneagram Path Type 3

Summary

Do you try to win admiration and recognition by being charming, likable, achieving, and shape-shifting into what others find most valuable? Do you feel burdened to appear successful, impress the people around you, and live under constant pressure to measure your worth by external achievement and what others think? These are characteristics of your Enneagram path Type 3 part.

This part is efficient, effective, competent, adaptable, goal-oriented, competitive, driven, and charming. It likes to perform and is very conscious of the image you portray to others. It supports your main type by creating supportive and loyal connections with others through your accomplishments, determination, and ability to excel.

How to Recognize Misaligned Traits of Enneagram Path Type 3

- Do you arrogantly believe that you alone are seeing all the possible scenarios?
- Do you keep busy to avoid feeling anxious?
- Do you refuse to try something new if failure is a possibility?
- Are you worried about your self-image and what others might be thinking of

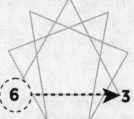

you, using your charm and likable persona to establish support and alliances?

How to Recognize Aligned Traits of Enneagram Path Type 3

- Do you know how to direct, respect, and trust yourself?
- Do you meet your goals by devising more effective and efficient ways to accomplish them?
- Do you act bravely for others and yourself without getting trapped in worst-case thinking or allowing your inner committee to sabotage your actions?

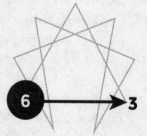

- Do you delight in your accomplishments, knowing that you con-tributed to something great?

Enneagram Path Type 9

Summary

During conflicts, can you see both sides to an issue and help bridge the gap between people? When you feel overwhelmed, do you numb out and find comfort in familiar routines? These are characteristics of your Enneagram path Type 9 part.

This part is warm, loving, caring, and focused on affirming and supporting others' agendas. It will merge and accommodate others' desires while losing sight of what you want to keep the peace and not disrupt your relationships. It supports your main type by being more trusting, encouraging you to rest, and helping you see others' viewpoints with more grace and receptivity.

How to Recognize Misaligned Traits of Enneagram Path Type 9

- At times, do you deal with stress by shutting down?
- Do you sometimes forget who you are because you've chosen security in peaceful loyalty to others over your own passions and desires?
- When you are overwhelmed, do you stubbornly resist others' demands and use passive-aggressive behaviors to avoid confrontations?
- Do you express irritation when others interrupt or disturb you or insist you get out of your comfortable routines or cozy environment?

How to Recognize Aligned Traits of Enneagram Path Type 9

- Do you take time to relax and enjoy moments with emotional peace, enabling your mind to slow down?
- Can you empathize with others and extend compassion to them?
- Do you develop secure relationships by being calm, stable, and less reactive?
- When trusting your inner guidance, do you reassure and support others with encouragements and affirmations?

Type 6: AWARE Exercise

Awaken

Awaken to the fact that your inner committee is not the Holy Spirit. What misaligned part of your heart is leaning on the inner committee for guidance? What is the inner committee feeling and saying to it right now? Is your anxiety causing any tension or pain in your body? Are your thoughts spinning through worst-case scenarios or how to plan for a future event?

Welcome

Welcome and extend kindness to yourself and your misaligned parts without guilt or shame, knowing that the Holy Spirit will always support you, guide you, and keep you safe. Recognize that this part of your heart is both a gift and a burden. Remain curious and nonjudgmental, releasing any anxiety or fear to Christ.

Ask

Ask the Holy Spirit to help you interpret what your misaligned part is trying to communicate and the motives behind it. How is it trying to protect your Wounded Child part? Resist the urge to reach out to a trusted authority figure. Then ask the Holy Spirit to give you great insights, wisdom, and discernment to trust yourself and make the right decision.

Receive

Receive Jesus' full provision for you as His cherished child. He sought you out and restored you to His family, and nothing can separate you from His loving-kindness and protection. You have a secure relationship with Him, and He will fiercely guard, guide, and protect you.

Engage

Engage yourself, your relationships, and your circumstances in a new way, knowing that you belong to Christ and are safe in His eternal care and protection. From this aligned place, you can experience the deep peace and rest that only comes from trusting in Christ's love for you. Then you can bless the world with your courage and loyalty.[2]

Gospel Self-Talk

"Because of Christ's work on my behalf, I am safe and secure. I can loosen my grip on needing to scan the horizon to predict and plan for worst-case scenarios. I can come to Christ and ask for His protection and guidance, trusting that He will answer! He gives me all I need and will never lead me astray or abandon me. It is a delight for Him to protect me, His Beloved Child. Therefore, I can receive His peace, which will calm my racing mind. Because I have the Holy Spirit, I can be more discerning and self-assured and generously give to others from a place of security and abundance."[3]

Type 6 EIP

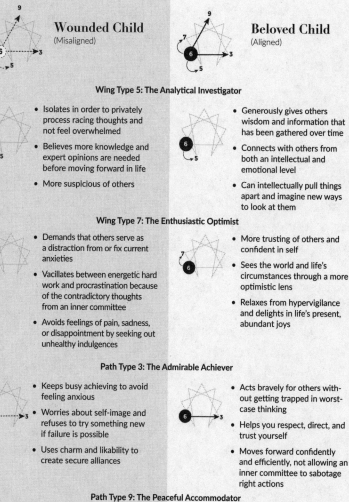

Wounded Child
(Misaligned)

Beloved Child
(Aligned)

Wing Type 5: The Analytical Investigator

- Isolates in order to privately process racing thoughts and not feel overwhelmed
- Believes more knowledge and expert opinions are needed before moving forward in life
- More suspicious of others

- Generously gives others wisdom and information that has been gathered over time
- Connects with others from both an intellectual and emotional level
- Can intellectually pull things apart and imagine new ways to look at them

Wing Type 7: The Enthusiastic Optimist

- Demands that others serve as a distraction from or fix current anxieties
- Vacillates between energetic hard work and procrastination because of the contradictory thoughts from an inner committee
- Avoids feelings of pain, sadness, or disappointment by seeking out unhealthy indulgences

- More trusting of others and confident in self
- Sees the world and life's circumstances through a more optimistic lens
- Relaxes from hypervigilance and delights in life's present, abundant joys

Path Type 3: The Admirable Achiever

- Keeps busy achieving to avoid feeling anxious
- Worries about self-image and refuses to try something new if failure is possible
- Uses charm and likability to create secure alliances

- Acts bravely for others without getting trapped in worst-case thinking
- Helps you respect, direct, and trust yourself
- Moves forward confidently and efficiently, not allowing an inner committee to sabotage right actions

Path Type 9: The Peaceful Accommodator

- Deals with stress by shutting down and numbing out
- Stubbornly resists others' demands and uses passive-aggressive behaviors to avoid confrontations
- Reacts negatively to interruptions and disturbances to comfortable routines

- Takes time to relax and allow the mind to slow down
- Reassures and supports others instead of seeking self-security
- Less reactive and more independent, trusting in inner guidance

6

SIXTEEN

Type 7: Enthusiastic Optimist

Playful | Excitable | Versatile
| Scattered | Escapist

Core Motivations

Core Fear
Being deprived, trapped in emotional pain, limited, or bored; missing out on something fun.

Core Desire
Being happy, fully satisfied, and content.

Core Weakness
Gluttony: feeling a great emptiness inside and having an insatiable desire to "fill yourself up" with experiences and stimulation in hopes of feeling completely satisfied and content.

Core Longing
To hear and believe, "You will be taken care of."

Primary Perspective

To achieve your core motivations, your primary focus of attention is escaping negative emotions to pursue positive emotions. You resist feeling pain, sadness, boredom, anxiety, or emptiness because you believe those emotions will bring you great harm. The satisfaction you get from focusing on fun and exciting experiences is only a temporary fix, leaving you always on the hunt for more.

Summary Overview

God created you to reveal His enthusiasm and playfulness. You radiate optimism in all situations and live life big, always eager to enjoy all the new experiences this world offers. You see endless possibilities and innovation all around you. Unfortunately, sin disrupted the world and brought great sorrow and difficulty. When life is hard, you experience anxiety and a deep need to avoid pain at all costs. You quickly escape to things that bring you joy and distract you from the negative emotions you fear.

While you radiate positivity, internally you are always longing for more and fearful of missing out. To you, life is like cotton candy, super sweet to the taste but quickly disappearing and leaving you unsatisfied. The cost of pursuing your need for adventure, happiness, and stimulating experiences is the inability to enjoy the present moment and feel satisfied with what you already have. Your relationships also suffer because people believe you value new experiences more than them, and you're unable to walk through challenging emotions and pain together.

The good news is that Jesus sees your struggle and delights in taking care of you. He will fill you up with His living water, which never runs dry. Jesus came to restore your joy and fulfill your longings. When your heart is aligned with the gospel and you learn to take your anxieties to Christ and rest in Him, you become more grounded in the present moment and savor it with a grateful heart. From this place, you can walk with others through both the highs and lows of life. Your receptive and thoughtful qualities emerge, and when combined with your natural creativity and energy, you inspire others and make the world a better place.

Type 7: Enneagram Internal Profile (EIP)

THE WOUNDED CHILD (MISALIGNED TYPE 7)

Summary

As a child, you longed to hear that "you will be taken care of" from your authority figures. You felt frustrated because your deep desires for fun and stimulation were shot down or not fully met, so you had to rely on yourself for these things.

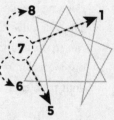

You constantly moved toward excitement, thrills, positivity, and fun to avoid anything unpleasant (including tedious chores or punishments). You knew what you wanted and set out to obtain and experience it to make yourself happy and satisfied.

Your Wounded Child part falsely believes that it's not okay to depend on others for anything. It longs to be truly satisfied and content. As an adult, your core longing remains the same: to hear from others that "you will be taken care of."

False Messages the Wounded Child Believes Are True

- "If I get what my heart currently desires, I will be okay."
- "I am on my own to take care of my needs and to find complete satisfaction in life."
- "I must reframe anything negative and remain positive so others don't trap me into hopelessness and pessimistic thinking."

- "All that I need can be found in the next fun and exciting adventure or event."

Misaligned Attributes

- When your Wounded Child part is activated, it fears and believes it is being deprived, trapped in emotional pain, limited, bored, and missing out on something fun and life-giving.
- The Wounded Child reacts and does its best to radiate positivity and reframe anything negative in hopes of experiencing joy, abundance, and a content heart. The problem is that the more you believe satisfaction is in the future, the more you miss out on experiencing the blessings and joys of the present moment.
- The Wounded Child part of your heart struggles to see and experience the abundant life you already have, which causes it to seek out more. Unfortunately, this does not work and only compounds your problems.

The Beloved Child (Aligned Type 7)

Summary

Only when your Beloved Child part is leading your heart can your misaligned parts loosen their grip on trying to find contentment apart from Christ. Your Beloved Child reminds them that they can experience soul satisfaction in what Christ has already given them, and nothing can take that away.

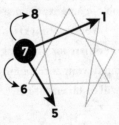

Your Beloved Child knows it has all of Christ's blessings, joy, and benefits, allowing your heart and mind to savor the present moment with a grateful heart. You can finally rest because you no longer need to seek out what you already have.

When your heart is aligned with the gospel, you experience a deep joy that surpasses understanding. You can be present with people in both the highs and lows, experiencing the fullness of life together.

True Messages the Beloved Child Believes

- "When I come and partake in the life-giving water Christ offers me, I experience a full and content heart."
- "I can depend on Christ to take care of me in difficult times."
- "I don't need to escape or reframe painful experiences since Christ is with me and will provide me with peace and assurance."
- "Christ credits to me His righteousness and blessings so I can experience His radiance, joy, and abundance and bless others with the overflow."

Aligned Attributes of the Beloved Child

- Can you slow down your mind to experience all the blessings that are right before you?
- Are you thoughtful and aware of others' needs, emotions, and desires, generously sharing the overflow of your joy, enthusiasm, and creativity?
- Trusting that Christ will take care of your needs, can you walk through life's lows and feel your difficult emotions?
- Are you more reliable and willing to complete necessary tasks, even if they're mundane?

CONNECTING TYPES

EIP Reminder: We all use all nine types to some degree. Therefore, the descriptions to follow reflect a combination of your main type's characteristics and your connecting types' characteristics. Out of their own core motivations, our four connecting types (wings and Enneagram paths either aligned or misaligned) use their respective strategies to attempt to meet our main type's core motivations, which still reign supreme.[1]

7

Wing Type 6

Summary

Do you have a curious, responsible, and problem-solving part of you that is loyal and collaborates well with people? Do you seek out the advice and insights of others to help you obtain loyal connection, security, and guidance? These are characteristics of your wing Type 6 part.

This part is reliable, trustworthy, and a natural troubleshooter. It supports your main type by helping you collaborate with others to reach your goals and be a more committed, loyal, and faithful friend.

How to Recognize Misaligned Traits of Wing Type 6

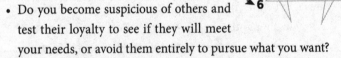

- Do you express your anxieties, insecurities, and dissatisfaction when something or someone is hindering you from getting what you want?
- Do you become suspicious of others and test their loyalty to see if they will meet your needs, or avoid them entirely to pursue what you want?
- Are you so preoccupied with your desires that you try to predict anything that might get in the way of obtaining them?
- When you are struggling, do your anxieties cause you to lose focus, become scattered, and doubt yourself?

How to Recognize Aligned Traits of Wing Type 6

- Do you take your anxieties and insecurities to God, trusting that He will care for your needs and give you clarity, courage, and strength to handle life's challenges?
- Can you see your circumstances with immense clarity and make accurate conclusions on how to solve an issue?
- Are you more warm, vulnerable, faithful, committed, witty, and

engaging, possessing a team-player mindset that can ask for help and advice?

- Are you more committed to your beliefs, viewpoints, and relationships than fulfilling your newest passion?

Wing Type 8

Summary

Do you have a quick mind and passion for life that leads to incredible life experiences? Do you push your way through obstacles, and even people, to get what you desire? These are characteristics of your wing Type 8 part.

This part is self-reliant, protective, independent, strong, and blunt, and has a take-charge attitude. It supports your main type by using its passion, determination, and strength to help you gain all that your heart desires.

How to Recognize Misaligned Traits of Wing Type 8

- Do you demand that others meet your needs for excitement, fun, and stimulation?
- Do you find yourself passionately plowing a path to gain your desires with little regard for those in your way?

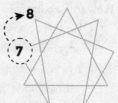

- Does your intense energy cause you to seek out activities and passions that give you an adrenaline high?
- Do you feel a need to protect yourself from those who might betray, harm, control, or deprive you of what you desire?

How to Recognize Aligned Traits of Wing Type 8

- Do you see your "failures" as positive opportunities to try something new, better, and different?
- Are you willing to endure hardships with a "can do" confidence and energetic drive to make life better for yourself and others?

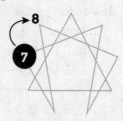

- Are you a natural leader who is decisive, confident, and able to quickly delegate your team in ways that allow them to thrive and excel?
- Are you courageous and willing to put yourself in harm's way to ensure safety and provide protection for those you lead?

Enneagram Path Type 1

Summary

Do you have a strong sense of responsibility and obligation to do the right thing and improve yourself and the world? Do you sometimes tell people what the ethical, moral, accurate, and appropriate way of doing things is? These are characteristics of your Enneagram path Type 1 part.

This part is serious, objective, more emotionally self-controlled, and critical of yourself and others. It focuses on improving and reforming the world by noticing what is wrong and insisting that it is made right.

How to Recognize Misaligned Traits of Enneagram Path Type 1

- Do you impose restrictions and limitations on yourself to be more productive?
- Are you sometimes irritable and critical of yourself and your circumstances?
- Do you notice and point out imperfections in yourself, others, and the world, which lead to you micromanaging?
- Do you get upset with people who are preventing you from experiencing your ideal desires?

How to Recognize Aligned Traits Enneagram Path Type 1

- Do you accept life as it is (both good and bad) and live for a higher purpose?
- Can you focus on your top priority and complete it on time without getting distracted?
- Can you slow down and use your wisdom,

accuracy, and creativity to meet your goals, making sure things are done right?

- Do you take ownership of your responsibilities, even if they are not fun?

Enneagram Path Type 5

Summary

Do you bring profound observations and innovations to the world by combining your passions with your intellectual insights? Do you procrastinate on projects because you fear you don't have all the information and resources you need? These are characteristics of your Enneagram path Type 5 part.

This part is intellectual and observes life with curiosity and a craving to know more. It fears it lacks inner resources and that too much interaction with others will lead to catastrophic depletion. Therefore, it withdraws from others to recharge. It supports your main type by helping you slow down and process your thoughts, emotions, and needs.

How to Recognize Misaligned Traits of Enneagram Path Type 5

- Are you fiercely independent, building up boundaries to protect yourself from others being too invasive or limiting in your life?
- Do you need to sort out your feelings by using your intellect before moving forward in life?
- Do you grow tired of constantly feeling like you need to be positive?
- Do you find yourself becoming secretive and isolating yourself from others to recharge your internal battery?

How to Recognize Aligned Traits of Enneagram Path Type 5

- Are you remarkably creative and able to combine your intellectual insights and passion to produce stunning original works,

sometimes pulling things apart and con-
ceptualizing new ways to look at them from
a creative viewpoint?

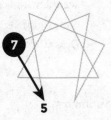

- Can you connect with others from both
  an intellectual and passionate place and
  generously give them the insights you have
  gathered over time?
- Do you become more accepting of all of life—the good and bad,
  happy and sad?
- Do you place more value on wisdom and discipline versus finding
  the next fun experience?

Type 7: AWARE Exercise

Awaken

Awaken to your belief that the future holds the satisfaction and contentment you long for. What misaligned part of your heart is telling you this false
message right now? Have you asked this part what it is feeling? Do you feel any
tension or pain in your body? What difficult emotions are you ignoring? Are
your thoughts being pulled away to the next exciting thing you have planned?

Welcome

Welcome and extend kindness to yourself and your misaligned part
without guilt or shame, knowing that Jesus sees your needs and says they
are not a problem for Him. Recognize that this part of your heart is both a
gift and a burden. Remain curious and nonjudgmental, especially toward
the difficult emotions you typically flee from.

Ask

Ask the Holy Spirit to help you interpret what your misaligned part
is trying to communicate and the motives behind it. How is it trying to

protect your Wounded Child part? Resist the urge to distract yourself from this exercise with something more fun or stimulating. Then ask the Holy Spirit to help you savor the gifts you have but often overlook so you can slow down and experience inner joy and peace.

RECEIVE

Receive the quiet and stillness as a beautiful gift that enables your heart to experience God's love for you. Here your heart will experience joy, radiance, and abundance deeper than you ever thought possible.

ENGAGE

Engage yourself, your relationships, and your circumstances in a new way, from a heart resting in the truth that your needs are not a problem for God. From this aligned place, you can trust that Christ is with you as you wade through the challenges and joys of life. He satisfies your deepest cravings, and from the overflow of His living water, you can extend love and care to others.[2]

Gospel Self-Talk

"Because of Christ's work on my behalf, I am not alone to provide for my needs and desires. I can loosen my grip on avoiding boredom and emotional pain because Christ provides for me out of His immense love. I can come to Him and ask to be filled with His living water, knowing He will give me what my heart craves! It is a delight for Him to bring contentment to my heart in unexpected ways. Therefore, I can slow down my mind, process my feelings, and surrender my anxieties to Him. From this grounded place, I can walk with others through both the highs and lows of life and inspire the world with the endless possibilities and innovation I see all around me."[3]

7

Type 7 EIP

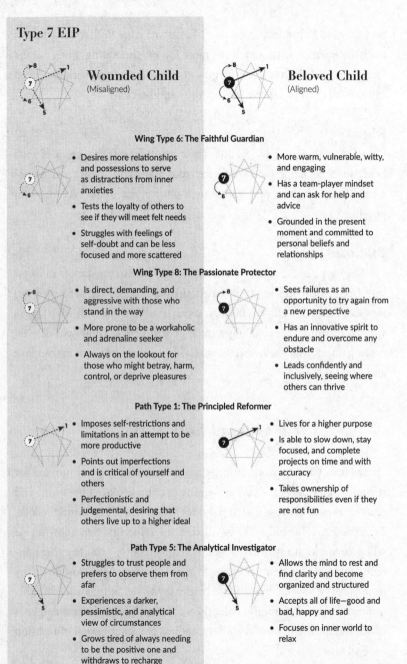

Wounded Child
(Misaligned)

Beloved Child
(Aligned)

Wing Type 6: The Faithful Guardian

- Desires more relationships and possessions to serve as distractions from inner anxieties
- Tests the loyalty of others to see if they will meet felt needs
- Struggles with feelings of self-doubt and can be less focused and more scattered

- More warm, vulnerable, witty, and engaging
- Has a team-player mindset and can ask for help and advice
- Grounded in the present moment and committed to personal beliefs and relationships

Wing Type 8: The Passionate Protector

- Is direct, demanding, and aggressive with those who stand in the way
- More prone to be a workaholic and adrenaline seeker
- Always on the lookout for those who might betray, harm, control, or deprive pleasures

- Sees failures as an opportunity to try again from a new perspective
- Has an innovative spirit to endure and overcome any obstacle
- Leads confidently and inclusively, seeing where others can thrive

Path Type 1: The Principled Reformer

- Imposes self-restrictions and limitations in an attempt to be more productive
- Points out imperfections and is critical of yourself and others
- Perfectionistic and judgemental, desiring that others live up to a higher ideal

- Lives for a higher purpose
- Is able to slow down, stay focused, and complete projects on time and with accuracy
- Takes ownership of responsibilities even if they are not fun

Path Type 5: The Analytical Investigator

- Struggles to trust people and prefers to observe them from afar
- Experiences a darker, pessimistic, and analytical view of circumstances
- Grows tired of always needing to be the positive one and withdraws to recharge

- Allows the mind to rest and find clarity and become organized and structured
- Accepts all of life—good and bad, happy and sad
- Focuses on inner world to relax

Type 8: Passionate Protector

ASSERTIVE | SELF-CONFIDENT | INTENSE | BIG-HEARTED | CONFRONTATIONAL

Core Motivations

CORE FEAR

Being weak, powerless, harmed, controlled, vulnerable, manipulated, and left at the mercy of injustice.

CORE DESIRE

Protecting yourself and those in your inner circle.

CORE WEAKNESS

Lust/excess: constantly desiring intensity, control, and power; pushing yourself willfully on life and people to get what you want.

CORE LONGING

To hear and believe, "You will not be betrayed."

8

Primary Perspective

To achieve your core motivations, your primary focus of attention is protecting yourself and those closest to you from being betrayed, blindsided, controlled, harmed, or treated unjustly. You don't want anyone to have power over you (physical, emotional, or financial), so you put on an intimidating, protective armor that makes you powerful, controlling, and unwilling to back down. You believe that if you reveal your tender heart behind the armor, others will take advantage of your vulnerability and harm you.

Summary Overview

God created you to reveal His strength and passion. You engage life with confident intensity and a determination to make things happen for yourself and the greater good.

Unfortunately, sin brought injustice and vulnerability to our world. You feel an intense need to protect yourself against this betrayal and powerlessness by always putting up an invincible exterior to safeguard your inner tenderness.

You struggle to believe that you will not be betrayed. In your attempt to fulfill your longing for power and justice, you can become too blunt, confrontational, insensitive, domineering, and even vengeful. While other types fear people and become passive, you fear people and become aggressive. You think, *I'll control them before they can control me.* Inevitably, this causes you to live in denial, suppressing your vulnerable emotions and sacrificing intimacy so your weaknesses can't be discovered and used against you. Your armor causes you to miss out on the intimacy and support you were created for.

The good news is, Jesus came to earth to bring justice and protect you. He will never betray you. Jesus came to restore our world by calling out injustices and rescuing the vulnerable, and He invites you into that process. When your heart is aligned with the gospel, and you learn to take your longing to Christ and surrender to Him your fear of betrayal, you can allow people to see your vulnerability and compassionate strength. From that place, you can protect the innocent from injustice, empower others, and use your decisive and assertive leadership skills to be a powerful change agent in the world.

Type 8: Enneagram Internal Profile (EIP)

THE WOUNDED CHILD (MISALIGNED TYPE 8)

Summary

As a child, you longed to hear that "you will not be betrayed" from your authority figures. You experienced harm or betrayal (or saw this occur to someone close to you), so you put on a strong armor to protect your tender heart from ever being vulnerable again.

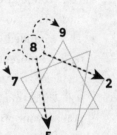

You became an adult at an early age to protect and provide for yourself or your family. You overwhelmed and exacerbated authority figures with your strong will, determination, impulsivity, and willfulness. If you felt strongly about something, you'd voice it directly and would not back down until you got what you wanted.

Your Wounded Child part falsely believes that it is not okay to trust or be vulnerable with anyone. It longs for someone else to be in charge so you can finally rest and experience the carefree childhood you missed out on. As an adult, your core longing remains the same: to hear from others that "you will not be betrayed."

8

False Messages the Wounded Child Believes Are True

- "It's not okay to be vulnerable or to trust anyone."
- "I must be in control of the situation and people before they can control and harm me."
- "I am the only one who can lead well, do what's best, and protect others from harm."
- "I must use my strength, intensity, passion, and quickness to show people that I am not to be underestimated."

Misaligned Attributes

- When your Wounded Child part is activated, it believes you are seen as weak, powerless, and vulnerable. It fears you will be controlled and harmed through manipulation, injustice, and betrayal.
- The Wounded Child reacts and does its best to protect you and those closest to you from being harmed and blindsided.
- The Wounded Child struggles to acknowledge and accept your tender, innocent, and vulnerable side and increases your armor to challenge and harm others before they have the opportunity to hurt you. Unfortunately, not only does this not work, but it only compounds your problems.

THE BELOVED CHILD (ALIGNED TYPE 8)

Summary

Only when your Beloved Child part is leading your heart can your misaligned parts loosen their grip on needing to wear protective armor. Your Beloved Child reminds them that Jesus chose to be betrayed, beaten, controlled, and killed so you can experience ultimate freedom, protection, and justice.

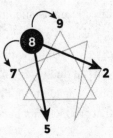

Your Beloved Child accepts that you are a weak and finite human being who cannot completely protect yourself from being harmed, controlled, or betrayed. Because Christ went through betrayal for you, you can vulnerably place your trust in Him since Romans 8:38–39 says that nothing can separate you from the love, provision, and protection you have in Christ.

When your heart is aligned with the gospel, you trust that you will not be betrayed or forsaken by Christ. From this firm foundation, you courageously share your vulnerable heart with others and plow paths of justice for the vulnerable.

True Messages the Beloved Child Believes

- "Following Christ's example, I can be both vulnerable and strong, which leads to the intimate and supportive relationships I long for."
- "Because I am the King's Beloved Child, I am provided for and lack nothing. Therefore, I can put my trust in His sovereign plan for my life and wait for His direction."
- "Christ will never betray or forsake me. I have a true advocate whom I can trust, and I can rest in His leadership."
- "I can extend to others the same love, tenderness, protection, and justice I receive from Christ."

Aligned Attributes of the Beloved Child

- You open your heart and vulnerably share how much you care for others.
- Because God protects you, values you, and is patient with you, you extend that same grace and kindness to others, especially those you lead.
- You can walk through life's challenges with a restful heart that surrenders to God's will and perfect timing.
- You notice and speak up for the vulnerable, plowing a path toward justice.

8

Connecting Types

EIP Reminder: We all use all nine types to some degree. Therefore, the descriptions to follow reflect a combination of your main type's characteristics and your connecting types' characteristics. Out of their own core motivations, our four connecting types (wings and Enneagram paths either aligned or misaligned) use their respective strategies to attempt to meet our main type's core motivations, which still reign supreme.[1]

Wing Type 7

Summary

Do you find yourself being more enthusiastic, optimistic, fun, and full of joyful passion? Do you fear being limited, deprived, or held back from getting what you desire? These are characteristics of your wing Type 7 part.

This part is excitable, spontaneous, distracted, impatient, and more social and outgoing. It anticipates future events as exciting, fun possibilities you can't miss out on. It supports your main type by helping you woo others and giving you a quick mind, which increases your confidence and passion for going after and getting what you want.

How to Recognize Misaligned Traits of Wing Type 7

- Do you spend money on fun and exciting "escape hatches" (unhealthy indulgences) to distract you from life's difficulties?
- Do you believe that you are the only one who is strong enough, passionate enough, and able to carry others through life's challenges?
- Do you make big promises and exaggerate what is possible to convince others to follow your lead?
- At times are you impatient, impulsive, and demanding, and do you express what you want with little regard to how it affects others?

How to Recognize Aligned Traits of Wing Type 7

- Do you experience moments of grace and joy, which enable your heart to be more vulnerable and trusting of others?

- Are you more joyful, spontaneous, playful, and capable of making the impossible possible?

- Do you bless others with your assertive energy and enthusiastic confidence?

- Are you gifted at leadership, seeing where others can thrive and encouraging them to become all they can be?

Wing Type 9

Summary

Do you sometimes avoid conflicts and tension by stubbornly withdrawing? Can you see, understand, and have compassion for differing perspectives, even though you are confident in your own? These are characteristics of your wing Type 9 part.

This part is more open and receptive to others' viewpoints and interacts with more kindness and compassion. It supports your main type by giving you quiet strength, steadfastness, and tender leadership skills that encourage others to excel in their strengths.

How to Recognize Misaligned Traits of Wing Type 9

- Do you ever withdraw, accommodate, or people-please to avoid conflict or tension?

- Are you sometimes less aware of how you feel because you're focused on accomplishing what you desire?

- Do you ignore or suppress feelings of anger and irritation so you can keep your relationships less turbulent and more peaceable?

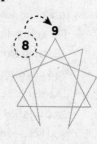

- Do you ever quietly dig in your heels and become stubborn until the other person gives in to your way of doing things?

How to Recognize Aligned Traits of Wing Type 9

- Do you recognize that others need your kindness, empathy, compassion, and tenderness as much as your strength?
- Are you more patient, understanding, and gracious to others' needs, desires, and opinions?
- Are you more adaptable, accommodating, and easygoing when expressing what you want or need?
- Can you mediate and harmonize groups by bringing people together under your gentle leadership and actively seeking ways to bring peace and healing to the world?

Enneagram Path Type 2

Summary

Do you create dependencies so others need you? Are you more outwardly emotionally demonstrative, helpful, friendly, nurturing, and generous? These are characteristics of your Enneagram path Type 2 part.

This part is helpful, friendly, cheerful, energetic, talkative, and engaging. It focuses on connecting you with others in hopes of experiencing their appreciation, gratitude, affection, and love.

How to Recognize Misaligned Traits of Enneagram Path Type 2

- Do you believe you have to earn love and affection from others by helping, supporting, and advising them?
- Do you hide your own needs and emotions, fearing they will threaten your relationships and keep others from giving you the appreciation you desire?

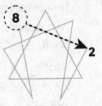

- Do you take offense when others don't help and care for you in the same way you love and support them?
- Do you assume that all your motives and actions are pure with no hidden agendas?

How to Recognize Aligned Traits of Enneagram Path Type 2

- Do you instinctively know how to make others feel special, seen, and supported?
- Can you be vulnerable and share your tender heart by humbly serving others?
- Are you warmly responsive and generous with your time, talents, abilities, and social connections?
- Are you more empathetic and aware that sometimes you need to pause in your pursuit of justice to tend to immediate wounds and needs?

Enneagram Path Type 5

Summary

Do you bring profound observations and innovations to the world by combining your passions and intellect? Do you withdraw from others to collect all the information and resources you need to accomplish what you desire? These are characteristics of your Enneagram path Type 5 part.

This part is intelligent, wise, innovative, and a curious observer that craves to know more. It fears that others will drain you of all your energy, emotional reserves, and resources. Therefore, it withdraws from others to recharge and protect your resources.

How to Recognize Misaligned Traits of Enneagram Path Type 5

- Are you fiercely independent, building up boundaries to protect yourself from others who try to control you?

- Before moving forward, do you use your intellect to sort out your feelings and desires?
- Do you grow tired of always being the protective one and need time to detach and tend to your own needs?
- Do you find yourself becoming secretive and more isolated from others to protect yourself from betrayal or depletion because you are alone to care for and protect yourself?

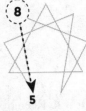

How to Recognize Aligned Traits of Enneagram Path Type 5

- Can you combine your intellectual insights with your intense passion to produce original works that profoundly bless the world?
- Do you generously give others the helpful insights and information you have gathered over time?
- Can you connect with others from both an intellectual and passionate level?
- Are you more aware of your inner world, knowing when to relax and recharge before your body experiences exhaustion or illness?

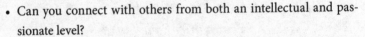

Type 8: AWARE Exercise

Awaken

Awaken to your belief that you will be betrayed and that you must protect your tender heart with armor. What misaligned part of your heart is telling you this false message right now? Have you asked this part what it is feeling? Do you feel any tension or pain in your body or a fire in your gut? Are your thoughts being pulled away from your vulnerability and toward ways you can protect yourself by controlling others?

WELCOME

Welcome and extend kindness to yourself and your misaligned part without guilt or shame, knowing that Jesus was betrayed and understands your deepest fears. Recognize that this part of your heart is both a gift and a burden. Remain curious and nonjudgmental, releasing your fear and anger to Christ.

ASK

Ask the Holy Spirit to help you interpret what your misaligned part is trying to communicate and the motives behind it. How is it trying to protect your Wounded Child part? Resist any urge to push forward to get what you desire. Then ask the Holy Spirit to help you rest in Christ's protection, leadership, and care.

RECEIVE

Receive the truth that nothing can separate you from Christ's love and provision. You can let go of always being the strong leader and reveal your tender heart. Allow the Holy Spirit to remind you that Jesus loved you so much that He allowed Himself to be betrayed and then die a vulnerable, painful death so you can be completely secure and provided for.

ENGAGE

Engage yourself, your relationships, and your circumstances in a new way, from a heart resting in your Father's strength and care, knowing that He always has your back. From this aligned place, you can approach life with childlike innocence and carefree joy. Then others will experience your tender strength, passion, and determination to plow a path for the greater good.[2]

Gospel Self-Talk

8

"Because of Christ's work on my behalf, I am protected and have an advocate. I can loosen my grip on needing to always protect myself from being harmed, blindsided, controlled, and betrayed. Christ knows I am finite and weak and cannot save myself. He went to great lengths to save me, and He will not allow anyone or anything to come between us now. Therefore, I can hang up my armor because He is stronger and delights in protecting me. I can now rest, reveal my vulnerable heart, and experience the intimacy I was created for. From this overflow of love and provision, I can bring Christ's justice and passion to the world."[3]

Type 8 EIP

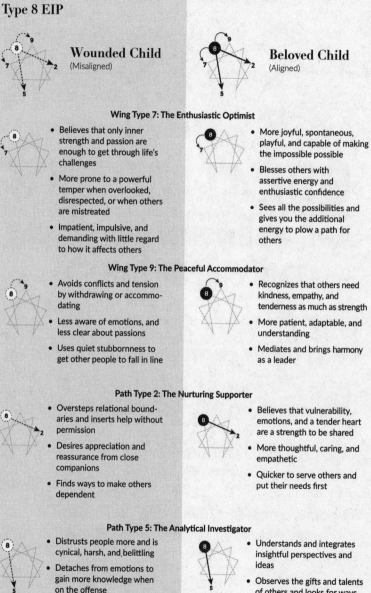

Wounded Child
(Misaligned)

Beloved Child
(Aligned)

Wing Type 7: The Enthusiastic Optimist

- Believes that only inner strength and passion are enough to get through life's challenges
- More prone to a powerful temper when overlooked, disrespected, or when others are mistreated
- Impatient, impulsive, and demanding with little regard to how it affects others

- More joyful, spontaneous, playful, and capable of making the impossible possible
- Blesses others with assertive energy and enthusiastic confidence
- Sees all the possibilities and gives you the additional energy to plow a path for others

Wing Type 9: The Peaceful Accommodator

- Avoids conflicts and tension by withdrawing or accommodating
- Less aware of emotions, and less clear about passions
- Uses quiet stubbornness to get other people to fall in line

- Recognizes that others need kindness, empathy, and tenderness as much as strength
- More patient, adaptable, and understanding
- Mediates and brings harmony as a leader

Path Type 2: The Nurturing Supporter

- Oversteps relational boundaries and inserts help without permission
- Desires appreciation and reassurance from close companions
- Finds ways to make others dependent

- Believes that vulnerability, emotions, and a tender heart are a strength to be shared
- More thoughtful, caring, and empathetic
- Quicker to serve others and put their needs first

Path Type 5: The Analytical Investigator

- Distrusts people more and is cynical, harsh, and belittling
- Detaches from emotions to gain more knowledge when on the offense
- More secretive and cerebral and less physically assertive and action oriented

- Understands and integrates insightful perspectives and ideas
- Observes the gifts and talents of others and looks for ways to help them thrive
- Pauses before reacting to think through the best path forward

8

Type 9: Peaceful Accommodator

THOUGHTFUL | REASSURING | RECEPTIVE
| ACCOMMODATING | RESIGNED

Core Motivations

CORE FEAR
Being in conflict, tension, or discord; feeling shut out and overlooked; losing connection and relationship with others.

CORE DESIRE
Inner stability and peace of mind.

CORE WEAKNESS
Sloth: remaining in an unrealistic and idealistic world to keep the peace, remain easygoing, and not be disturbed by your anger; falling asleep to your passions, abilities, desires, needs, and worth by merging with others to keep peace and harmony.

9

CORE LONGING
To hear and believe, "Your presence matters."

Primary Perspective

To achieve your core motivations, your primary focus of attention is accommodating others to keep harmony in your relationships and give you peace of mind. You struggle with inertia, merging with other people's passions, desires, and callings instead of moving toward your own. You decide to blend in or stay in the background because you fundamentally believe that your presence doesn't matter much to others, so you shouldn't assert or promote yourself.

Summary Overview

God created you to reveal His tranquility and unity. You are easygoing, nonjudgmental, calm, empathetic, and patient. You can see all points of view, which makes you a natural peacemaker and agent of reconciliation, and you long for harmony in the world. Unfortunately, sin disrupted our world and brought chaos. You believe it is your responsibility to ensure that people experience peace and that everyone is respected and heard, which causes you to focus too much on others, losing your identity in the process.

You appear relaxed, but inside, you feel frustrated and overlooked. In your attempt to fulfill your need for peace and comfort, you withdraw or numb your feelings, dreams, and desires and "go along to get along." You become conflict-avoidant, indecisive, easily overwhelmed, and numb to your life. This eventually backfires in your relationships when people get frustrated by your passivity, stubbornness, unwillingness to be bothered, emotional unavailability, and passive-aggressive responses, resulting in the conflict you desperately wanted to avoid.

The good news is, Jesus came to bring true peace to the world, and He says your voice matters. Jesus came to restore harmony and wake you up to the great purpose He has planned for you. When your heart is aligned with the gospel, you believe you matter and can make a difference in the world. You find your own passion and calling and move toward it with boldness and confidence. From this place, you also realize that true peace comes from entering into conflict, not avoiding it. You genuinely engage with others, bridging differences and bringing people together to achieve true harmony.

Type 9: Enneagram Internal Profile (EIP)

The Wounded Child (Misaligned Type 9)

Summary

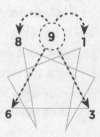

As a child, you longed to hear that "your presence matters" from your authority figures. You could feel and identify the energy, moods, and well-being of your family. Any relational tensions overwhelmed you, so you made every effort to create peace and harmony.

Your efforts to make others happy led you to merge with others and completely forget yourself in the process. When tensions arose, you would accommodate, numb out, shut down, withdraw, or disassociate, neglecting your own desires, passions, and needs in the process.

Your Wounded Child part falsely believes that it is not okay to assert yourself or think much of yourself. It longs to be noticed, appreciated, and able to speak up and follow your own path. As an adult, your core longing remains the same: to hear from others that "your presence matters."

False Messages the Wounded Child Believes Are True

- "It's not okay to assert my viewpoints or go after my passions and desires."

- "I make sure everyone else is good and okay so I can be okay, which means I must keep my relationships peaceful and intact by accommodating everyone else's needs, desires, and agendas."
- "I am not good enough. I must try harder to make others happy and pleased with me."
- "I must always maintain a humble, gentle, and peaceable demeanor and never boast, promote myself, or think highly of myself."

Misaligned Attributes

- When your Wounded Child part is activated, it fears and believes its presence and voice don't matter, and it must accommodate others' desires, passions, and agendas to avoid conflict.
- The Wounded Child reacts and does its best to merge with others to keep the peace. The problem is that the more you accommodate people, the more you lose your voice and ability to live your life independent of others' opinions.
- The Wounded Child part of your heart struggles to acknowledge that your life and calling matter and are vital to this world. This causes it to withdraw or merge, losing its sense of self in the pursuit of peace. Unfortunately, not only does this not work, but it only compounds your problems.

THE BELOVED CHILD (ALIGNED TYPE 9)

Summary

Only when your Beloved Child part is leading your heart can your misaligned parts loosen their grip on needing to accommodate others to maintain harmony. Your Beloved Child reminds them that Jesus created you with a vital voice and mission. He calls you to bring your full self to all of life.

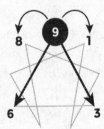

Your Beloved Child knows it is fully seen by Christ and never overlooked. You matter so much to Him that He came to earth to guarantee you will always have an intimate, eternal relationship with Him. He desires you to live out of this love and bless others with your voice, viewpoints, and abilities.

When your heart is aligned with the gospel, you can experience a deep knowing that your presence matters. No longer hiding or minimizing yourself, you generously show up to bless others with your incredible gifts of empathy, compassion, tenderness, peace, encouragement, and kindness.

True Messages the Beloved Child Believes

- "Christ created me to uniquely use my gifts, desires, and perspective to be a vital part of His unfolding purposes."
- "I bless the world when I show up fully and use my voice."
- "Because I see all viewpoints and have a nonjudgmental presence, others feel safe around me, which brings them a sense of peace and rest they normally don't experience."
- "I will greatly bless the world when I am both confident and humble, loving and direct, tender and strong."

Aligned Attributes of the Beloved Child

- No longer merging with others, you assert your presence and live with the confidence that you have much to offer the world.
- You set up healthy boundaries in your relationships because you respect yourself and what you need, all the while bringing empathy and harmony to others without merging with them in the process, which inspires and comforts them.
- You regularly share your thoughts, viewpoints, and opinions with others, trusting that they matter.
- You set goals and boldly follow through with what you believe God is calling you to do.

9

CONNECTING TYPES

EIP Reminder: We all use all nine types to some degree. Therefore, the descriptions to follow reflect a combination of your main type's characteristics and your connecting types' characteristics. Out of their own core motivations, our four connecting types (wings and Enneagram paths either aligned or misaligned) use their respective strategies to attempt to meet our main type's core motivations, which still reign supreme.[1]

Wing Type 1

Summary

Do you feel a strong sense of responsibility to do the ideal and right thing? Do you feel a burden to be perfect in your relationships and struggle with self-condemnation when others are upset with you? These are characteristics of your wing Type 1 part.

This part is objective, detail-oriented, logical, serious, and more emotionally self-controlled. It focuses on improving the world and the lives of others by being fair and treating everyone with equal kindness and respect.

How to Recognize Misaligned Traits of Wing Type 1

- Are you quick to judge and condemn others while justifying yourself based on your high standards, principles, and morals?
- Do you passive-aggressively show your impatience and judgments in your body language?
- Do you struggle with self-condemnation and guilt, particularly if you feel you didn't make someone happy?
- Are you internally conflicted between upholding and voicing your moral principles versus needing to maintain peace and harmony with others?

How to Recognize Aligned Traits of Wing Type 1

- Are you more motivated to pursue your calling because being a good steward of God's gifts is the right thing to do?
- Are you an excellent mediator who focuses on improving the lives of others by combining your principles and relational warmth?
- Do you use your wisdom and discernment to establish healthy boundaries and not merge with others but stay independent?
- Are you more principled and intentional with asserting your presence, voice, passions, and opinions?

Wing Type 8

Summary

Do you feel more self-confident and speak your viewpoints and opinions? Can your anger erupt when you or others are being overlooked or mistreated? These are characteristics of your wing Type 8 part.

This part is resourceful, driven, decisive, and a natural leader. It is a champion of yourself and others by leading the way, providing protection, and plowing a path. It supports your main type by giving you the confidence to assert your kindness and generous heart to benefit others and the world.

How to Recognize Misaligned Traits of Wing Type 8

- Do you become passive-aggressive, irritable, frustrated, or stubborn if you feel overlooked or betrayed?
- Are there times you are more controlling and demand that others listen to you?
- Do you struggle to stay tender, patient, and

9

gracious when you feel others are being disrespected, bullied, or harmed?

- Do you avoid vulnerability, fearing that others will take advantage of you and manipulate you into accommodating their agendas and desires?

How to Recognize Aligned Traits of Wing Type 8

- Are you more self-confident in all the abilities God gave you, and do you pursue and accomplish them for the greater good?
- Can you vulnerably share your emotions and needs with directness and emotional balance?
- Are there times you become more independent, assertive, and self-affirming, and you express what you need or want?
- Can you shift your focus from people-pleasing and merging with others to doing what is best for everyone, including yourself?

Enneagram Path Type 3

Summary

Do you feel more confident in your abilities and invest in your development? Do you strive for acceptance, validation, and admiration from others? These are characteristics of your Enneagram path Type 3 part.

This part is outgoing, affirming, friendly, and self-assured and does not want to be seen as a failure or worthless. It supports your main type by creating connections with others through accomplishments and winning their affection by shape-shifting to their desires.

How to Recognize Misaligned Traits of Enneagram Path Type 3

- Do you ignore or suppress your emotions and identity so you can focus on achieving?

- When someone exposes your weaknesses or failures, do you feel shame and believe you are worthless, incompetent, and not good enough?
- Do you people-please not only to maintain harmony but also to gain more value in the eyes of others?
- Are you sometimes aware that you overencourage to win the admiration of others?

How to Recognize Aligned Traits of Enneagram Path Type 3

- Do you take time to discover the desires and talents God created you with and invest in your development?
- Are you more confident and energetic and do you go after the things that bring you joy and bless others?
- Do you try to understand your authentic self by developing a healthy relationship with your inner world?
- Can you stop procrastinating, stick to a plan, and accomplish your goals?

Enneagram Path Type 6

Summary

Do you have a loyal spirit that strives to benefit others by trouble-shooting problems? Do you sometimes doubt yourself and seek support and advice from those you trust? These are characteristics of your Enneagram path Type 6 part.

This part anticipates how circumstances could go wrong and how this can affect your interactions with others. It scans the horizon to plan and prepare for possible threats to you and those you are loyal to. It supports your main type by helping you remain present in your relationships by being reliable, faithful, and courageous.

9

How to Recognize Misaligned Traits of Enneagram Path Type 6

- Do you express your frustration, dissatisfaction, self-doubt, and dread when anxiety rises?
- Do you have a strong internal or external reaction when someone blames or accuses you of something?
- When you sense something is not right, do you become suspicious of others and test their loyalty?
- Do you fear that others will abandon you and you will be alone?

How to Recognize Aligned Traits of Enneagram Path Type 6

- Do you take your insecurities to God, trusting that He will give you the clarity and strength you need to handle life's many challenges?
- Are you less accommodating but still loyal, cooperative, and focused on the well-being of others?
- Do you demonstrate your courage by stepping out of your comfort zone into unfamiliar areas?
- Are you committed to your own development, intentionally becoming more self-aware and awake to your passions?

Type 9: AWARE Exercise

Awaken

Awaken to your belief that your presence doesn't matter and you must merge with others to maintain harmonious relationships. What misaligned part of your heart is telling you this false message right now? Have you asked this part what it is feeling? Do you feel any tension or pain in your body when you think about pursuing your desires? Are you ignoring any difficult thoughts or emotions because addressing them might cause tension in a relationship?

WELCOME

Welcome and extend kindness to yourself and your misaligned parts without guilt or shame, knowing that Jesus sees you and values your voice, passions, and desires. Recognize that this part of your heart is both a gift and a burden. Remain curious and nonjudgmental; release to Christ any feelings of frustration from being overlooked.

ASK

Ask the Holy Spirit to help you interpret what your misaligned part is trying to communicate and the motives behind it. How is it trying to protect your Wounded Child part? Resist any urge to dissociate or numb out. Then ask the Holy Spirit to help you find your voice and pursue the gifts He has given you.

RECEIVE

Receive Christ's peace and unending pursuit of you, resting in the truth that your presence matters greatly to Him. Allow the Holy Spirit to remind you of Jesus' perfect example of being bold yet gentle. He was the Prince of Peace, yet wasn't afraid to cause conflict or tension to accomplish His greater purpose.

ENGAGE

Engage yourself, your relationships, and your circumstances in a new way, from a heart resting in the truth that your presence and calling are vital to God's plan. From this aligned place, you can show up to life, bridge differences, and bring people true peace and harmony.[2]

9

Gospel Self-Talk

"Because of Christ's work on my behalf, my presence matters. I can loosen my grip on needing to accommodate others to keep the peace and make them happy. I can set up healthy boundaries by saying no without feeling bad about it. I know Christ uniquely created me to bless others with my presence, passions, and abilities, and He is asking me to show up to life. I will no longer hoard or hide the gifts God has blessed me with but reveal them to the world. I love and respect myself by bravely stepping forward, knowing God will meet me there. By finding my voice and sharing my full self with others, I can follow in Christ's footsteps and bring true peace and harmony to the world."[3]

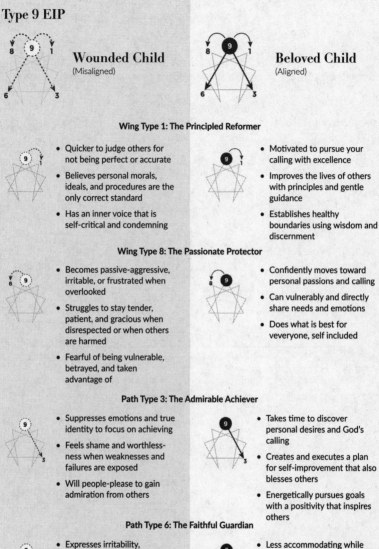

Type 9 EIP

Wounded Child
(Misaligned)

Beloved Child
(Aligned)

Wing Type 1: The Principled Reformer

- Quicker to judge others for not being perfect or accurate
- Believes personal morals, ideals, and procedures are the only correct standard
- Has an inner voice that is self-critical and condemning

- Motivated to pursue your calling with excellence
- Improves the lives of others with principles and gentle guidance
- Establishes healthy boundaries using wisdom and discernment

Wing Type 8: The Passionate Protector

- Becomes passive-aggressive, irritable, or frustrated when overlooked
- Struggles to stay tender, patient, and gracious when disrespected or when others are harmed
- Fearful of being vulnerable, betrayed, and taken advantage of

- Confidently moves toward personal passions and calling
- Can vulnerably and directly share needs and emotions
- Does what is best for veveryone, self included

Path Type 3: The Admirable Achiever

- Suppresses emotions and true identity to focus on achieving
- Feels shame and worthlessness when weaknesses and failures are exposed
- Will people-please to gain admiration from others

- Takes time to discover personal desires and God's calling
- Creates and executes a plan for self-improvement that also blesses others
- Energetically pursues goals with a positivity that inspires others

Path Type 6: The Faithful Guardian

- Expresses irritability, dissatisfaction, and self-doubt when anxious
- Has a strong internal or external reaction when blamed
- Fears the relational abandonment of others

- Less accommodating while still loyal and caring for the well-being of others
- Demonstrates courage by stepping out of comfort zone into unfamiliar areas
- More committed to persevering through challenges to benefit self and others

9

Acknowledgments

OUR KIDS: Nathan and Libby McCord, we are so thankful for both of you, for your kindness, patience, and willingness to embrace what we were learning all these years. You are a true gift and blessing to us.

OUR FAMILY: Jerald and Johnnie McCord, Dr. Bruce and Dana Pfuetze, and Dr. Mark and Mollie Pfuetze, you are all a foundation of love and support, a launching pad for us to live out our calling given to us by God. We respect you and honor you. You have loved us well. Thank you for graciously giving us permission to share our stories so we can help others better understand the power of the gospel and the impact of the Enneagram.

OUR "YOUR ENNEAGRAM COACH" TEAM: You helped turn our pastoral ministry into a global ministry, bringing the gospel to thousands. You are a gift from our Father.

OUR EXECUTIVE TEAM: Thank you Robert Lewis (chief strategy officer), Justin Barbour (chief financial officer), Suzie Barbour (chief operating officer), and Neil Samudre (chief marketing officer).

OUR TEAM: Thank you Taylor Simon (executive assistant), Christina Sheer (director of operations), Abby Ortiz (operations & customer experience manager), Brandon Billings (customer experience), Mark Christianson (customer experience), and Brian Lee (coaching & product).

Contributors to More Than Your Number: Thank you Jane Butler (design), Lydia Craig (content writer and contributor to part 3 of the book), and Adam Breckenridge (director of coaching & product).

OUR COLLABORATIVE WRITER: John Driver, you greatly helped us organize and clarify our message, making it so much more accessible to our readers. Your professionalism honed our story and insights so that others can engage in the same transformative journey we have experienced using the Enneagram Internal Profile. Without you, this book would not have been written. What began as a professional partnership has turned into a dear friendship.

OUR LITERARY AGENTS: Thank you, Wolgemuth & Associates, for your partnership, wisdom, and diligent work to help us find the right home for this important project: Robert Wolgemuth, Andrew Wolgemuth, Erik Wolgemuth, and Austin Wilson.

OUR PUBLISHER: We are incredibly grateful to have the excellent team at W Publishing Group (Thomas Nelson, HarperCollins Christian Publishing) as our partner in taking this message to people around the world. Thank you Damon Reiss, Kyle Olund, Carrie Marrs, Whitney Bak, Caren Wolfe, Allison Carter, Kerri Daly, and the entire editorial and marketing team.

OUR FRIENDS: Kyle and Pamela Turner—you have been such a gift to us during our time in Tennessee. You have been present as we have worked through our own personal story and the origins of principles in this book.

Dan Gurley—thank you for your encouragement and presence as you and I (Jeff) have walked out the principles of EIP in our lives. I could not be more grateful to you.

OUR SPIRITUAL TEACHERS AND THE AUTHORS WE HAVE LEARNED FROM: We are so thankful for your books, sermons, messages, and training. May our efforts honor your work: Dr. Alison Cook, Kimberly Miller, Dr. Richard Schwartz, Serge, and Dr. Jay Earley.

OUR ENNEAGRAM TEACHERS AND COACHES: Thank you for all you have done ahead of us Katherine Fauvre, Ian Cron, Suzanne Stabile, Ginger Lapid-Bogda, Russ Hudson, Don Riso, Jessica Dibb, Helen Palmer, Dr. David Daniels, Marilyn Vancil, and Elizabeth Wagele.

Notes

Introduction: My Good Shepherd

1. With sensitivity, please know that we are not referring to dissociative identity disorder or multiple personalities. Understanding this, the pages ahead will continue to expand this idea of "parts" with increasing clarity.
2. Dane Ortlund, *Gentle and Lowly: The Heart of Christ for Sinners and Sufferers* (Wheaton, IL: Crossway, 2020), 122.

Chapter 1: The Wounded Child and the Beloved Child

1. Our process is not a substitution for seeing mental health professionals via counseling, therapy, or psychiatric intervention. These are helpful paths you can simultaneously take alongside your own work with the Enneagram.
2. Many of these clues are similar to helpful insights written in the book *Sonship*. Serge, *Sonship* (Greensboro, NC: New Growth Press, 2013), 23–24.

Chapter 2: Recognizing the Fog Within

1. A variation of this quote was cited in Robert Edward Luccock, *If God Be for Us: Sermons on the Gifts of the Gospel* (Harper: New York, 1954), 38.
2. Groundbreaking work by Richard Schwartz speaks to this concept in his development of Internal Family Systems, the role of which we will reference in later chapters. Richard C. Schwartz and Martha Sweezy, *Internal Family Systems Therapy*, 2nd ed. (New York: The Guilford Press, 2020).
3. For Enneagram enthusiasts who utilize the Tritype®, the three types that make up your Tritype are equally important. But for the sake of this book, we will only be focusing on the types directly connected to your main type.
4. In his paradigm of Internal Family Systems, Richard Schwartz uses terms

like *befriend* and *exile* to describe the way we might interact with varying parts within us.

5. Again, you can visit https://www.yourenneagramprofile.com/resources to learn more about determining your own individual Enneagram type.

Chapter 3: Waking the Beloved Child

1. Alison Cook and Kimberly Miller, *Boundaries for Your Soul* (Nashville: Thomas Nelson, 2018), 27.

Chapter 4: Activating Your Internal GPS with the Enneagram

1. Even though we list the core longing as the last of the core motivations in Your Enneagram Coach materials, as you have seen, we often discuss core longing first because it is the best place to initiate conversations on these topics.

Chapter 5: The Health of Your Enneagram Type

1. Jerry Bridges, *The Discipline of Grace* (Colorado Springs: NavPress, 2006), 248, Kindle edition.

Chapter 6: Beginning Your Enneagram Internal Profile

1. A full list of each type's primary strategy will be explored in chapter 7.

2. This list was partially inspired by chapter-by-chapter concepts found in Marilyn Vancil, *Self to Lose, Self to Find: Using the Enneagram to Uncover Your True God-Gifted Self* (New York: Convergent, 2020).

Chapter 7: Understanding the Parts of Your Enneagram Internal Profile

1. Our Tritype (developed by Katherine Fauvre) and our triads are also parts worth exploring, especially for those who want to take a deeper dive via additional resources, personal coaching, and the like.

2. Note that Jeff's parts are not named in the aligned and misaligned versions as Beth's were. Each of us can name our parts in unique ways, and it is not necessary to assign adjectives to each, unless we are inclined to do so.

Chapter 8: Unpacking AWARE

1. Timothy Keller, *The Meaning of Marriage: Facing the Complexities of Commitment with the Wisdom of God* (2011; repr., New York: Penguin Books, 2016), 44.
2. Dane Ortlund, *Gentle and Lowly* (Wheaton, IL: Crossway, 2020), 205.
3. Ortlund, 35.
4. Thomas Goodwin, *The Heart of Christ* (Louisville, KY: GLH Publishing, 2015), 36.
5. Jerry Bridges, "Preach the Gospel to Yourself," chap. 3 in *The Discipline of Grace* (Colorado Springs: NavPress, 2006).
6. Bridges, *The Discipline of Grace*, 27, 59.
7. Brennan Manning, *Abba's Child: The Cry of the Heart for Intimate Belonging* (Colorado Springs: NavPress, 1994), 28, Kindle edition.
8. Dan Zink, "A Model to Guide Us" (lecture, Marriage and Family Counseling, Covenant Theological Seminary, St. Louis, MO, spring 2002).

Chapter 9: Walking Through AWARE

1. The original quote reads as follows: "It is by going down into the abyss / that we recover the treasures of life. // Where you stumble, / there lies your treasure. // The very care you are afraid to enter / turns out to be the source of / what you are looking for." Diane K. Osbon, ed., *Reflections on the Art of Living: A Joseph Campbell Companion* (New York: HarperPerennial, 1995), 24.
2. Jerry Bridges, *The Discipline of Grace,* (Colorado Springs, CO: NavPress, 2006),157.

Chapter 10: Type 1: Principled Reformer

1. Feel free to explore the core motivations of the other parts throughout the EIP sections in part 3.
2. For additional resources to help you walk through the AWARE exercise, visit https://www.yourenneagramprofile.com/resources.
3. Visit https://www.yourenneagramprofile.com/resources to access additional downloadable resources for working through your own EIP.

Chapter 11: Type 2: Nurturing Supporter

1. Feel free to explore the core motivations of the other parts throughout the EIP sections in part 3.

2. For additional resources to help you walk through the AWARE exercise, visit https://www.yourenneagramprofile.com/resources.

3. Visit https://www.yourenneagramprofile.com/resources to access additional downloadable resources for working through your own EIP.

CHAPTER 12: TYPE 3: ADMIRABLE ACHIEVER

1. Feel free to explore the core motivations of the other parts throughout the EIP sections in part 3.

2. For additional resources to help you walk through the AWARE exercise, visit https://www.yourenneagramprofile.com/resources.

3. Visit https://www.yourenneagramprofile.com/resources to access additional downloadable resources for working through your own EIP.

CHAPTER 13: TYPE 4: INTROSPECTIVE INDIVIDUALIST

1. Feel free to explore the core motivations of the other parts throughout the EIP sections in part 3.

2. For additional resources to help you walk through the AWARE exercise, visit https://www.yourenneagramprofile.com/resources.

3. Visit https://www.yourenneagramprofile.com/resources to access additional downloadable resources for working through your own EIP.

CHAPTER 14: TYPE 5: ANALYTICAL INVESTIGATOR

1. Feel free to explore the core motivations of the other parts throughout the EIP sections in part 3.

2. For additional resources to help you walk through the AWARE exercise, visit https://www.yourenneagramprofile.com/resources.

3. Visit https://www.yourenneagramprofile.com/resources to access additional downloadable resources for working through your own EIP.

CHAPTER 15: TYPE 6: FAITHFUL GUARDIAN

1. Feel free to explore the core motivations of the other parts throughout the EIP sections in part 3.

2. For additional resources to help you walk through the AWARE exercise, visit https://www.yourenneagramprofile.com/resources.

3. Visit https://www.yourenneagramprofile.com/resources to access additional downloadable resources for working through your own EIP.

Chapter 16: Type 7: Enthusiastic Optimist

1. Feel free to explore the core motivations of the other parts throughout the EIP sections in part 3.
2. For additional resources to help you walk through the AWARE exercise, visit https://www.yourenneagramprofile.com/resources.
3. Visit https://www.yourenneagramprofile.com/resources to access additional downloadable resources for working through your own EIP.

Chapter 17: Type 8: Passionate Protector

1. Feel free to explore the core motivations of the other parts throughout the EIP sections in part 3.
2. For additional resources to help you walk through the AWARE exercise, visit https://www.yourenneagramprofile.com/resources.
3. Visit https://www.yourenneagramprofile.com/resources to access additional downloadable resources for working through your own EIP.

Chapter 18: Type 9: Peaceful Accommodator

1. Feel free to explore the core motivations of the other parts throughout the EIP sections in part 3.
2. For additional resources to help you walk through the AWARE exercise, visit https://www.yourenneagramprofile.com/resources.
3. Visit https://www.yourenneagramprofile.com/resources to access additional downloadable resources for working through your own EIP.

About the Authors

Beth and Jeff McCord are the founders of Your Enneagram Coach, a global community designed to be a safe place to explore the tool of the Enneagram from a well-studied, practically engaged, and deeply gospel-centered approach. Through their leadership of a vast network of coaches and followers, they teach and guide individuals, couples, families, leaders, and organizations toward self-awareness and into the life-enhancing growth that only Christ can bring. Their mission is to help people see themselves with astonishing clarity so they can break free from self-condemnation, fear, and shame by knowing and experiencing the unconditional love, forgiveness, and freedom found in Christ.

In addition to their live marriage events, weekly podcast, and ever-evolving offerings of curriculum and courses, Beth and Jeff are bestselling authors of *Becoming Us*. Beth has authored ten other books, and Jeff is a former pastor with more than twenty years of diverse ministry experience in shepherding, counseling, and leading. They live in Nashville, Tennessee, and have two grown children, Nate and Libby.

About the Collaborators

JOHN DRIVER, MS, is an award-winning writer and collaborator of more than twenty-five books. As an author, he has been featured on *Good Morning America (GMA3)*, SiriusXM Radio, and numerous other media outlets and podcasts. A former teacher with a history degree from the University of Tennessee, he lives near Nashville with his wife and daughter. He serves as the executive and teaching pastor at The Church at Pleasant Grove and hosts the weekly podcast *Talk About That*.

LYDIA J. CRAIG lives in Nashville with her husband and three kids. In the second grade, she fell in love with writing, which led her to pursue her master's degree in library science. Along with working as a content writer for Your Enneagram Coach, she also writes middle-grade fiction.

JANE BUTLER is an award-winning designer who weaves creativity and digital solutions to communication challenges. As a cofounder of Well Refined, a boutique marketing firm, she has collaborated with a variety of artists, non-profits, organizations, and businesses across North America. Jane lives a minimalist lifestyle in New York City with her husband and three children.

Don't Miss Your
Bonus Gifts

One book couldn't hold all of Beth and Jeff's
insights, so they created digital resources
just for you. Download your FREE tools
today to enhance your understanding of
More Than Your Number.

Claim your bonus tools at
yourenneagramprofile.com/resources

Take the Next Step in Your Journey with the Enneagram

Ready to go deeper in your understanding of your Enneagram Internal Profile? Join Beth and Jeff for an innovative course that teaches you how to create an Enneagram Internal Profile for your specific Type.

Get access at yourenneagramprofile.com/course

From the Publisher

GREAT BOOKS
ARE EVEN BETTER WHEN THEY'RE SHARED!

Help other readers find this one:

- Post a review at your favorite online bookseller

- Post a picture on a social media account and share why you enjoyed it

- Send a note to a friend who would also love it—or better yet, give them a copy

Thanks for reading!